REVISIONS

REVISIONS

A Series of Books on Ethics

Volume 3

Revisions:
Changing Perspectives in Moral Philosophy

EDITED BY

Stanley Hauerwas
AND
Alasdair MacIntyre

UNIVERSITY OF NOTRE DAME PRESS
NOTRE DAME   LONDON

Library of Congress Cataloging in Publication Data

Main entry under title:

Revisions

(Revisions ; v. 3)
1. Ethics—Addresses, essays, lectures.
2. Christian ethics—Addresses, essays, lectures.
I. Hauerwas, Stanley. II. MacIntyre, Alasdair.
III. Series: Revisions (Notre Dame, Ind.) ; v. 3.
BJ1012.C454 .R441983   170   82-40386
ISBN 0-268-01614-3
ISBN 0-268-01617-8 (pbk.)

Contents

Preface

Ethics is in vogue. Professional associations in areas such as medicine and engineering revise codes, set up committees and sponsor conferences. Legislatures enforce standards with conscientious vigor. Courses in moral philosophy, in Christian ethics, bioethics, environmental ethics and business ethics multiply in colleges, in divinity schools and in professional schools. Foundations are generous in their funding. It might be expected that we, one of us a teacher of moral theology and the other of moral philosophy, would be saluting this development with enthusiastic approval. But we are in fact apprehensive and suspicious. Why so?

This is not the first time that ethics has been fashionable. And history suggests that in those periods when a social order becomes uneasy and even alarmed about the weakening of its moral bonds and the poverty of its moral inheritance and turns for aid to the moral philosopher and theologian, it may not find those disciplines flourishing in such a way as to be able to make available the kind of moral reflection and theory which the culture actually needs. Indeed on occasion it may be that the very causes which have led to the impoverishment of moral experience and the weakening of moral bonds will also themselves have contributed to the formation of a kind of moral philosophy and a kind of moral theology which are unable to provide the needed resources. How far this is the case in the present situation we are not sure; but that it is the case to some not unimportant degree we are quite certain. In the two introductory essays each of us has explained in a little detail the nature of our concerns and preoccupations in this respect in the context of the recent history or our respective disciplines. We hope that what we have said there will make it clear why we think it important to republish in this collection the particular set of essays that we have chosen.

Acknowledgments

We are most grateful to Miss Iris Murdoch and to the editor and publishers of *Encounter* for permission to reprint "Against Dryness"; to the Warden of Wadham College, the editor of *Mind* and the publishers of *Mind*, Basil Blackwell, for permission to reprint "Fallacies in Moral Philosophy"; to Miss Iris Murdoch, Dr. Marjorie Grene, editor of *The Anatomy of Knowledge*, and to its publishers, Routledge & Kegan Paul and the University of Massachusetts Press, for permission to reprint "On 'God' and 'Good' "; to Professor Edmund Pincoffs, the editor of *Mind* and Basil Blackwell for permission to reprint "Quandary Ethics"; to Professor J. B. Schneewind and to Professor A. Phillips Griffiths, Director of the Royal Institute of Philosophy in whose third volume of Philosophy Lectures *Knowledge and Necessity* "Moral Knowledge and Moral Principles" first appeared, for permission to reprint that paper; to Professor Frithjof Bergmann, Professor Alastair Hannay, editor of *Inquiry*, and to Universitetsforlaget, its publisher, for permission to reprint "The Experience of Values"; to Professor Quentin Bell and to the Principal of Bretton Hall College, where "Bad Art" was first delivered as a Foundation Lecture, for permission to reprint it; to Professor Peter Berger and to the editor and publisher of the *Archives Européennes de Sociologie* for permission to reprint "On the Obsolescence of the Concept of Honor"; to Professor Richard J. Mouw and the editors of the *Journal of Medicine and Philosophy* for permission to reprint "Biblical Revelation and Medical Decisions"; to Professor Annette Baier and the editors of the *Canadian Journal of Philosophy* for permission to reprint "Secular Faith"; to Mr. Dwight Macdonald for permission to reprint Mary McCarthy's translation of "The Iliad or the Poem of Force," which first appeared in *Politics*; and to Professor Herbert Fingarette and the editors of the *Hastings Law Journal* for permission to reprint "The Meaning of Law in the Book of Job."

We would particularly like to thank the authors who have accepted unusually low fees in order to assist the University of Notre Dame in keeping the price of this book down and in keeping it in print for as long as it seems likely to be useful.

1

Moral Philosophy: What Next?

Alasdair MacIntyre

The inability of philosophers to reach agreement is notorious. And this inability extends to disagreement over how to characterise their disagreements and as to which of their disagreements are central to their discipline and which peripheral. No one will therefore expect an account and an evaluation of some part of philosophy to command universal assent or anything remotely like it among those professionally engaged in that part of the discipline. For such an account and evaluation will itself necessarily embody some particular partisan philosophical standpoint. It will itself be both an expression of and an occasion for disagreement within the conflicts of which it is a chronicle.

Contemporary moral philosophy is likely to suffer even more from this endemic inability to agree than are such other subdisciplines as logic or epistemology; for differing standpoints within moral philosophy have always been closely related to differing moral standpoints. And our own is one of those periods in the history of morality when the deepest moral divisions exist in areas of central human concern: social justice, war, sexuality, the uses of technology. Just because this is the case, those who cannot avoid confronting the resulting dilemmas are forced into formulating their problems with an unusual degree of articulateness and theoretical depth. Moral philosophy, in a way and to a degree that has some but few historical parallels, has become recognized by those who are not professional philosophers as an important form of inquiry. So recently among physicians, corporate executives, the military, and engineers there has emerged a serious wish to discover what moral philosophy has to contribute at the level of practice. And, in the face of this, the state of the discipline has become a matter of more than academic importance.

The choice of essays for this volume reflects the shared conviction of the editors that moral philosophy has had too narrow a focus in recent decades and that the ways in which this collection differs systematically from others which represent the standard fare of the discipline are an index of the ways in which that focus needs to be corrected. It is highly possible that not a single one of our contributors agrees with us on this point. It may well be the case that each of them understands the importance of what they have written very differently from the way in which we do, and it is certainly the case that our contributors disagree with each other as well as with us on many issues. What underlies our principle of selection is the belief that individually these essays supply an important counterbalance and corrective to some dominant trend and that collectively they would, if what they have to teach were taken seriously, enlarge the discussion so as to rescue it from some of its present frustrations and inadequacies.

I hasten to add that neither of us believes that what we take to be frustrations and inadequacies are the outcome of any lack of intellectual power and distinction. The best writing in ethics among those who have established their views as dominant in the field has had the effect that it has had in key part because of such power and distinction. What we do, however, believe is that it has too often drawn upon increasingly impoverished traditions, both in morality and in philosophy. And some evidence at least that that is the case is provided by the contrast between what has happened in moral philosophy in recent decades and what has happened in philosophy at large.

One way of writing the history of recent philosophy in the English-speaking world would be as a systematic dismantling of the positions taken by the logical positivists of the Vienna Circle and their immediate intellectual heirs. The relatively brief period during which those positions were dominant—the dominance of a position in philosophy is not so much a matter of how widely it is accepted as of how widely the need is felt *either* to defend *or* to attack it—marked not only the apparent victory of certain specifically philosophical theses (concerning, for example, the verification principle, the analytic/synthetic distinction, and the relationship of theoretical to observation statements), but also the high point of the ascendancy within philosophy of a still powerful cultural ideology, that of *scientism*. It is of the essence of this ideology, as it was of logical positivist philosophy, to make a particular (and in fact erroneous) interpretation of the procedures and structures of the natural sciences normative for the understanding of rationality. Whatever does not conform to the canons, not of the natural sciences, but of the natural sciences positivistically understood, lies beyond the realm of rational discourse. What is thereby excluded from the realm of rational discourse? Any area, according to such positivists as Carnap and Ayer, in which the function of discourse is to express feelings and attitudes; and it was to this area that they consigned the utterances of poetry, theology, and morality. Almost fortuitously, it happened that there soon became available in English a systematically argued account of the nature of morality in precisely the terms required by the positivists, albeit one which itself derived from a rather different intellectual background, that of the criticism of G. E. Moore's ethics. I am referring of course to the emotivist account contained in C. L. Stevenson's *Ethics and Language,* first published in 1945, but propounded somewhat earlier by Stevenson in a number of articles. It is not surprising then that for a short period Stevenson's analysis of the meaning of such statements as "This is good" as roughly equivalent to "I approve of this; do so as well" seemed philosophically attractive. But its predominance was short lived.

What Stevenson's emotivism seemed fatally to ignore and to obscure was the place of reasoning in ordinary moral discourse. And a great deal of analytical postpositivist moral philosophy since 1945 has partly in consequence been preoccupied with the character of the logical relationships that inform such reasoning. The inquiries embodying this preoccupation have certainly thrown a good deal of light on important points of detail concerning moral argument, but in retrospect they have perhaps chiefly been remarkable—especially considering the high standards of rigor which have marked their pursuit—for what they have not (or at least not yet) achieved, and this in some salient respects.

First they have failed to secure agreement even on central issues: Is there a sense in which some distinctively moral injunctions can be expressed only by categorical imperatives, or could morality be a system of hypothetical imperatives? Are there undeniably factual premises from which undeniably moral conclusions follow? In giving good reasons for acting as morality requires, may we or must we move in the chain of reason-giving ultimately to desires and interests of a kind prior to moral considerations? Must all moral judgments be universalizable? On such issues contemporary moral philosophers of notable distinction continue to disagree with one another, and this disagreement is not merely of

the kind that is endemic in all philosophy. For the outcome of that
dismantling of logical positivist positions which has taken place in
the philosophy of language and the philosophy of science, by contrast, has been the formulation and elaboration of new, highly
original and seminal insights; new accounts of naming and
reference, of intensionality and of the place of incommensurability
in scientific theory choice have led to new philosophical alignments.
The crucial contemporary disagreements in these areas—although
they are in some ways, as always in philosophy, the heirs and successors to earlier philosophical conflicts—embody what are evident-
ly significant philosophical advances, even if it is still far from clear
what their long-term impact will be. It implies no disrespect to the
major participants in recent inquiries in moral philosophy to remark
that in their work it has been quite otherwise. Both rigor and imaginative brilliance have been shown in developing what are
essentially older positions in new ways; but the key points of
disagreement remain obstinately where they were. Such innovation
as there is, is only in the detail.

    In consequence we have a number of equally impressive and
mutually incompatible recent accounts of the status and justification of moral rules, all of them reviving central themes and doctrines of seventeenth- and eighteenth-century moral philosophy.
Contractarianism, universalizability, nonutilitarian naturalism, and
utilitarianism (and more complex views that blend versions of these,
such as Hare's synthesis of universalizability and utilitarianism) all
provide examples of contemporary renderings of earlier originals.
But such progress as each of these inquiries makes is almost entirely internal to the positions originally adopted by their protagonists,
so that characteristically each view has been developed from some
earlier to some later version (as, for example, with Hare's prescrip-
tivist utilitarianism, Foot's naturalism, and Rawls's rationalism).
Nothing seems to have been achieved toward any resolution of the
major disagreements between the protagonists, and very little has
been written that philosophers working outside moral philosophy
are likely to recognize as characterized by philosophical inventiveness of a kind that could be important to their own inquiries.

    This lack of philosophical progress is matched by the relative in-
ability of recent moral philosophy to throw any special light upon
the problems of our practical moral life. Consider for example those
dilemmas of contemporary medical practice that have been
engendered by scientific and technological advance. One notable instance concerns the problem of whether to take the surgical and
medical actions necessary to preserve the life of a *spina bifida* in-

fant. Some such infants are in fact able to grow up to enjoy a disabled but essentially normal life; the majority, however, will be little more than a cause of suffering to themselves and to those burdened with their care. But we cannot now predict what the outcome will be in individual cases. We are not at present able to tell which *spina bifida* infants will flourish and which will not. Hence the choice is *either* to preserve the life of all, thus maximizing pain and suffering, *or* to preserve the life of none, thus depriving of life a number of human beings with as much capacity for a fulfilled human life as most of us. If we choose the former, we violate those rules which enjoin us all, and more especially physicians and surgeons, to prevent and reduce the pain and suffering of others; if the latter, that rule which enjoins us all and more especially physicians and surgeons to prevent the loss of innocent human life.

Notice the dilemma arises *not* because two contingently incompatible claims can be supported by reasons that can be shown to be equally compelling, but because we do not in our contemporary moral culture apparently have the resources to evaluate the rational strength of the rival claims. It is not, so to speak, that we are able to weigh the rival claims on some moral set of scales and that they turn out to be of equal weight; it is rather that there are no scales. And, lacking such, all talk of "the balance of moral considerations" is bound to be vacuous. But what does it mean to say that there are no scales?

The problem is not that we lack abundant means for justifying the claims to authority of particular moral rules. The problem is perhaps that we have all too many such means and that they provide quite disparate and incommensurable forms of justification. So we find in ordinary moral discourse the use of justifying arguments framed in terms of universalizability or of contractarianism or of utilitarianism, some of these latter invoking act-utilitarianism, others different versions of rule-utilitarianism. If I ask why I ought to tell the truth, I may be told that since I believe that others ought not to lie to me, I have logically committed myself to the view that in relevantly similar circumstances I ought not to lie to them; or that if I lie to others, I will pay the price of ceasing to be treated as a member of the community of the mutually trustworthy; or that obedience to a rule enjoining truth-telling is more generally productive of utility than any alternative rule; and so on. There are all too many answers, each with a good deal of plausibility in its own terms.

But turn now to the question: How are we to proceed when rules conflict? When, whatever rule we normally observe concerning truth-telling, contingent circumstances make it impossible to do both what that rule enjoins and what some other rule—for example, the rule that enjoins us to prevent suffering, which we also normally observe—enjoins, which of the two rules is to be accorded precedence? Here by contrast we find no clear answers: all utilitarian answers turn out to be either vacuous or arbitrary; nonutilitarianism answers are equally barren. That is to say, we do not lack for rational justifications of particular rules; but we do not know how to organize these into a hierarchy whose form would exhibit some overarching unity in our moral lives. We are, so it appears, rationally impotent in the face of genuine dilemmas, where rival rules embody considerations whose authority competes for our allegiance. And this is precisely the situation in which the physician and the surgeon find themselves in such cases as that of the *spina bifida* child.

It is natural to inquire if this inability, even of sophisticated moral agents, to solve the problems presented by such contemporary dilemmas and the lack of progress in recent moral philosophy that I have noted may not be related. Perhaps contemporary morality has certain specific features from which both the theoretical sterility and the practical impasses arise. But this suggestion cannot be investigated without first undertaking a historical and comparative inquiry so that we can identify the specifically contemporary features of the morality dominant in our culture and society and discover what differentiates this morality from that of other times and places, including in those times and places the various predecessors of modernity in the ancient, medieval, and renaissance worlds.

The need for this type of inquiry has until very recently been systematically ignored within moral philosophy; it has been left to social anthropologists and sociologists to concern themselves with the varieties of moral practice and discourse and to historians to concern themselves with narratives of moral change. But although work as various as that of Rodney Needham, Maria Ossowska, and Carolly Erickson has provided a large mass of philosophically relevant material, their findings are rarely framed in a way that would provide direct answers to philosophers' questions. Perhaps partly because of this, and because of the pressures exerted by the conventional ordering of the academic division of labor, moral philosophers have continued talking confidently of *the* moral point of view and *the* language of morals, rather than asking of any particular moral concept or belief "Whose concept or belief is this?" and "What is the particular historical and social setting in which it arose and flourished?"

I have already remarked on the way in which the themes and procedures of recent moral philosophers revive, indeed are very often restricted to, themes and procedures of seventeenth- and eighteenth-century European moral philosophy. And this contemporary confidence in the single and unitary character of morality is part of our inheritance. But for writers in the seventeenth and eighteenth century this confidence was founded on a belief which they took to have empirical confirmation, that fundamental human nature is one and the same amidst all social and cultural change and that morality is single and unitary because it is the expression of this single and unitary human nature. Hobbes, Hutcheson, Hume, Smith, Diderot, and Kant may all disagree about the characteristics of that fundamental human nature, or about how they come to be expressed in morality, or indeed about both of these; but on the invariance of human nature they do agree. And so their treatment of morality as single and unitary has a rational foundation. With recent moral philosophers any sense of the need for this kind of rational foundation for their inquiries seems to have been lost; identification of *the* moral is consequently presented as a relatively unproblematic matter and certainly not as one requiring extended historical investigation. Yet such investigation need proceed only a little way for it to become clear that modern European morality has at least three highly specific features.

The first is that it is post-theistic. We inhabit a morality which only relatively recently was detached from some version of biblical religion. It is usually taken for granted that the relationship of contemporary morality to theism is merely and unimportantly historical. Contemporary moral philosophers do not so much quarrel with Kant's claim that judgments which express the moral law presuppose a belief in a *summum bonum* that is unwarranted unless God exists; they simply ignore it. But clearly this response to Kant is a symptom of a more general blindness to the nature of certain key features of moral discourse. It is, for example, centrally important that such words as "ought" and "should" in our normal discourse are given a peculiar force when they are used to express the notions of being "obliged" or "bound" or "required" to perform some particular action or type of action. And this force is given to them by the fact that in such contexts these expressions are given the sense that they have when we assert that such-and-such is required by law or that the law is such that we are bound or obliged to do such-and-such. This point has been made cogently by G. E. M. Anscombe ("Modern Moral Philosophy," *Philosophy*, 1958, pp. 1–19), who goes on to remark

To have a *law* conception of ethics is to hold that what is needed for conformity with the virtues, failure in which is the mark
of being bad *qua* man (and not merely, say, *qua* craftsman or
logician)—that what is needed for *this*, is required by divine
law. Naturally it is not possible to have such a conception
unless you believe in God as a law-giver; like Jews, Stoics and
Christians. (p. 6)

It follows, as Miss Anscombe notes, that when such expressions are employed, with that kind of import, by those who do not
believe in a divine lawgiver, what we have to deal with is a survival,
a fragment from a larger whole.

Failure to recognize this may lead, on the one hand, to attempts
to supply some nontheistic account of what it is to be obliged or
bound or required which will still preserve the sense and force of
"ought" and "should" that they originally acquired in theistic contexts, or on the other, to find some other sense and force for these
words when used to make judgments of moral import. And it is
perhaps this failure to recognize how much of the "ordinary
language" of contemporary morality is a survival from theism that
underlies a corresponding failure to reckon with the fact that each of
these two alternatives embodies a different kind of moral project. In
consequence, adherents of the two parties are often not offering
rival accounts of one and the same subject matter, but rival ways of
revising and reformulating that subject matter in the interests of
rival goals. What is going on is therefore, to a greater extent than is
admitted, a work of construction. What is presented as participa-
tion in the unified enterprise of describing and analyzing morality is
in fact often enough engagement in assorted enterprises of inven-
tion.

Of course it is not only in respect of its theistic past that a good
deal of modern morality can be rightly understood as a fragmented
survival. It is characteristic of most modern morality that it does not
presuppose—or at least its theorists tend to unite in denying that it
presupposes—any agreement on what constitutes the good life for
human beings. For the most part either it is deontological in form or
it is utilitarian, and utilitarianism in its latest versions has had to
recognize the heterogeneity and variety of human wants. A wide
measure of disagreement on goods and large disagreement on
whether it is possible to speak of *the* good is generally taken for
granted. But it was not always so. We inhabit a culture which was
at an earlier stage informed by a shared belief in a *summum bonum*.

And that belief had classical, in particular Aristotelian, as well as biblical, sources. They combined to provide morality with a point and a purpose, in virtue of which the moral life could be treated as an intelligible pursuit for a rational being. But when shared belief in the *summum bonum* is lost, the question of the point and purpose of morality also becomes one for which answers have to be invented, and to which naturally enough rival and incompatible answers are given.

In light of these considerations it is not surprising that morality should become a matter of choices, a matter about which each individual has to make his or her own decisions. And the kind of philosophical theory according to which underlying each moral judgment there is a choice that the agent has made—a type of choice in which the individual is at the most fundamental level unconstrained by good reasons, precisely because his or her choice expresses a decision as to what is to count as a good reason for him or her—provides at once a rationale for what many ordinary moral agents take to be their situation and the latest, most radical version of a thesis about morality that has its origins in the eighteenth-century divorce of moral philosophy from philosophical psychology. Hume and Smith are the last great moral philosophers who make a theory of the virtues central to moral philosophy; and correlatively they are the last great moral philosophers for whom moral psychology is at the heart of moral theory. For the virtues, however conceived, always must stand in some determinate relationship to the passions, and any cogent account of the virtues requires at its foundation a cogent account of the passions and their relationship to reason. From Plato to Smith the recognition that this is so does not falter. But toward the end of the eighteenth century not only does the theory of the virtues cease to be a central preoccupation of moral philosophy, but to a very large degree the problems of morality are formulated so that philosophical psychology has to be irrelevant to our understanding of morality. Bentham and his immediate heirs constitute the most important exception to this generalization; but from the time of Sidgwick onward even utilitarians practice ethics in this peculiarly modern way, a way whose progenitors are Kant in Germany and Reid in Scotland.

According to Reid the will may be determined either by 'animal motives' or by 'rational motives'. When the will is determined by animal motives, it is our desires which determine what we do. When the will is determined by rational motives, it is the obligations which we perceive ourselves to have which determine our actions.

The freedom of the will consists in the fact that the choice between being determined by one type of motive or by the other is itself undetermined. Similarly in Kant the will may either be a self-determined rational will or a will determined by the inclinations, which are what they are because our physical constitution is what it is, and the freedom of the will consists in the fact that the choice between these two types of determination is not itself further determined. This conception of an undetermined choice as the initiating point of moral agency is, of course, in both Reid and Kant, combined with a belief in the objectivity of the moral law. But when the epistemological bases of those beliefs come to be undermined, when Kant's appeal to universalizability is shown to be vacuous by Hegel, and Reid's appeal to the objectivity of the principles of common sense is discredited by Mill, what is left is a conception of fundamental choice remarkably like that advanced by Kierkegaard in *Either-Or*. And such a conception is in turn remarkably close to that which is so central to contemporary moral theory and practice.

What, in part at least, led both Reid and Kant to distinguish sharply between moral considerations and considerations arising from the passions was, of course, a reaction against Hume's moral philosophy. Reid and Kant had both inherited from their respective Protestant traditions a conception of moral judgment as an expression of conformity to an objective moral law. And both saw clearly that if the passions were what Hume said they were, and if morality was a matter of the passions in the way that Hume said it was, then moral judgment must be what Hume said it was; but moral judgment as characterized by Hume could not be an expression of conformity to an objective moral law. Since they did not dissent substantially from Hume's view of the passions, they naturally enough concluded that morality could not be a matter of the passions.

The self's capacity for choice thus emerged as its salient moral characteristic; and later writers have so focused upon that characteristic that it has sometimes appeared as though it were the self's only, or almost its only, moral characteristic. The consequence has been a deeply impoverished view of the relevant dimensions of character and agency. But the emphasis upon choice was harmful not only in the area of moral psychology. For what were taken to be chosen were principles or rules. And the basic character of choice is linked to the fundamental role assigned to principles or rules. Therefore, a major preoccupation of moral philosophy becomes the discussion of what principles or rules to choose, of what the logical status of principles or rules is, and how to make such choices. And it is precisely in this area central to recent analytic moral philosophy that, as I noted at the outset, so little progress has been made and so much radical disagreement remains. But we can now understand why it is not surprising; for this particular area of inquiry is largely, if not entirely, defined by a concern with two highly problematic concepts—concepts whose problematic character can only be understood in the light of their emergence from a particular complex moral and philosophical history. So behind the notion of choice there lies the discarding of a moral psychology which was not only presupposed by any substantial theory of the virtues, but which was required by any theory of goods as characteristic objects of human desire and aspiration. And behind the notion of principles there lies the discarding of a belief in divine law, obedience to which was once understood as required if we are to achieve our *summum bonum* as human beings.

To have recognized this is already to have sketched one possible program of inquiry for the moral philosopher: how far and in what ways might it be possible to repair the argumentative structures that underpinned our moral tradition in the past? And how far is its loss irremediable? (This is the program on which I made a beginning, although only a beginning, in *After Virtue* and in my Carlyle Lectures, forthcoming as *The Transformations of Justice*.) But it also raises a set of large questions about what is likely to be omitted or obscured in our contemporary apprehension of moral reality by an understanding too exclusively informed by the modern concepts of *choice* and *principle*. The essays in this book have central importance for their part in answering this latter question. Every one of them can function as a corrective to recent tendencies, and indeed some of them, most notably perhaps the essays by Stuart Hampshire and Iris Murdoch, have already so functioned. But none of them, not even these, has as yet been accorded quite the full importance and attention it deserves. This is not, of course, to say that there are not other bodies of philosophical writing of high importance in this respect. I think especially of the contributions both to moral questions directly and to a wide range of philosophical questions relevant to ethics by G. E. M. Anscombe and of the equally remarkable but very different contributions by Peter Geach. The former have happily become available in her *Collected Philosophical Papers* (University of Minnesota Press) and the latter are available in part in his book *The Virtues* (Cambridge University Press). Professor Geach preferred that we not include his "Good and Evil"

(*Analysis*, 17,2 [December, 1956], pp. 33–42) for reasons to which we are entirely sympathetic.

It will, of course, be immediately clear that those philosophers whose writings we have identified as supplying a badly needed corrective do not necessarily agree with each other or with Anscombe or Geach or with Stanley Hauerwas or with me. But to some significant degree they do cooperate, perhaps inadvertently, in delineating new directions and possibilities, and they do so, not exclusively but in large part, by pointing to deficiencies in what has been until recently the dominant perspective in moral philosophy. What then are the crucial distortions of moral reality which that perspective encourages?

The first is a highly misleading form of contrast between the realm of moral judgment and the realm of factual judgment, and correspondingly between the activities involved both in making and in responding to moral judgments, on the one hand, and the activities involved in making and in responding to judgments of perception and scientific judgments. In its crudest forms this contrast is a simple consequence of the view that moral judgments, whether on particular situations or concerning general principles, are always expressions of some underlying choice by the agent who makes the judgment, when that view is held in conjunction with the belief that factual judgments, such as judgments of perception or scientific judgments, have no such basis. Disagreement over facts is, on this view, always capable of resolution, at least—to use a phrase often relied upon by its advocates—in principle, by consulting ordinary sense experience, or by using the scientific procedures of observation and experiment. Disagreement over moral issues cannot be similarly resolved precisely because it rests upon differences of attitude and choice rather than upon different beliefs as to what is the case. What this set of distinctions suggests, and philosophy in so suggesting reinforces a good deal that is commonly taken for granted, is that in any situation the moral agent has two distinct tasks: to apprise him or herself of the facts of the matter and then only secondly to decide what moral judgment to make. Morality enters in only *after* questions of fact have been settled. And this is surely a crucial mistake and a mistake with two different sources, one concerning the moral agent's tasks and one concerning the character of moral judgments.

The moral agent's tasks do not and cannot begin only after questions of fact have been settled. For, as both Simone Weil and

Iris Murdoch have insisted, one *sine qua non* of human goodness is the ability to see things as they are; and to see things as they are is a morally difficult task. "The chief enemy of excellence in morality," says Iris Murdoch, "(and also in art) is personal fantasy: the tissue of self-aggrandizing and consoling wishes and dreams which prevents one from seeing what is there outside one." And of the question about what parts of the self can "be preserved, through the exercise of virtue and through grace," Simone Weil says that "this whole question is fraught with temptations to falsehood, temptations that are positively enhanced by pride, by shame, by hatred, contempt, indifference, by the will to oblivion or to ignorance." A part of moral philosophy and moral psychology must therefore be concerned with how we do come to see things as they are, the variety of ways in which we may fail, the variety of causes of failure, and the kind of discipline that can overcome these obstacles. How do we learn to see differently?

Herbert Fingarette says of the Book of Job that it is "not an argument but a book of transformed perspectives." Both his paper and Simone Weil's suggest the place of dramatic poetry in any inquiry which reflects upon such transformation. Fingarette's discussion of retribution links what he has to say about this to a topic much treated of in conventional moral philosophy.

Frithjof Bergmann provides a systematic, general philosophical argument against the view that our experience is what it would have to be if the distinction between facts and values were what some philosophers have said it is. In so doing he identifies a second source of the mistake of thinking that an agent's moral tasks begin only after questions of fact have been settled. This source is the thesis that moral thinking is radically different in kind from scientific or other thinking about questions of fact. It is certain versions of this thesis that are challenged in two very different ways by Stuart Hampshire in "Fallacies in Moral Philosophy" and by J. B. Schneewind in "Moral Knowledge and Moral Principles." Both put in question the role moral principles have been supposed to play in our moral thinking on the view that has been dominant and do so in a way that makes their discussions relevant to what has been going on elsewhere in philosophy. Bergmann in his paper connects the kind of analysis that Schneewind carries through to Murdoch's emphasis upon the importance of a realistic moral vision and at the same time opens up a large area for future debate. Obedience to the categorical principles of morality based on a particular view of their logical status as first principles, may, so he argues, itself blind us. Moral principles, on Bergmann's view—and it is not at all a consequentialist view—are like the precepts of art and thus "subject to revision." Schneewind's argument points in the same direction. But then, what kind of authority does, for example, the injunction that forbids the taking of innocent life possess? Richard J. Mouw's paper provides, quite incidentally to its central purpose, a very different kind of answer to this question with his account of the way in which divine commandments can enter into the moral life. And in so doing he makes clear what is also the plain implication of a number of other essays, that there is no sphere of morality independent of the agent's metaphysical or theological (or antitheological) view of the world and, more particularly, of God and the self.

The question of God is raised one way or another in the essays by Murdoch, Fingarette, and Mouw. It is addressed directly from an atheistic standpoint by Annette Baier, who confronts the question of the links between moral commitment and belief in God in the light of David Gauthier's argument that Locke was right in thinking that "the taking away of God . . . in thought dissolves all," at least insofar as it dissolves any rational belief in duties or obligations whose justification requires, as an essential component, a general performance of which one cannot be otherwise assured (David Gauthier, "Why Ought One Obey God, Reflections on Hobbes and Locke," *Canadian Journal of Philosophy* 7 (1977), pp. 425–46). Baier's argument suggests that the only alternative to being theological is being antitheological. And if she is correct, then the comfortable assumption that questions about God can be put on one side at the level of moral decision (as assumption that extends far beyond moral philosophy) will have to be abandoned.

The question of the identity of the self as moral agent and of the different ways in which that identity can be envisaged is raised in Peter Berger's essay, an essay which makes the sociological dimension of moral inquiry clear. Berger's contrast between the presuppositions of traditional conceptions of honor and those of modern conceptions of dignity challenges the attempt so characteristic of the dominant tendencies in moral philosophy to portray the moral agent in terms of an abstract universal rationality divorced from all social particularity. It suggests, in fact, that this kind of portrait may show us, not the moral agent as such, but the moral agent suffering from certain peculiar afflictions of modernity. And Berger once again raises the question of the relationship of the way in which the self is understood to belief in God.

It ought by now to be clear that two themes in tension with one another run through many of the essays. On the one hand there is a strong wish to question the place of rules in moral life; on the other, a sense of the absolute demands of morality. The tension becomes explicit in the complex argument of Edmund Pincoffs' "Quandary Ethics," whose starting-point is a quarrel both with a certain conception of what a moral problem is and with the twin theses that moral problems are central to the moral life and ought to be accorded a central place in moral philosophy. It is not surprising that themes and arguments from a number of the other essays reappear in Pincoffs' reordering of the categories of moral thinking.

Finally, a number of the essays touch upon the parallels between or the relationship of morality and art. What is written about art by philosophers is rarely helpful here. But Quentin Bell's "Bad Art," with its thesis that "bad art arises from a failure of sentiment" and its illuminating discussion of the relationship of the artist to social norms and expectations, ought to be on every moral philosopher's bookshelf. We hope very much that this book will put it there.

I hope that I have said enough to make it clear that it is not just that the authors of the essays in this book have large disagreements with one another, sometimes explicit, often implicit. It is even the case that their work points us in quite different directions for future inquiry. What the essays have in common, however, is the presentation of considerations which radically undermine a good deal that has been central to moral philosophy. They force upon us the necessity of radical revision in a number of different ways.

2

On Keeping Theological Ethics Theological

Stanley Hauerwas

1. THE ETHICAL SIGNIFICANCE OF SAYING SOMETHING THEOLOGICAL

"Say something theological," is a request, as Gustafson notes, theologians frequently hear.[1] Such a request, often made in a more oblique manner, may be entirely friendly, as the inquirer—possessed by an archaeological curiosity in still living antiquities—simply wants an example of a religious relic. More likely, however, the request is really a challenge: "Say something theological in a way that convinces me that you are not talking nonsense." Such a challenge thus assumes that anyone using theological language seriously—that is, as though that language is essential for telling us about how things are or how we ought to be—bears the burden of proof.

This is particularly the case in matters having to do with ethics. For even though at a popular level many continue to assume there must be a close connection between religion and morality, this has not been compellingly evidenced on the philosophical level. Indeed the persistence of such an assumption only testifies how hard it is to kill certain habits of thought. For the assumption that there is a strong interdependence between religion and morality is but the remains of the now lost hegemony of Christianity over Western culture. That many still persist in assuming religion is essential to motivate us to do the good is an indication, however, that no satisfactory alternative has been found to replace Christianity, as world view and cult, in sustaining the *ethos* of our civilization. We, therefore, find ourselves in the odd situation where many of our society's moral attitudes and practices are based on Jewish and Christian beliefs that are thought to be irrelevant or false in themselves. This situation does not provide an argument for the continued viability of religious practices, but only an indication that as a culture we still have not fully faced the implications of generating a genuine secular morality.

Our culture's lingering failure to find an adequate substitute for Christianity has presented theologians with a temptation almost impossible to resist. Even if they cannot demonstrate the truth of theological claims, they can at least show the continued necessity of religious attitudes for the maintenance of our culture. Of course it would be unwise to continue to use the explicit beliefs derived from the particular historic claims associated with Christianity (and Judaism) as the basis of a secular morality. Such beliefs bear the marks of being historically relative and contingent. If religion is to deserve our allegiance, so the thinking goes, it must be based on the universal. Thus, theologians have sought, at least since the Enlightenment, to demonstrate that theological language can be translated into terms that are meaningful and compelling for those who do not share Christianity's more particularistic beliefs about Jesus of Nazareth. In short, theologians have tried to show that we do not need to speak theologically in order to "say something theological," as other forms of speech are really implicitly religious. After all, hasn't talk of God always really been but a way to talk about being human?[2]

Even though this understanding of the theological task is relatively recent, there is ample precedent for this endeavor in Christian tradition. As early as the second century, Christians felt their faith contained enough in common with the nonbeliever to legitimate an apologetic strategy. Moreover, such a strategy seems required by a faith that claims a strong continuity between the God who redeems and the God who creates. Thus Christians should not be surprised to find their specific religious beliefs confirmed by the best "humanistic alternatives."

Without denying some continuity between recent theological strategies and some modes of past Christian theology, it is equally important that we see the fundamental differences. The apologist of the past stood in the church and its tradition and sought relationship with those outside. Apologetic theology was a secondary endeavor because the apologist never assumed that you could let the questions of unbelief order the theological agenda. But now the theologian stands outside the tradition and seeks to show that selected aspects of that tradition can no longer pass muster from the perspective of the outsider. The theologian thus tries to locate the "essence," or at least what is essential to religion, in a manner that frees religion from its most embarrassing particularistic aspects. Ironically, just to the extent this strategy has been successful, the more theologians have underwritten the assumption that anything said in a theological framework cannot be of much interest. For if what is said theologically is but a confirmation of what we can know on other grounds or can be said more clearly in non-theological language, then why bother saying it theologically at all? Of course there may still be reason to keep theologians around to remind us of what people used to believe, or to act as a check against the inevitable perversities of those in our culture who persist in the more traditional forms of religious practice and belief, but theology as such cannot be considered a serious intellectual endeavor. Nor is this meant to deny that theologians may have important insights concerning general human and moral issues, but that situation testifies to their individual intelligence and insight rather than their particular theological convictions or training.

For example, much of the recent work in "medical ethics" has been done by theologians, but their prominence in that area has been purchased largely by demonstrating that they can do "medical ethics" just as well as anyone who is not burdened by a theological agenda. As a result it is very hard to distinguish between articles in medical ethics written by theologians and those written by non-theologians except that often the latter are better argued. It is telling that the article in this book defending the significance of theological convictions for ethical reflection on medicine was written by a philosopher.

The absence of articles by theologians in this anthology is not accidental or due to the prejudice of the editors. The prejudice, if there was one, was one in the opposite direction. We very much wanted to include more theologically informed articles. But most of the articles that are theologically explicit lacked appropriate intelligibility for a general readership;[3] and, as I have suggested, most of the articles written by theologians failed to be sufficiently theological. Thus we had to use articles written by nontheologians that at least suggest what difference theological convictions might make for how we think and, more importantly, for how we live.

It seems doubly odd that this anthology lacks articles by theologians, since many of the issues raised by articles have often been more thoroughly discussed by theologians both past and present. For example, running through these essays is the constant question: to what extent is ethics analogous to law? For centuries Christian theologians have discussed that question and at no time more intensely than the Reformation. That discussion has had rich results, for Christian thinkers have consistently maintained that the law is not sufficient to depict the Christian moral life.[4] In a related manner many of these essays challenge too optimistic assumptions about humanity and moral rationality. Nowhere in modern literature have such assumptions been more decisively challenged than by Reinhold Niebuhr.[5] And still further these essays suggest that ethicists must free themselves from their fascination with quandaries and rules, and pay more attention to the virtues and character. Again religious traditions provide rich resources for such an analysis and some theologians, for example, James Gustafson, have developed well-argued accounts of ethics so understood.[6] Yet each of these significant developments in theology has largely been ignored outside the theological community. Why is that the case?

At least part of the fault can be attributed to the sheer prejudice of many secular thinkers. They are simply ignorant of the disciplined nature of theological reflection and assume any reflection informed by religious claims cannot possibly be intelligible. But I suspect that there is a further reason, not so easily addressed, that is internal to how theological reflection about ethics has been done in our time. The lack of attention to theological reflection about the moral life is partly due to the inability of Christian theologians to find a sufficient medium to articulate their own best insights for those who do not share their convictions. In order to understand why that is the case it will be necessary to describe the development of Christian ethics during this century. For it is only against this historical background that we can understand the failure of Christian ethics to command attention, and furthermore, why that failure should not be perpetuated, since those convictions still offer a powerful resource for ethical reflection, even for those who find they are unable to envision and construe the world through them.

2. THE DIFFICULTY OF KEEPING CHRISTIAN ETHICS CHRISTIAN[7]

The very idea of Christian ethics as a distinct discipline is a relatively recent development. Of course, Christians have always had a lot to say about moral matters, but neither in their practical discourse nor their more systematic reflections did they try to make ethics a subject separable from their beliefs and convictions. The Church fathers did not write ethics *per se*; rather their understanding of theology shaped their view of the moral life. Prior to the Enlightenment, the notion that there might be an independent realm called "morality" to which one must try to determine one's relation religiously and theologically simply did not exist.

The story of the development of "Christian ethics" as a distinct field, at least in the Protestant context, has two different strands—one philosophical and the other more pastoral. The first begins in Europe, especially in Germany, where Protestant liberalism tried to save the soul of theology by rescuing its essence—the fatherhood of God and the brotherhood of man. The great exponent of this solution, of course, was Kant who, with his characterically admirable clarity, maintained that

> since the sacred narrative, which is employed solely on behalf of ecclesiastical faith, can have and, taken by itself, ought to have absolutely no influence upon the adoption of moral maxims, and since it is given to ecclesiastical faith only for the vivid presentation of its true object (virtue striving toward holiness), it follows that this narrative must at all times be taught and expounded in the interests of morality; and yet (because the common man especially has an enduring propensity within him to sink into passive belief) it must be inculcated painstakingly and repeatedly that true religion is to consist not in the knowing or considering of what God does or has done for our salvation, but in what we must do to become worthy of it.[8]

Thus morality becomes the "essence" of religion, but ironically it is understood in a manner that makes positive religious convictions secondary.

The other part of our story does not begin with such an explicit intellectual agenda, but involves a group of Protestant pastors in the late nineteenth and early twentieth centuries and their attempt to respond to the economic crisis of their people.[9] These men challenged the widespread assumption that poverty was the fault of the poor. Taking their bearings from the prophetic traditions of the Hebrew Scripture, they preached against political and economic structures which they believed were the roots of poverty. In the process they thought they discovered an old truth that had been lost through centuries of Christian accommodation with the status quo—namely that the essential characteristic of the Christian religion is its insistence on organic unity between religion and morality, theology and ethics.[10] For Christian salvation consists in nothing less than

> an attitude of love in which we would freely coordinate our life with the life of our fellows in obedience to the loving impulses of the spirit of God, thus taking our part in a divine organism of mutual service. God is the all-embracing source and exponent of the common life and good of mankind. When we submit to God, we submit to the supremacy of the common good. Salvation is the voluntary socializing of the soul.[11]

The "social gospel," as we learned to call this movement, cared little for the development of Christian ethics as a reflective mode of discourse. Rather Christian ethics meant for them the mobilization of the energy and power of the church for social renewal. That does not mean they were unsophisticated, for they were deeply influenced by Protestant liberalism, particularly the Kantianism of Albrecht Ritschl. Thus they were adamant in their opposition to all eschatologies that might justify passive Christian response to societal injustice. The social gospel sought "to develop the vision of the Church toward the future and to cooperate with the will of God which is shaping the destinies of humanity."[12] The social gospelers did not think of Christian ethics as a theoretical discipline concerned with the relation of religion and morality; rather Christian ethics was understood to be the exploration of those strategies that could best help to build "a social order in which the worth and freedom of every least human being will be honored and protected; in which the brotherhood of man will be expressed in the common possession of the economic resources of society; and in which the spiritual good of humanity will be set high above the private profit interests of materialistic groups."[13]

Yet with the social gospel for the first time serious courses began to be taught in American Protestant seminaries in Christian ethics—though they were often called Christian sociology. Taking their inspiration from the social gospel, these courses tended to be primarily concerned with why Christians should be committed to social justice and what economic and social strategy best accomplished that end. As a result, one of the central agendas of Christian ethics, still very much present, was a concern to make use of the social sciences for social analysis and action.[14] A Christian ethicist often became but a social scientist with a religious interest.

More importantly, however, this emphasis meant that the primary conversation partners for most Christian ethicists were not philosophers but social scientists.

It was not long, however, before some of the more naive theological and social assumptions of the social gospel began to be questioned in the light of experience and historical criticism. For example, the social gospel's conviction that "the first step in the salvation of mankind was the achievement of the personality of Jesus"[15] was rendered problematic by the increasing knowledge that the Gospels do not pretend to portray Jesus "the way he really was." Thus the attempt of liberal Protestantism to free Jesus from past "schemes of redemption," to base his divine quality not in metaphysical questions but on the free and ethical acts of his personality, ironically failed to meet the challenge of a critical approach to Scripture.

Moreover the social strategy of the social gospel was soon called into question by the change of attitude occasioned by World War I and the intractability of many social problems with regard to unambiguous solutions. In spite of their trenchant criticism of American capitalism, the social gospelers were after all completely committed to American progressive ideology and policies. They never doubted the uniqueness of the American experience nor entertained any critical doubt about the achievement of the American ideal, which they saw as nothing less than the realization of the Kingdom of God. The only question was how to bring the economic institutions of American life under the same spirit of cooperation that our political institutions had already achieved. The primary difference between "saved and unsaved organizations" for the social gospel is that the former are democratic and the latter are autocratic and competitive. Their attempt to turn American business into worker cooperatives was but the continuing attempt to create and secure "saved institutions."[16]

Though often more realistic and theologically profound than these aims suggest, it was clear that the movement started by the social gospel required a new theological rationale as well as social strategy.[17] "Christian ethics" became the discipline pledged to find just such a rationale and strategy. The great figure representing this project was Reinhold Niebuhr, who began his long career as a social gospel advocate, became its most powerful critic, and was quite possibly the last publically accessible and influential theologian in America. Niebuhr seemed to be saying something theological that was compelling to a wide range of people, including people in government, but as we shall see his accomplishment was fraught with ambiguity.

Niebuhr's criticism of the social gospel originally centered on his increasing dissatisfaction with its optimistic view of social institutions and change. His own experience as a pastor in Detroit during the great labor struggles taught him to distrust any idea that institutions qua institutions are capable of moral transformation, much less salvation.[18] Rather, under the influence of Marx, he began to appreciate the necessity of power and coercion as essential for achieving, not a saved society, but at least one that might be more relatively just.

Niebuhr's theological transformation was at least partly the result of his having to wrestle with the implications of this changed perspective on social action. Theologically, how can we come to terms with living in a world which might well require us to kill for a relative political good, and with the full knowledge that any achievement of some justice that may require violence necessarily results in some injustice. Thus Niebuhr came to conclude "the tragedy of human history consists precisely in the fact that human life cannot be creative without being destructive, that biological urges are enhanced and sublimated by demonic spirit and that this spirit cannot express itself without committing the sin of pride."[19]

Though by education a theological liberal, Niebuhr found the liberal optimistic understanding of mankind insufficient to sustain his social vision. He turned to that line of Christian theology represented by Augustine, Luther, and Kierkegaard, who emphasized humanity's fallenness and the need for a redemption not of human making. What we need to sustain us in the struggle for social justice is not, as the social gospel presumed, a grand idealistic vision, but a forgiveness which is necessarily a "moral achievement which is possible only when morality is transcended in religion."[20] Thus, for Niebuhr, Jesus' cross represents the ultimate sacrificial love that will always call into question every social and political order. Such a cross is necessary to sustain moral action in an inherently unjust world, for only as it stands on the edge of history do we have the basis for a hope that does not result in either despair or utopianism.[21]

Under Niebuhr's influence, the agenda of Christian ethics became, for many, the attempt to develop those theological, moral, and social insights necessary to sustain the ambiguous task of achieving more relatively just societies. Although this would seem to indicate a decisive break with his social gospel forebears, in fact

Niebuhr continued their most important theological and social presuppositions. Like them he assumed that the task of Christian ethics was to formulate the means for Christians to serve their societies, particularly American society. His understanding and justification of democracy was more sophisticated, but like the social gospelers he never questioned that Christianity has a peculiar relationship to democracy. For Niebuhr and the social gospelers the subject of Christian ethics was America.[22] They differed only on how nearly just such a society could be and the theological presupposition necessary to understand and sustain social involvement.

Niebuhr, far more than was seen at the time, continued to be essentially a liberal theologian. His emphasis on the sinfulness of man in his magisterial *Nature and Destiny of Man* led many to associate him with the "neo-orthodox" movement of Bultmann, Brunner, and Barth. Yet Niebuhr never shared Barth's theological rejection of liberalism as a basic theological strategy; he, like Bultmann, continued liberal theology's presumption that theology must be grounded in anthropology. Thus, his compelling portrayal of our sinfulness, which appeared *contra* liberal optimism, only continued the liberal attempt to demonstrate the intelligibility of theological language through its power to illuminate the human condition. In spite of Niebuhr's personally profound theological convictions, many secular thinkers accepted his anthropology and social theory without accepting his theological presuppositions.[23] And it is not clear in doing so that they were making a mistake, as the relations between Niebuhr's theological and ethical positions were never worked out with total clarity.

It was becoming increasingly apparent that Christian ethics must be written in a manner that allowed, and perhaps even encouraged, the separation of ethics from its religious roots. Perhaps this seems an odd result for a movement that began by asserting the "organic unity" between religion and ethics, but it was a development that was a necessary outgrowth of the social gospel commitments. The social gospelers were able to make direct appeals to their religious convictions to justify their social involvement, because in the late nineteenth century they could continue to presuppose that America was a "religious" or even a "Christian civilization and country." Niebuhr, more aware of our religious pluralism as well as the secular presuppositions underlying the American experience, attempted to provide a theological rationale for why Christians should not seek to make their theological commitments directly relevant for social policy and strategy. Even though he appeared extremely critical of the Lutheran law-Gospel distinction, in fact, he drew on the resources of that tradition, now reinterpreted in existential categories, to justify an understanding of justice and its attainment that did not require any direct theological rationale. Niebuhr's views prevailed for no other reason than that they were more in accord with the changing social and religious situation in America. American society was increasingly becoming a pluralist and secular society.[24] As a result Christian theologians, particularly as they dealt with social issues, felt it necessary to find ways in which their ethical conclusions could be separated from their theological framework. In the hope of securing societal good, the task of Christian ethics thus became the attempt to develop social strategies which people of goodwill could adopt even though they differed religiously and morally.

Therefore, even though Niebuhr criticized the Catholic natural law tradition for "absolutizing the relative," he nonetheless was a natural law thinker. Only the natural law, through which justice was defined, involves "not so much fixed standards of reason as they are rational efforts to apply the moral obligation, implied in the love commandment, to the complexities of life and the fact of sin, that is, to the situation created by the inclination of men to take advantage of each other."[25] In fact, Niebuhr's understanding of the "law of love" as an unavoidable aspect of the human condition, was in many ways a powerful attempt to provide a natural theology that could make the cross intelligible as a symbol of human existence.[26]

If Reinhold Niebuhr's work resulted in an ambiguous account of Christian ethics, in many ways his brother's work proved to be a more decisive challenge for that task. H. Richard Niebuhr was less concerned with the difficulties of sustaining the social imperatives of the social gospel; instead he tended to pursue the theological difficulties that the social gospel had occasioned. Deeply influenced by Troeltsch, he was acutely aware that the social gospeler's attempt to move directly from their theological convictions to social strategies was fraught not only with social ambiguities but with theological difficulties. Moreover, he was increasingly doubtful of any position which assumed that God could be used to underwrite mankind's interests, even if those interests were most impressive.

Under H. Richard Niebuhr's influence it became the business of Christian ethics to find the most adequate conceptual means to explicate what kind of moral implications might follow from Christian convictions.[27] Thus, Christian theologians began to give more serious attention to what philosophers were doing, hoping they would supply just such conceptual tools. But the kind of philosophical ethics to which Niebuhr's students looked had exactly the opposite effect. They learned from those philosophical sources that there was an inherent problem in trying to move from theological claims to normative recommendations, for in doing so one commits the "supernaturalistic fallacy."[28] As a result, theological ethicists began to pay even less attention to positive theological claims and instead attempted to show that formally a theological basis for ethics was not inherently incoherent and, in particular, that theological claims could underwrite anti-relativist and objectivist concerns.[29] In the hands of some, Christian ethics became but another form of meta-ethics. In the process, it became just as ahistorical as its philosophical counterpart.

That was certainly not a result which would have made H. Richard Niebuhr happy. Even though in his work Christian ethics was less an aid to action than an aid to understanding, he did not want Christian ethics to lose its theological agenda. On the contrary, his attempt to focus attention on the question "What is going on?" rather than "What we should do?" was an attempt to keep theological questions primary for ethical reflection. It was H. R. Niebuhr's task to show that the former question could only be answered adequately in theological terms. Thus in the *Responsible Self* he maintained the central Christian claim is "God is acting in all actions upon you. So respond to all actions upon you as to respond to his action."[30]

For H. R. Niebuhr the problem was not how to secure justice in an unjust world, but rather how to account for moral activity amid the relativities of history. His theological project was to provide a theological interpretation of the relativity of our existence so that the knowledge of our finitude was relativized by our relation to a God who alone deserves our complete loyalty. For H. R. Niebuhr the task of Christian ethics was a theological task, but, ironically, his own theology made it difficult to keep Christian ethics Christian. For the very idea of "Christian ethics" suggested a far too narrow conception of God to do justice to the relativities of our existence.[31]

In spite of the undeniable influence of Barth on H. R. Niebuhr, the influence of Schleiermacher was stronger. He strongly reacted against the Christocentrism of Barth, but just as importantly, like his brother he continued the liberal project to secure the intelligibility of theological discourse by demonstrating how it reflects as well as describes the human condition. Therefore while differing deeply with his brother on particular theological issues, he remained essentially in the tradition of Calvinism, as opposed to Reinhold's Lutheranism, but in many ways the structure of their theologies was similar. H. Richard Niebuhr's *The Responsible Self* was an attempt to analyze the inherent relatedness of human to human, human to nature, human and nature to God and yet to provide a satisfactory account of our need for an achievement of unity for the self. Such unity, he tried to show, at least made intelligible the confession by some of belief in a God who enters a covenant with his creation.[32]

The recent history of Christian ethics has largely been the story of the attempt to work out the set of problems bequeathed to us by the social gospel and the Niebuhrs. The other figure in the drama of late has been Roman Catholic moral theology. Under the impetus of Vatican II, Roman Catholic moral theologians have increasingly made contact with their Protestant counterparts in hopes they could learn from them how to put their natural law commitments in a more compelling theological framework. Protestant thinkers, struggling with the failure of their own tradition to develop discriminating forms of argument, looked to the Catholic casuistical tradition for help in thinking about such issues as marriage, abortion, and war. No thinker better represents this tendency of Protestant thinkers than Paul Ramsey. For Ramsey continues to assume that the task of Christian ethics is to address the American body politic. Yet now the issue is not the transformation of that polity but how the ethos that underwrites that polity can be sustained under the increasing onslaught of relativistic and consequential moral theories. The heir of both Niebuhrs, Ramsey found that neither the Niebuhrs nor Protestant thought in general provided the framework appropriate for disciplined ethical argument. Thus Ramsey looked to the Catholic tradition for principles to structure arguments that, at least in principle, would be publicly acceptable. Still, the influence of the Niebuhrs meant that Ramsey could not accept Roman Catholic assumptions about the relative autonomy of natural law and morality. As a result, his work clearly manifests the tension inherent in the development of Christian ethics—namely, a concern to provide a theological account of the moral life while at the same time underplaying the significance of theology for purposes of public discussion.[33]

Much of Ramsey's perspective on this wider set of issues was set by the situation ethics debate of the 1950s and '60s. Against

Joseph Fletcher's acceptance of act-utilitarianism as the most appropriate expression of Christian love, Ramsey insisted that Christian love must be in-principled. Moreover, the principles he thought best expressed or embodied their love were very much like the traditional Roman Catholic prohibitions against unjust life-taking, lying, sexual misconduct, and so on. Thus Ramsey maintained that Christian ethics, as well as Christian responsibility to maintain the best moral insights of Western civilization, was clearly aligned with deontological normative theories and against all consequentialism.[34]

Perhaps it is hard to see how this agenda has anything in common with the social gospel, but in many interesting ways Ramsey stands in continuity with that project. Even though he does not seek to underwrite a social activism that the social gospelers thought was required by the "organic unity between religion and ethics," Ramsey nonetheless shares their assumption that the first subject of Christian ethics is how to sustain the moral resources of American society. Moreover, like Reinhold Niebuhr he assumes that project requires an account sufficient to underwrite a politics of realism in which we see that we may well have to kill in the name of a lesser evil; but unlike Niebuhr, Ramsey sought to provide, through a theological reinterpretation of the just war tradition, a control on realism's tendency to consequentialism.[35]

Ramsey claims that what makes ethics Christian is that theological convictions are necessary to sustain the deontological commitments of our culture. Therefore, in Ramsey's work in such areas as medical ethics, most of the theology can be done in the "Preface" of his books. As a result, even many of those who are sympathetic with Ramsey's construal of the ethos of medicine in deontological terms see no reason why those deontological commitments require Ramsey's peculiar theological views about the significance of covenant love to sustain that ethos. Or again many may well side with Ramsey against the act-utilitarianism of Fletcher, but see no reason why that debate involves theological questions, since it is simply a straightforward philosophical matter involving whether a coherent deontological or teleological normative theory can be defended. All the talk about love by both Fletcher and Ramsey is but a confusion of the issue.

Therefore, contemporary theologians find themselves in a peculiar situation. Increasingly they turned to philosophical sources to help them illumine the logic of their ethical commitments, but just to the extent they did so it became harder to say what, if anything, Christian ethics had to contribute to discussions in ethics.

What they failed to see was that the very philosophical sources from which they drew to clarify the nature of their normative claims made it difficult to suggest how religious convictions might challenge just those philosophical frameworks. Thus theologians assumed, along with their philosophical colleagues, that ethics must basically be about dealing with quandaries, the only question being whether Christian convictions are more basically deontological or teleological or some as yet unspecified combination of the two.

The distinctive nature of theological ethics continued to be shown not in its philosophical expression, but rather in the range of interests each theologian addressed. By continuing to draw on the inspiration of the social gospel, the theologian continued to be concerned about questions of social and economic justice, marriage and the family, the status of the nation state, that hitherto had tended to be ignored by the philosopher. Yet, with the work of Rawls and the rise of journals such as *Philosophy and Public Affairs*, the theologian could no longer even claim that mark of distinction. The only alternatives left seemed to be to retreat to working in a confessional stance or analyzing the methodological issues and alternatives for understanding how theological ethics has been or should be done.

Much of the later work has been done by James Gustafson—a student of H. R. Niebuhr—who has sought through careful analysis of historical and current options within theological ethics to keep the discourse alive.[36] Though much of Gustafson's work is descriptive, his concerns are primarily constructive. It is, therefore, not accidental that Gustafson began to direct attention to the importance for ethics of the "sort of persons we are," of character and virtue, as the appropriate context for assessing the significance of theological language for ethical behavior.[37]

Above all, Gustafson's work is centered on the question "Can Ethics be Christian?" For him the Christian theologian's ethical task is done for the sake of a community which shares a set of common experiences and beliefs about God and his particular revelation in Jesus Christ.

The Christian community is not, however, the exclusive audience. Since the intention of the divine power for human wellbeing is universal in its scope, the historically particular medium through which that power is clarified for Christians also has universal significance. The theologian engaged in the task of "prescriptive" ethics formulates principles and values that can guide the actions of persons who do not belong to the Christian community. They will be persuasive to others, however, on the basis of supporting reasons different from those that Christians might respond to. In effect, the theologian moves from the particular Christian belief to a statement of their moral import in a more universal language. These statements will be persuasive to nonreligious persons only by the cogency of the argument that is made to show that the "historical particularity" sheds light on principles and values that other serious moral persons also perceive and also ought to adhere to. Indeed, since the Christian theologian shares in the general moral experiences of secular people, and since one facet of this work that is theologically warranted is the inferring of principles and values from common experience, he or she need not in every practical circumstance make a particular theological case for what is formulated. The theologian ought, however, to be able to make a Christian theological case if challenged to do so.[38]

Gustafson's reasoning is based on his theological belief that God's purposes are for "the well being of man and creation," and thus on most occasions the reasons that justify any moral act would justify the moral acts of Christians. The only case he can give that might be an exception to this is some Christians' commitment to nonviolent resistance to evil, since the justification of such a response clearly must rely on appeal to cetain "religious" reasons that go beyond what we mean by morality.[39]

If this is all that is to be gained by speaking theologically about morality, then one may well question if it is worth the effort. As I have tried to show through this brief history of the development of the "discipline" of Christian ethics, the primary subject theologically became how to keep Christian ethics Christian. This situation is no doubt partly the result of the changing historical and sociological stance of the churches vis-à-vis American society. For as that society increasingly becomes secular, Christians, insofar as they endeavor to remain political actors, must attempt to translate their convictions into a nontheological idiom. But once such a translation is accomplished, it becomes very unclear why they need the theological idiom in the first place.

The difficulty of making and keeping Christian ethics Christian, however, derives not only from social strategies, but, as we have seen, also from theological difficulties. For the recovery of the ethical significance of theological discourse was part of a theological movement within Protestantism that in large measure sought to avoid the more traditional particularistic claims of Christianity. Ironically, just to the extent that the development of Christian ethics as a field was a success, it reinforced the assumption that more positive theological convictions had little purchase on the way things are or should be. It is no wonder, therefore, that the dominant modes of philosophical ethics received little challenge from the theological community. Indeed, exactly to the contrary, theologians and religious thinkers have largely sought to show that the modes of argument and conclusions reached by philosophical ethicists are no different from those reached by ethicists working with more explicit religious presuppositions. The task of Christian ethics, both socially and philosophically, was not revision but accommodation.

3. A REVISION OF THEOLOGICAL ETHICS

I have tried to suggest why the development of Christian ethics during this century provided no significant alternative to the dominant modes of ethical reflection done by philosophers. To be sure there are aspects in the work of Rauschenbusch, the Niebuhrs, Ramsey, and Gustafson that stand in sharp contrast with the accepted mode of doing philosophical ethics. But it is simply the case that their work has failed to influence or even to be taken very seriously by others working in ethics in a nontheological context.

Of course part of the reason for that is more sociological than intellectual. Religion has increasingly become marginal in our culture, both politically and intellectually. Those types of religion that attempt to assert their relevancy in the social and political realm do so with a crudeness that only underwrites the general assumption that our society will do better to continue to relegate religious concerns to the private and subjective realm. This same kind of relegation has occurred in the intellectual realm, often with much less good reason. Few modern intellectuals feel the obligation to read the better work done in theology, because they prejudicially assume that theology must inherently be a form of special pleading.

As I suggested at the beginning, attempts to address this prejudice on its own terms are doomed to failure. The more theologians seek to find the means to translate theological convictions into terms acceptable to the nonbeliever, the more they substantiate the view that theology has little of importance to say in the area of ethics. It seems that the theologian is in a classical "no win" situation. Yet I think in many ways this is not the case. It may be that theology can make a virtue of necessity. In many ways the social and intellectual marginality of the church in our culture is an intellectual resource that can provide the opportunity to recover some of the more important aspects of Christian reflection, particularly concerning morality. As I have tried to suggest, the very development of "Christian ethics" as a branch of theology was inspired by an attempt to reawaken Christian social responsibility. But the very terms of that reawakening and its underlying theology had already accommodated itself far too much to the secular ethos. Therefore, in spite of the significant advances in Christian reflection represented by the development of Christian ethics, in many ways it failed to represent adequately the resources for ethical reflection within the Christian tradition. Thus one of the ironies is that many of the challenges represented by the essays in this book could have been made, and perhaps made even more forcefully, from a theological perspective. But they were not, and they were not because Christians generally and theologians in particular continued to assume that they had built a home within Western civilization that they had a stake in continuing.

As a result Christians have not provided themselves with an adequate understanding of their own convictions, and they have not contributed as they should to the ongoing discussion in which any person concerned to live better must engage. Our work in ethics as theologians has often come to resemble what Quentin Bell in his essay describes as "bad art." For like the artist who produces "bad art," theologians have accepted an account of the "social good" that fails to manifest the struggle inherently necessary for any good that is worth pursuing.

It is odd that Christians, of all people, could have made that mistake, since who could know better than they that the moral good is not an achievement easily accomplished by the many, but a demanding task that only a few master. Christians have not been called to do just the right, to observe the law, though doing the right and observing the law are not irrelevant to being good. Rather for Christians the moral life, at least scripturally, is seen as a journey through life sustained by fidelity to the cross of Christ, which brings a fulfillment no law can ever embody. Thus Aquinas says there is a twofold element in the Law of the Gospel. There is the chief element, namely, the grace of the Holy Ghost bestowed inwardly. And as to this the New Law justifies. Hence Augustine says: "There (that is, in the Old Testament) it is given in an inward manner, that they might be justified." The other element of the Evangelical Law is secondary; namely the teachings of faith, and those commandments which direct human affections and human actions. And as to this, the New Law does not justify. Hence the Apostle says: "The letter killeth, but the spirit quickeneth" (II Cor. 3:6), and Augustine explains this by saying that the letter denotes any writing that is external to man, even that of the moral precepts such as are contained in the Gospel. Therefore the letter, even of the Gospel would kill, unless there were the inward presence of the healing grace of faith.[40]

From such a perspective Christian thinkers, above all, should have been among the first to criticize the attempt to model the moral life primarily on the analogy of the law. Instead, fearing moral anarchy, like our philosophical colleagues, Christian thinkers assumed that questions of "right" were more primary than questions of good, that principles were more fundamental than virtues, that morality to be coherent required some one principle from which all others could be derived or tested, that the central task of moral reflection was to help us think straight about quandaries, and that we had to see the world as neatly divided into facts and values, rather than an existence filled with many valuational possibilities, some of which may well be in conflict. Perhaps most ironical, Christian theology attempted to deny the inherent historical and community-dependent nature of our moral convictions in the hopes that our "ethics" might be universally persuasive.

But as Schneewind reminds us, the justification of our moral principles and assertions cannot be done from the point of view of anyone, but rather requires a tradition of moral wisdom. Such a tradition is not a "deposit" of unchanging moral "truth," but is made up of the lives of men and women who are constantly testing and changing that tradition through their own struggle to live it. The maintenance of such a tradition requires a community across time sufficient to sustain the journey from one generation to the next. The Christian word for that community is church.[41]

It is my suspicion that if theologians are going to contribute to reflection on the moral life in our particular situation, they will do so exactly to the extent they can capture the significance of the church for determing the nature and content of Christian ethical reflection. This may seem an odd suggestion, for it seems such a move would only make the theologian that much further removed from being a serious conversation partner. It is assumed, by theologian and philosopher alike, that any distinctive contribution of theological ethics must begin with beliefs about God, Jesus, sin, etc., and the moral implications of those beliefs. And of course there is much truth to that. Yet the problem with putting the matter in that way is that such "beliefs" look like descriptions of existence, some kind of primitive metaphysics, that you must then try to analyze for their moral implications. To force Christian moral reflection into such a pattern is to make it appear but another philosophical account of the moral life.

But that is exactly what it is not. For Christian beliefs about God, Jesus, sin, the nature of human existence, and salvation are intelligible only if they are seen against the background of the church—i.e., a body of people who stand apart from the "world" because of the peculiar task of worshipping a God whom the world knows not. This is a point as much forgotten by Christian theologians as by secular philosophers, since the temptation is to make Christianity another "system of belief." Yet what was original about the first Christians was not the peculiarity of their beliefs, even beliefs about Jesus, but their social inventiveness in creating a community whose like had not been seen before. To say they believed in God is true but uninteresting. What is interesting is that they thought that their belief in God as they had encountered him in Jesus required the formation of a community distinct from the world exactly because of the kind of God he was. You cannot know what kind of God you disbelieve in, from a Christian perspective, unless you see what kind of community is necessary to worship him across time. The flabbiness of contemporary atheism is, thus, a judgment on the church's unwillingness to be a distinctive people.

Therefore, when asked to say something theological, especially when the questioner is seeking to understand the ethical significance of religious convictions, we should perhaps not say with Gustafson "God," but "Church." For the criticism of the emphasis in contemporary ethics on law, on rights, on principles, on quandaries, on facts distinguished from values, made by many of the essays in this book, is the result of trying to write ethics for anyone, as if ethics can be abstracted from any community. It is not surprising that the law becomes the primary analogue for such an ethic, as law is often seen as the minimal principles needed to secure order between people who share little in common. Ethics, like law, thus becomes the procedural means to settle disputes and resolve problems while leaving our individual "preferences" and desires to our own choice. To say more about morality requires not simply a conception of the good, but a tradition that carries the virtues necessary for training in movement toward the good.

That such is the case accounts for the peculiar incompleteness of many of the essays in this volume. They rightly criticize the thinness of much of contemporary ethical theory; yet they offer no persuasive alternative. Perhaps that is why, despite the power of their philosophical arguments, these essays, many of which have been published for many years, have had so little effect on the way philosophical ethics continues to be done. They point to the need for "revision," but the social and political practices necessary for that revision to be institutionalized are missing. Moreover, any attempts to create them appear utopian or totalitarian. Of course, appeals can be made to particular individuals as paradigms of the kind of moral life envisioned by these essays, but moral geniuses are never sufficient to sustain our best moral convictions. For sustenance we need a community to direct attention toward, and sustain the insights of, those who have become more nearly good.

As Christians we believe we not only need a community, but a community of a particular kind to live well morally. We need a people who are capable of being faithful to a way of life, even when that way of life may be in conflict with what passes as "morality" in the larger society. Christians are a people who have learned that belief in God requires that we learn to look upon ourselves as creatures rather than as creators. This necessarily creates a division between ourselves and others who persist in the pretentious assumption that we can and should be morally autonomous. Of course Christians are as prone to such pretensions as non-Christians. What distinguishes them is their willingness to belong to a community which embodies the stories, the rituals, and others committed to worshipping God. Such a community, we believe, must challenge our prideful pretensions as well as provide the skills for the humility necessary for becoming not just good, but holy.

Theologians, therefore, have something significant to say about ethics, but they will not say it significantly if they try to disguise the fact that they think, write, and speak out of and to a distinctive community. Their first task is not, as has been assumed by many working in Christian ethics and still under the spell of Christendom, to write as though Christian commitments make no difference in the sense that they only underwrite what everyone already in principle can know, but rather to show the difference those commitments make. At least by doing that, philosophers may have some idea how the attempt to avoid presuming any tradition or community may distort their account of the moral life as well as moral rationality. Our task as theologians remains what it has always been—namely to exploit the considerable resources embodied in particular Christian convictions which sustain our ability to be a community faithful to our belief that we are creatures of a graceful God. If we do that, we may well discover that we are speaking to more than just our fellow Christians, for others as a result may well find we have something interesting to say.

Of course, it may still be objected that such an ethic, insofar as it entails beliefs in God and claims about his relation to Israel and Jesus Christ, cannot be valid, because such beliefs are inherently incoherent. There is no quick or easy response to such a challenge, since many different kinds of reasons are given for assuming the invalidity of belief in God and they can only be addressed one at a time. But at least if the agenda were the kind suggested by Baier's, Weil's, and Fingarette's essays, we would have a basis for a discussion.

Baier rightly calls our attention to the need for the virtues of faith and hope to sustain the moral enterprise. Her secular faith in the possibility of a community of just persons is in fact nothing less than a counterchurch. Moreover, there is much to be said for such a faith (and hope) as well as its reasonableness. But there is a peculiar tension between her account of such a faith and Murdoch's claim that moral philosophy cannot escape the fact that sin must be recognized as an unavoidable aspect of the human condition. If Murdoch is right to challenge the optimistic assumption that goodness comes through knowing the right principles and thinking clearly, then Baier has provided us with insufficient grounds to place our faith in a future community of just persons. That is not to say belief in God is necessary to counter our sinfulness, but rather that our sinfulness at least helps us understand why a people who believe in the kind of God Christians worship find they must in some ways be a separate people—that is, a people who have at least pledged to live righteously.

More profoundly, Weil challenges a secular faith as she recognizes that we live in a world that simply is not governed by man. Rather, our lives are determined by forces that are all the more coercive because we assume that we possess them rather than they possessing us. The faith necessary to sustain the moral life, therefore, is not simply a hope in the possibility of a community of just persons, but much more; it is a faith that would sustain us through the suffering that seems to be an inherent requirement for anyone who wishes to be not just law-abiding, but good.

For as Weil suggests, the only means of breaking the possession of force over our lives is the respect of life in another when we have to castrate ourselves of all yearning for it. Such a commitment is heartbreaking, for it requires a generosity that is, as she suggests, "godlike." It is testimony of those who seem to possess such generosity that finally they are such not by their own power, but by a gift of a greater power. Certainly such testimony does not compel belief in God, or even mean that the power which provides such a gift is necessarily the same as the one whom Christians believe moves the sun and the stars, but it at least provides the basis for the serious consideration of such a faith.

Only if God is such a power is he worthy of belief. For only in such a power, as Fingarette indicates, can we face the wild and untamed nature of our existence and yet still sustain the moral endeavor. What such a power requires is that we face the truth—a truth perhaps too awesome to sustain Baier's faith in a community of just people—that the power that grasps us, that the power that gifts us with a generosity that is frightening, is God—and we are not. Such a God, as Gustafson suggests, did not bring us into being and create our world for our survival and flourishing.[42] Rather the truth, and it is a truth with immense ethical implications, is that we live truthfully when we learn to see our lives as a glorification of God.

If theologians wrote their ethics presupposing such a God, they might well find that they have something interesting to contribute to discussion of the morally worthy life. Rather than spending our time on questions of the supernaturalistic fallacy or the relation of religion and morality, we must deal, as Murdoch suggests, with questions of truth and why we are so hesitant to face the world without illusion. If we dealt with those questions, we might well find that what we have to say theologically has more significance than we had anticipated.

NOTES

1. James Gustafson, "Say Something Theological," 1981 *Nora and Edward Ryerson Lecture* (Chicago: University of Chicago, 1981), p. 3. Gustafson notes that he has the presence of mind to say "God."

2. This development is as true of Roman Catholics as it has been of Protestant theology. See, for example, Thomas Sheehan's review of Karl Rahner's *Foundations of Christian Faith*, in which he applauds Rahner's attempt to carry out Feuerbach's program of transforming theology into anthropology. Of course, the odd thing about Sheehan's enthusiasm for this move is that Feuerbach assumed that to do so was the agenda of atheism, not theism. "The Drama of Karl Rahner," *New York Review of Books*, February 4, 1981, pp. 13-14.

3. For example, we would have liked to have used John Howard Yoder's, "What Would You Do If...? An Exercise in Situation Ethics," *Journal of Religious Ethics* 2, 1 (Fall 1974), pp. 81-106, but felt that his argument's effectiveness required the reader to be more familiar with Yoder's ecclesiological presuppositions than could be assumed.

4. See, for example, Ed Long's fine article "Soteriological Implications of Norm and Context," in *Norm and Context in Christian Ethics*, edited by Gene Outka and Paul Ramsey (New York: Scribner's, 1968), pp. 265-296.

5. In particular, see Reinhold Niebuhr, *The Self and the Dramas of History* (New York: Scribner's, 1955).

6. James Gustafson, *Can Ethics Be Christian?* (Chicago: University of Chicago Press, 1975).

7. I am keenly aware of the inadequacy of the brief overview of the development of Christian ethics over the last century. Not only do I leave out of the account many of the main actors, even those I treat are not analyzed with the nuance they deserve. I hope soon to write a more adequate book-length account that will do justice to this complex story. However, for the purposes of this essay I thought it worthwhile to tell the history in a somewhat contentious manner, since my interests are more systematic than historical. Moreover, I am certainly ready to defend the interpretive features of my account, even though I have not taken the time here to document them adequately.

8. Immanuel Kant, *Religion Within the Limits of Reason Alone*, translated with an introduction by Theodore Greene and Hoyt Hudson (New York: Harper, 1960), p. 123.

9. C. H. Hopkins, *The Rise of the Social Gospel in American Protestantism, 1865-1915* (New Haven: Yale University Press, 1940).

10. Walter Rauschenbusch, *A Theology for the Social Gospel* (Nashville: Abingdon Press, 1945), p. 140.

11. Ibid., pp. 98-99.

12. Ibid., p. 210.

13. Ibid., p. 224.

14. For example, in his fine article on one of the early social gospelers, Francis Greenwood Peabody, David Little observes that "like many of his contemporaries, Peabody recommended wide exposure to the methods of social science as the basis for sound moral action. Since the ethical aims of true religion and manifest pattern of social development were believed to be rooted in one and the same phenomenon, inductive empirical investigation of social life could only complement and enrich the moral task. He is very

clear about this: 'Ethics is finally social science and social science is ethics. Ethics is the end of sociology.' " "Francis Greenwood Peabody," *Harvard Library Bulletin* 15, 3 (July 1967), pp. 287-300.

15. Rauschenbusch, p. 151.

16. Rauschenbusch, pp. 112-113.

17. For a particularly able defense of Rauschenbusch see Max Stackhouse's, "The Continuing Importance of Walter Rauschenbusch," which introduces Rauschenbusch's *The Righteousness of the Kingdom* (Nashville: Abingdon Press, 1968), pp. 13-59.

18. Niebuhr's reflections on his change of mind can be found in his *Leaves from the Notebook of a Tamed Cynic* (New York: Living Age Books, 1957). See also Niebuhr's, "Intellectual Autobiography," in *Reinhold Niebuhr: His Religious, Social, and Political Thought*, ed. Charles Kegley and Robert Bretall (New York: Macmillan, 1956), pp. 1-24.

19. Reinhold Niebuhr, *The Nature and Destiny of Man*, (New York: Scribner's, 1941), 1:10-11.

20. Reinhold Niebuhr, *An Interpretation of Christian Ethics* (New York: Living Age Books, 1956), p. 201. It is interesting that Niebuhr's stress on forgiveness as the hallmark of Christian ethics is not carried forward in his later work. Rather his emphasis is almost entirely on self-sacrificial love. It is my hunch that Niebuhr was much closer to being right by focusing on forgiveness than love as the more important for the systematic display of Christian ethics.

21. In his *Christian Realism and Liberation Theology* (Maryknoll: Orbis Books, 1981) Dennis McCann suggests that rather than providing a strategy for social action Niebuhr is best interpreted as trying to form a "spirituality" necessary to sustain political activity. That seems to me to be a particularly fruitful way to read Niebuhr, as it helps account for the lack of any conceptually clear connections between Niebuhr's theological views and his strategic judgments.

22. See, for example, Niebuhr's *The Children of Light and the Children of Darkness* (New York: Scribner's, 1944) and *The Irony of American History* (New York: Scribner, 1962). This perhaps helps explain the oft-made observation that Niebuhr paid almost no attention to the social significance of the church—for finally, in spite of all the trenchant criticism he directed at America, America was in fact his church. Thus the criticism that Niebuhr failed to sustain his trenchant perspective in the last years of his life in some ways is misplaced, since it fails to note that Niebuhr from beginning to end was involved in a stormy love affair with America. In some ways the social gospelers were less accommodationist than Niebuhr in this respect; Rauschenbusch, in particular, assumed the necessity of the church to stand as a critic against American society.

The importance of America as the subject of Christian ethics can also be seen in the tendency of many Christian ethicists to think of ethics as a form of "American studies." H. R. Niebuhr's *The Kingdom of God in America* (New York: Harper, 1937) remains the classical text for this genre.

23. Niebuhr profoundly influenced such people as Hans Morganthau,
George Kennan, Arthur Schlesinger, Jr., and many others. It is, perhaps, a
mark of the instability of Niebuhr's position that often both sides of a
political issue, particularly in foreign affairs, can claim with some justice to
be Niebuhrians, the most recent example being the controversy surrounding Ernest Lefever's appointment in the Reagan administration.
24. Arthur Schlesinger documents this well in his "The Political
Philosophy of Reinhold Niebuhr," in *Reinhold Niebuhr: His Religious,
Social, and Political Thought,* pp. 125-150. Schlesinger rightly notes that
Niebuhr, the penetrating critic of the social gospel and of pragmatism, ended up "the powerful reinterpreter and champion of both. It was the triumph
of his own remarkable analysis that it took what was valuable in each,
rescued each by defining for each the limits of validity, and, in the end, gave
the essential purposes of both new power and vitality. No man has had as
much influence as a preacher in this generation; no preacher has had as
much influence in the secular world" (p. 149).
25. Reinhold Niebuhr, *Faith and History* (New York: Scribner's, 1951),
pp. 188-189.
26. Niebuhr's stress on the sinfulness of man leads some to forget that
for Niebuhr theology is still primarily anthropology. As a result Niebuhr
never answered satisfactorily how the cross of Jesus is necessary for our
understanding adequately why the cross is the most adequate symbol of
"the perfection of *agape* which transcends all particular norms of justice
and mutuality in history." (*Nature and Destiny of Man* 2:74).
27. For the best short introduction to H. R. Niebuhr's work see James
Gustafson, "Introduction," in H. R. Niebuhr, *The Responsible Self: An
Essay in Christian Moral Philosophy* (New York: Harper and Row, 1963),
pp. 6-41.
28. H. R. Niebuhr was not himself very taken with ethics done out of
the analytical tradition, but instead was influenced more by the pragmatist
tradition of Royce and Perry. However, a latter generation of students,
trained by Gustafson, turned increasingly to Moore, Ross, Hare, in attempts to think through the problems they had inherited from Niebuhr.
29. Art Dyck's enthusiasm for and theological justification of the
"ideal-observer" theory is a good example of this tendency. See his *On
Human Care: An Introduction to Ethics* (Nashville: Abingdon, 1977).
30. H. R. Niebuhr, *The Responsible Self,* p. 126.
31. For H. R. Niebuhr, Jesus is normative only as he "represents the
incarnation of radical faith," which is faith that "Being is God, or better,
that the principle of being, the source of all things and the power by which
they exist, is good, as good for them and good to them" (*Radical
Monotheism and Western Culture* [New York: Harper and Row, 1960], p.
38).
32. Thus he says, "Man responsive and responsible before nature, fitting his actions into those of nature; man responsive in political or economic
or cultural society as responsible citizen; responsible businessman, respon-

sible educator, responsible scientist, responsible parent, responsible church-man—such men we know and understand. But what ties all these respon-sivities and responsibilities together and where is the responsible *self* among all these roles played by the individual being? Can it be located within the self, as though by some mighty act of self-making it brought itself into being as one 'I' among these many systems of interpretation and response? The self as one self among all the systematized reactions in which it engages seems to be the counterpart of a unity that lies beyond, yet ex-presses itself in, all the manifold systems of actions upon it. In religious language, the soul and God belong together; or otherwise stated, I am one within myself as I encounter the One in all that acts upon me" (*The Respon-sible Self*, p. 122).

33. The theological side of Ramsey's work was more apparent in his ear-ly work where he was emphatic that "natural law" must be transformed by love. See in particular his *War and the Christian Conscience* (Durham, N.C.: Duke University Press, 1961). Ramsey's shift to the motif of covenant fidelity as the central metaphor for Christian reflection also seems to have been accompanied with a greater appreciation for the continuity between the "natural" covenants we find in our lives and that which God has made with us. As a result he is able to proceed with much less direct appeal to theological warrants. See, for example, his *The Patient as Person* (New Haven: Yale University Press, 1970).

34. Thus Ramsey argues that "Protestant Christian ethics is often too profoundly personal to be ethically relevant, if in this is included even a minimum of concern for the social habits and customs of a people. Ordinarily, we do not take Christian ethics with enough seriousness to illumine the path that men, women, and *society* should follow today. This suggests that only some form of rule-agapism, and not act-agapism, can be consistent with the elaboration of a Christian's social responsibilities. No social morality ever was founded, or ever will be founded, upon a situational ethic" (*Deeds and Rules in Christian Ethics* [New York: Scribner's, 1967], p. 20).

35. Ramsey's profound debt to Niebuhr can be most clearly seen in his *The Just War: Force and Political Responsibility* (New York: Scribner's, 1968). There Ramsey, like Niebuhr, argues that the failure of all peace movements is they presume the illusion that force can be avoided in politics and as a result only increase the likelihood of war. In contrast the just war tradition influenced by the theological insights of Augustine rightly sees that war can never be fought for peace, but only for more relative just ends. Thus Ramsey argues the ethos necessary to control violence through just war principles must ultimately draw on religious presuppositions. For only if you think death is not ultimate power over life can you be willing to ex-pose yourself to death and to kill others for the limited moral goods of political community.

36. See, for example, Gustafson's *Christian Ethics and the Community* (Philadelphia: Pilgrim Press, 1971) and *Theology and Christian Ethics*

(Philadelphia: Pilgrim Press, 1974), both of which are collections of his essays that attempt to bring some intellectual clarity to the activity of other Christian ethicists.

37. This emphasis, of course, is but an indication of Gustafson's indebtedness to H. R. Niebuhr's attempt to identify the central issue of Christian ethics as that of the "self." Unfortunately many of the interpreters of H. R. Niebuhr tend to stress more his account of "responsibility" and, as a result, fail to see that Niebuhr's primary concern was the "self."

38. Gustafson, *Can Ethics Be Christian?*, p. 163.

39. It is telling, I think, that in his recent constructive work, *Ethics from a Theocentric Perspective* (Chicago: University of Chicago Press, 1981) Gustafson thinks John Howard Yoder's sectarian stance to be the most intelligible alternative to his own position.

40. Thomas Aquinas, *Summa Theologia*, I–II.106.2 translated by Fathers of the English Dominican Province (Chicago: William Benton Publisher, 1952). Many others besides Aquinas could be quoted to substantiate this point. I purposely chose Aquinas, since many who defend a natural law approach to Christian ethics appeal to him as their primary authority. Yet as the quotation makes clear, Aquinas assumed that an adequate theological ethics could not be limited to or based on an analogy with law.

41. For a fuller account of this perspective see my *A Community of Character: Toward a Constructive Christian Social Ethic* (Notre Dame, Ind.: University of Notre Dame Press, 1981).

42. See Gustafson's *Ethics from a Theocentric Perspective*, vol. 1 (Chicago: University of Chicago Press, 1981). For a critical appraisal of this important book see my "God the Measurer," *Journal of Religion* (forthcoming).

3

Against Dryness:
A Polemical Sketch

Iris Murdoch

The complaints which I wish to make are concerned primarily with prose, not with poetry, and primarily with novels, not with drama; and they are brief, simplified, abstract, and possibly insular. They are not to be construed as implying any precise picture of "the function of the writer." It is the function of the writer to write the best book he knows how to write. These remarks have to do with the background to present-day literature, in Liberal democracies in general and Welfare States in particular, in a sense in which this must be the concern of any serious critic.

We live in a scientific and anti-metaphysical age in which the dogmas, images, and precepts of religion have lost much of their power. We have not recovered from two wars and the experience of Hitler. We are also the heirs of the Enlightenment, Romanticism, and the Liberal tradition. These are the elements of our dilemma: whose chief feature, in my view, is that we have been left with far too shallow and flimsy an idea of human personality. I shall explain this.

Philosophy, like the newspapers, is both the guide and the mirror of its age. Let us look quickly at Anglo-Saxon philosophy and at French philosophy and see what picture of human personality we can gain from these two depositories of wisdom. Upon Anglo-Saxon philosophy the two most profound influences have been Hume and Kant: and it is not difficult to see in the current philosophical conception of the person the work of these two great thinkers. This conception consists in the joining of a materialistic behaviourism with a dramatic view of the individual as a solitary will. These subtly

This essay from *Encounter* vol. 16, no. 1 (January 1961): 16–20 is reprinted by permission.

give support to each other. From Hume through Bertrand Russell, with friendly help from mathematical logic and science, we derive the idea that reality is finally a quantity of material atoms and that significant discourse must relate itself directly or indirectly to reality so conceived. This position was most picturesquely summed up in Wittgenstein's *Tractatus*. Recent philosophy, especially the later work of Wittgenstein and the work of Gilbert Ryle derivative therefrom, alters this a little. The atomic Humian picture is abandoned in favour of a type of conceptual analysis (in many ways admirable) which emphasises the structural dependence of concepts upon the public language in which they are framed. This analysis has important results in the philosophy of mind, where it issues in modified behaviourism. Roughly: my inner life, for me just as for others, is identifiable as existing only through the application to it of public concepts, concepts which can only be constructed on the basis of overt behaviour.

This is one side of the picture, the Humian and post-Humian side. On the other side, we derive from Kant, and also Hobbes and Bentham through John Stuart Mill, a picture of the individual as a free rational will. With the removal of Kant's metaphysical background this individual is seen as alone. (He is in a certain sense alone on Kant's view also, that is: not confronted with real dissimilar others.) With the addition of some utilitarian optimism he is seen as eminently educable. With the addition of some modern psychology he is seen as capable of self-knowledge by methods agreeable to science and common sense. So we have the modern man, as he appears in many recent works on ethics and I believe also to a large extent in the popular consciousness.

We meet, for instance, a refined picture of this man in Stuart Hampshire's book *Thought and Action*. He is rational and totally free except in so far as, in the most ordinary lawcourt and commonsensical sense, his degree of self-awareness may vary. He is morally speaking monarch of all he surveys and totally responsible for his actions. Nothing transcends him. His moral language is a practical pointer, the instrument of his choices, the indication of his preferences. His inner life is resolved into his acts and choices, and his beliefs, which are also acts, since a belief can only be identified through its expression. His moral arguments are references to empirical facts backed up by decisions. The only moral word which he requires is "good" (or "right"), the word which expresses decision. His rationality expresses itself in awareness of the facts, whether about the world or about himself. The virtue which is fundamental to him is sincerity.

If we turn to French philosophy we may see, at least in that section of it which has most caught the popular imagination, I mean in the work of Jean-Paul Sartre, essentially the same picture. It is interesting how extremely Kantian this picture is, for all Sartre's indebtedness to Hegelian sources. Again, the individual is pictured as solitary and totally free. There is no transcendent reality, there are no degrees of freedom. On the one hand there is the mass of psychological desires and social habits and prejudices, on the other hand there is the will. Certain dramas, more Hegelian in character, are of course enacted within the soul; but the isolation of the will remains. Hence *angoisse*. Hence, too, the special anti-bourgeois flavour of Sartre's philosophy which makes it appeal to many intellectuals: the ordinary traditional picture of personality and the virtues lies under suspicion of *mauvaise foi*. Again the only real virtue is sincerity. It is, I think, no accident that, however much philosophical and other criticism Sartre may receive, this powerful picture has caught our imagination. The Marxist critics may plausibly claim that it represents the essence of the Liberal theory of personality.

It will be pointed out that other phenomenological theories (leaving aside Marxism) have attempted to do what Sartre has failed to do, and that there are notable philosophers who have offered a different picture of the soul. Yes; yet from my own knowledge of the scene I would doubt whether any (non-Marxist) account of human personality has yet emerged from phenomenology which is fundamentally unlike the one which I have described and can vie with it in imaginative power. It may be said that philosophy cannot in fact produce such an account. I am not sure about this, nor is this large question my concern here. I express merely my belief that, for the Liberal world, philosophy is not in fact at present able to offer us any other complete and powerful picture of the soul. I return now to England and the Anglo-Saxon tradition.

The Welfare State has come about as a result, largely, of socialist thinking and socialist endeavour. It has seemed to bring a certain struggle to an end; and with that ending has come a lassitude about fundamentals. If we compare the language of the original Labour Party constitution with that of its recent successor we see an impoverishment of thinking and language which is typical. The Welfare State is the reward of "empiricism in politics." It has represented to us a set of thoroughly desirable but limited ends, which could be conceived in *non-theoretical terms*; and in pursuing it, in allowing the idea of it to dominate the more naturally theoretical wing of our political scene, we have to a large extent lost our theories. Our central conception is still a debilitated form of Mill's equation: happiness equals freedom equals personality. There should have been a revolt against utilitarianism; but for many reasons it has not taken place. In 1903 John Maynard Keynes and his friends welcomed the philosophy of G. E. Moore because Moore reinstated the concept of experience, Moore directed attention away from the mechanics of action and towards the inner life. But Moore's "experience" was too shallow a concept; and a scientific age with simple attainable empirical aims has preferred a more behaviouristic philosophy.

What have we lost here? And what have we perhaps never had? We have suffered a general loss of concepts, the loss of a moral and political vocabulary. We no longer use a spread-out substantial picture of the manifold virtues of man and society. We no longer see man against a background of values, of realities, which transcend him. We picture man as a brave naked will surrounded by an easily comprehended empirical world. For the hard idea of truth we have substituted a facile idea of sincerity. What we have never had, of course, is a satisfactory Liberal theory of personality, a theory of man as free and separate and related to a rich and complicated world from which, as a moral being, he has much to learn. We have bought the Liberal theory as it stands, because we have wished to encourage people to think of themselves as free, at the cost of surrendering the background.

We have never solved the problems about human personality posed by the Enlightenment. Between the various concepts available to us the real question has escaped: and now, in a curious way, our present situation is analogous to an eighteenth-century one. We retain a rationalistic optimism about the beneficent results of education, or rather technology. We combine this with a romantic conception of "the human condition," a picture of the individual as stripped and solitary: a conception which has, since Hitler, gained a peculiar intensity.

The eighteenth century was an era of rationalistic allegories and moral tales. The nineteenth century (roughly) was the great era of the novel; and the novel throve upon a dynamic merging of the idea of person with the idea of class. Because nineteenth-century society was dynamic and interesting and because (to use a Marxist notion) the type and the individual could there be seen as merged, the solution of the eighteenth-century problem could be put off. It has been put off till now. Now that the structure of society is less interesting and less alive than it was in the nineteenth century, and now that Welfare economics have removed certain incentives to thinking, and now that the values of science are so much taken for granted, we confront in a particularly dark and confusing form a dilemma which has been with us implicitly since the Enlightenment, or since the beginning, wherever exactly one wishes to place it, of the modern Liberal world.

If we consider twentieth-century literature as compared with nineteenth-century literature, we notice certain significant contrasts. I said that, in a way, we were back in the eighteenth century, the era of rationalistic allegories and moral tales, the era when the idea of human nature was unitary and single. The nineteenth-century novel (I use these terms boldly and roughly: of course there were exceptions) was not concerned with "the human condition," it was concerned with real various individuals struggling in society. The twentieth-century novel is usually either crystalline or journalistic; that is, it is either a small quasi-allegorical object portraying the human condition and not containing "characters" in the nineteenth-century sense, or else it is a large shapeless quasi-documentary object, the degenerate descendant of the nineteenth-century novel, telling, with pale conventional characters, some straightforward story enlivened with empirical facts. Neither of these kinds of literature engages with the problem that I mentioned above.

It may readily be noted that if our prose fiction is either crystalline or journalistic, the crystalline works are usually the better ones. They are what the more serious writers want to create. We may recall the ideal of "dryness" which we associate with the symbolist movement, with writers such as T. E. Hulme and T. S. Eliot, with Paul Valery, with Wittgenstein. This "dryness" (smallness, clearness, self-containedness) is a nemesis of Romanticism. Indeed it *is* Romanticism in a later phase. The pure, clean, self-contained "symbol," the exemplar incidentally of what Kant, ancestor of both Liberalism and Romanticism, required art to be, is the analogue of the lonely self-contained individual. It is what is left to the otherworldliness of Romanticism when the "messy" humanitarian and revolutionary elements have spent their force. The temptation of art, a temptation to which every work of art yields except the greatest ones, is to console. The modern writer, frightened of technology and (in England) abandoned by philosophy and (in France) presented with simplified dramatic theories, attempts to console us by myths or by stories.

On the whole: his truth is sincerity and his imagination is fantasy. Fantasy operates either with shapeless day-dreams (the journalistic story) or with small myths, toys, crystals. Each in his own way produces a sort of "dream necessity." Neither grapples with reality, hence "fantasy," not "imagination."

The proper home of the symbol, in the "symbolist" sense, is poetry. Even there it may play an equivocal role, since there is something in symbolism which is inimical to words, out of which, we have been reminded, poems are constructed. Certainly the invasion of other areas by what I may call, for short, "symbolist ideals," has helped to bring about a decline of prose. Eloquence is out of fashion; even "style," except in a very austere sense of this term, is out of fashion.

T. S. Eliot and Jean-Paul Sartre, dissimilar enough as thinkers, both tend to undervalue prose and to deny it any *imaginative* function. Poetry is the creation of linguistic quasi-things; prose is for explanation and exposition, it is essentially didactic, documentary, informative, Prose is ideally transparent; it is only *faute de mieux* written in words. The influential modern stylist is Hemingway. It would be almost inconceivable now to write like Landor. Most modern English novels indeed are not *written*. One feels they could slip into some other medium without much loss. It takes a foreigner like Nabokov or an Irishman like Beckett to animate prose language into an imaginative stuff in its own right.

Tolstoy, who said that art was an expression of the religious perception of the age, was nearer the truth than Kant, who saw it as the imagination in a frolic with the understanding. The connection between art and the moral life has languished because we are losing our sense of form and structure in the moral world itself. Linguistic and existentialist behaviourism, our Romantic philosophy, has reduced our vocabulary and simplified and impoverished our view of the inner life. It is natural that a Liberal democratic society will not be concerned with techniques of improvement, will deny that virtue is knowledge, will emphasise choice at the expense of vision; and a Welfare State will weaken the incentives to investigate the bases of a Liberal democratic society. For political purposes we have been encouraged to think of ourselves as totally free and responsible, knowing everything we need to know for the important purposes of life. But this is one of the things of which Hume said that it may be true in politics but false in fact; and is it really true in politics? We need a post-Kantian unromantic Liberalism with a different image of freedom.

The technique of becoming free is more difficult than John Stuart Mill imagined. We need more concepts than our philosophies have furnished us with. We need to be enabled to think in terms of degrees of freedom, and to picture, in a non-metaphysical, non-totalitarian, and non-religious sense, the transcendence of reality. A simpleminded faith in science, together with the assumption that we are all rational and totally free, engenders a dangerous lack of curiosity about the real world, a failure to appreciate the difficulties of knowing it. We need to return from the self-centred concept of sincerity to the other-centred concept of truth. We are not isolated free choosers, monarchs of all we survey, but benighted creatures sunk in a reality whose nature we are constantly and overwhelmingly tempted to deform by fantasy. Our current picture of freedom encourages a dream-like facility; whereas what we require is a renewed sense of the difficulty and complexity of the moral life and the opacity of persons. We need more concepts in terms of which to picture the substance of our being; it is through an enriching and deepening of concepts that moral progress takes place. Simone Weil said that morality was a matter of attention, not of will. We need a new vocabulary of attention.

It is here that literature is so important, especially since it has taken over some of the tasks formerly performed by philosophy. Through literature we can re-discover a sense of the density of our lives. Literature can arm us against consolation and fantasy and can help us to recover from the ailments of Romanticism. If it can be said to have a task, now, that surely is its task. But if it is to perform it, prose must recover its former glory; eloquence and discourse must return. I would connect eloquence with the attempt to speak the truth. I think here of the work of Albert Camus. All his novels were *written*; but the last one, though less striking and successful than the first two, seems to me to have been a more serious attempt upon the truth: and illustrates what I mean by eloquence.

It is curious that modern literature, which is so much concerned with violence, contains so few convincing pictures of evil.

Our inability to imagine evil is a consequence of the facile, dramatic and, in spite of Hitler, optimistic picture of ourselves with which we work. Our difficulty about form, about images—our tendency to produce works which are either crystalline or journalistic—is a symptom of our situation. Form itself can be a temptation, making the work of art into a small myth which is a self-contained and indeed self-satisfied individual. We need to turn our attention away from the consoling dream necessity of Romanticism, away from the dry symbol, the bogus individual, the false whole, towards the real impenetrable human person. That this person is substantial, impenetrable, individual, indefinable, and valuable is after all the fundamental tenet of Liberalism.

It is here, however much one may criticise the emptiness of the Liberal idea of freedom, however much one may talk in terms of restoring a lost unity, that one is forever at odds with Marxism. Reality is not a given whole. An understanding of this, a respect for the contingent, is essential to imagination as opposed to fantasy. Our sense of form, which is an aspect of our desire for consolation, can be a danger to our sense of reality as a rich receding background. Against the consolations of form, the clean crystalline work, the simplified fantasy-myth, we must pit the destructive power of the now so unfashionable naturalistic idea of character.

Real people are destructive of myth, contingency is destructive of fantasy and opens the way for imagination. Think of the Russians, those great masters of the contingent. Too much contingency of course may turn art into journalism. But since reality is incomplete, art must not be too much afraid of incompleteness. Literature must always represent a battle between real people and images; and what it requires now is a much stronger and more complex conception of the former.

In morals and politics we have stripped ourselves of concepts. Literature, in curing its own ills, can give us a new vocabulary of experience, and a truer picture of freedom. With this, renewing our sense of distance, we may remind ourselves that art too lives in a region where all human endeavour is failure. Perhaps only Shakespeare manages to create at the highest level both images and people; and even *Hamlet* looks second-rate compared with *Lear*. Only the very greatest art invigorates without consoling, and defeats our attempts, in W. H. Auden's words, to use it as magic.

4

Fallacies in Moral Philosophy

Stuart Hampshire

1. In 1912 there appeared in *Mind* an article by the late Professor Prichard entitled "Does Moral Philosophy rest on a Mistake?" I wish to ask the same question about contemporary moral philosophy, but to suggest different reasons for an affirmative answer. Most recent academic discussions of moral philosophy have directly or indirectly reflected the conception of the subject-matter of moral philosophy which is stated or implied in Professor Prichard's article; and this conception of the subject was in turn directly derived from Kant. Kant's influence has been so great, that it is now difficult to realise how revolutionary it was; yet I think that his main thesis, now generally accepted without question by philosophers as the starting-point of moral philosophy, had not been advocated, or even seriously entertained, by any philosopher who preceded him. I shall suggest that the *un-bridgeable* separation between moral judgments and factual judgments, which Kant introduced, has had the effect, in association with certain logical assumptions, of leading philosophers away from the primary and proper questions of moral philosophy.[1]

What I shall summarily call the post-Kantian thesis, now so widely accepted without question, is: there is an unbridgeable logical gulf between sentences which express statements of fact and sentences which express judgments of value and particularly moral judgments; this absolute logical independence, ignored or not clearly stated by Aristotle, must be the starting-point of moral philosophy, and constitutes its peculiar problem. Post-Kantian philosophers of different logical persuasions have, of course, given very different accounts of the logic and use of value judgments; but they have generally agreed in regarding the logical independence of moral and empirical beliefs as defining the main problem of ethics.

This essay from *Mind* 58 (1949): 466–82 is reprinted by permission.

If one reads the Nichomachean Ethics after reading the works of (for example) Professor G. E. Moore or Sir David Ross or Professor Stevenson, one has the impression of confronting a wholly different subject. The first point of difference can be tentatively expressed by saying that Aristotle is almost entirely concerned to analyse the problems of the moral *agent,* while most contemporary moral philosophers seem to be primarily concerned to analyse the problems of the moral *judge* or critic. Aristotle describes and analyses the processes of thought, or types of argument, which lead up to the *choice* of one course of action, or way of life, in preference to another, while most contemporary philosophers describe the arguments (or lack of arguments) which lead up to the acceptance or rejection of a moral *judgment about actions.* Aristotle's Ethics incidentally mentions the kind of arguments we use as spectators in justifying sentences which express moral praise and blame of actions already performed, while many contemporary moral philosophers scarcely mention any other kind of argument. Aristotle's principal question is—What sort of arguments do we use in practical deliberation about policies and courses of action and in choosing one kind of life in preference to another? What are the characteristic differences between moral and theoretical problems? The question posed by most contemporary moral philosophers seems to be—What do we mean by, and how (if at all) do we establish the truth of, sentences used to express moral judgments about our own or other people's actions?

The difference between these two approaches to the problems of moral philosophy emerges most clearly from the analogy between aesthetics and ethics to which allusion is made both in Aristotle's Ethics and also in most modern discussions of so-called value judgments (for example, by Sir David Ross in "The Right and the Good" and by Professor Ayer in "Language, Truth and Logic"). For Aristotle (as for Plato) the aesthetic analogy which illuminates the problem of moral philosophy is the analogy between the artist or craftsman's characteristic procedures in designing and executing his work and the similar, but also different procedures which we all use in designing and executing practical policies in ordinary life. For contemporary moral philosophers, largely preoccupied with elucidating sentences which express moral praise or blame (moral "judgments" in the sense in which a judge gives judgments), the relevant analogy is between sentences expressing moral praise or condemnation and sentences expressing aesthetic praise or condemnation. As aesthetics has become the study of the logic and language of aesthetic *criticism,* so moral philosophy has become largely the study of the logic and language of moral criticism.

No one will be inclined to dispute that the processes of thought which are characteristic of the artist or craftsman in conceiving and executing his designs, are essentially different from the processes of the critic who passes judgment on the artist's work; it is notorious that the processes involved in, and the gifts and training required for, the actual making of a work of art are different from those which are required for the competent appraisal of the work; the artist's problem is not the critic's problem. An aesthetician may choose—and in fact most modern aestheticians have chosen—to confine himself to an analysis of the characteristic arguments involved in arriving at a judgment about a work of art (theories of a special aesthetic emotion, of objective standards of taste, etc.). Alternatively he may analyse and characterise the creative process itself (theories of imagination, the relation of technique to conception, the formation of style, the nature of inspiration, etc.). He may decide that the two inquiries, though certainly distinguishable and separable, are in some respects complementary, or at least that there are some questions contained within the first which cannot be answered without a prior answer to the second. But, however complementary they may be, the first inquiry certainly does not include the second. Those who wish to distinguish more clearly the peculiar characteristics of artistic activity, will learn little or nothing from the typical aestheticians' discussions of the objective and subjective interpretations of critical aesthetic judgments. But it seems now to be generally assumed that to ask whether sentences expressing moral praise or blame are to be classified as true or false statements, or alternatively as mere expressions of feeling, is somehow a substitute for the analysis of the processes of thought by which as moral agents we decide what we ought to do and how we ought to behave. Unless this is the underlying assumption, it is difficult to understand why moral philosophers should concentrate attention primarily on the analysis of ethical terms as they are used in sentences expressing moral praise and blame; for we are not primarily interested in moral criticism, or even self-criticism, except in so far as it is directly or indirectly an aid to the solution of practical problems, to deciding what we ought to do in particular situations or types of situation; we do not normally perplex ourselves deeply in moral appraisal for its own sake, in allotting moral marks to ourselves or to other people. The typical moral problem is not a spectator's problem or a problem of classifying or describing conduct, but a problem of practical choice and decision.

But the aesthetic analogy may be misleading, in that the relation of the value judgments of the art critic to the characteristic problems of the artist or craftsman cannot be assumed to be the same as the relation of the sentences expressing moral praise or blame to the problems of the moral agent.[2] To press the analogy would be question-begging, although the validity of the analogy between the problems of ethics and aesthetics is so often assumed. Leaving aside the analogy, the issue is—Is the answer to the question "What are the distinguishing characteristics of sentences expressing moral praise or blame?" necessarily the same as the answer to the question "What are the distinguishing characteristics of moral problems as they present themselves to us as practical agents?"? Unless these two questions are identical, or unless the first includes the second, much of contemporary moral philosophy is concerned with a relatively trivial side-issue, or is at the very least incomplete. My thesis is that the answer to the second question must contain the answer to the first, but that, if one tries to answer the first question without approaching it as part of the second, the answer will tend to be, not only incomplete, but positively misleading; and that the now most widely accepted philosophical interpretations of moral judgments, their logical status and peculiarities, are radically misleading for this reason. They purport to be logical characterisations of moral judgments and of the distinguishing features of moral arguments, but in these characterisations the *primary* use of moral judgments (= decisions) is largely or even entirely ignored.

2. Suppose (what probably occurs occasionally in most people's experience) one is confronted with a difficult and untrivial situation in which one is in doubt what one ought to do, and then, after full consideration of the issues involved, one arrives at a conclusion. One's conclusion, reached after deliberation, expressed in the sentence "x is the best thing to do in these circumstances," is a pure or primary moral judgment (the solution of a practical problem). It is misleading to the point of absurdity to describe this sentence, as used in such a context, as meaningful only in the sense in which an exclamation is meaningful, or as having no literal significance, or as having the function merely of expressing and evoking feeling. It is also misleading to describe it as a statement about the agent's feeling or attitude; for such a description suggests that the judgment would be defended, if attacked, primarily by an appeal to introspection. It is surely misleading to describe the procedure by which such a judgment or decision is established as right as one of comparing degrees of moral emotion towards alternative courses of action. I am supposing (what is normal in such cases) that the agent has

reasoned and argued about the alternatives, and am asserting that he would then justify his conclusion, if it were attacked, by reference to these arguments; and a statement about his own moral feelings or attitudes would not be, within the ordinary use of language, either a necessary or sufficient justification. Therefore the characterisation of such judgments as purely, or even largely, reports of feelings or attitudes is at the least incomplete and misleadingly incomplete, because in this characterisation the typical procedures of deliberation on which the judgment is based are suppressed or ignored. It is also paradoxical and misleading to introduce the word "intuition," as another group of post-Kantian philosophers have done, in describing the procedure by which such a judgment is arrived at, or by which it is justified and defended; for the force of the word "intuition" is to suggest that the conclusion is not established by any recognised form of argument, by any ratiocinative process involving a succession of steps which are logically criticisable; the word "intuition" carries the suggestion that we do not, or even cannot, deliberate and calculate in deciding what we ought to do; but we always can and often actually do deliberate and calculate.

If the procedure of practical deliberation does not conform, either in its intermediate steps or in the form of its conclusions, with any forms of argument acknowledged as respectable in logical text-books, this is a deficiency of the logical text-books. Or rather it is a mistake in the *interpretation* of text books of logic to assume that they provide, or that they are intended to provide, patterns of all forms of reasoning or argument which can properly be described as rational argument. Arguments may be, in the ordinary and wider sense, rational, without being included among the types of argument which are ordinarily studied by logicians, since logicians are generally concerned exclusively with the types of argument which are characteristic of the *a priori* and empirical sciences. There are other patterns of argument habitually used outside the sciences, which may be described as more or less rational in the sense that they are more or less strictly governed by recognised (though not necessarily formulated) rules of relevance. If one criticises a sequence of sentences by saying that assertion or denial of the earlier members of the sequence is irrelevant to acceptance or rejection of their successors, then this sequence is being regarded as constituting an argument. Aristotle at least remarks that not all arguments are theoretical arguments, terminating in a conclusion which is intended as a statement, either factual or logically true;

there are also practical arguments—he naturally says "syllogisms"—
the form of which is similar in many respects to some types of
theoretical argument, but which are also characteristically different
in their form; in particular they differ in the form of their conclusion,
which is not a theoretical or true-or-false statement, but has the
distinctive form of a practical judgment, for example, "this is the
right action" or "this is the best thing to do," or "this ought to be
done."

Even when sentences containing moral terms are used by spectators (not agents) in contexts in which they seem to be in fact
associated with a purely emotional reaction to a decision or action,
it is misleadingly incomplete to characterise them as having the
logical force only, or largely, of expressions of, or statements about,
the speaker's or writer's feelings or attitudes. If a purely critical and
apparently emotional moral judgment of this kind is challenged and
needs to be defended and justified, it will be justified by the same
kind of arguments which one would have used as an agent in practical deliberation. If I am not prepared to produce such practical
arguments, pointing to what ought to have been done, I shall admit
that I am not making a genuine moral judgment, but merely expressing or reporting my own feelings; and I shall admit that it was
misleading to use the form of sentence ordinarily associated with
moral judgments, and not with expressions of feeling. Doubtless
many sentences containing moral terms are ambiguous, and may be
normally used both as expressions of practical judgments and as expressions of feeling; but the important point is that, if challenged
about our intentions, we are required to *distinguish* between such
uses; and our languages, by providing the distinctive quasi-
imperative form of the practical judgment, enable us to distinguish.
But moral philosophers, tacitly assuming that moral judgments
must be descriptive statements, have represented a moral problem
as a critic's or spectator's problem of proper classification and
description.

If, following Aristotle, one begins by describing how moral
problems differ both from technical and theoretical problems, one
will have begun to answer the question about the distinctive nature
of moral judgments, even in their purely critical use. But if one
begins by separating them from their context in practical deliberation, and considers them as quasi-theoretical[3] expressions of moral
praise and condemnation, the resulting characterisation of them
must be misleadingly incomplete.

3. The fact that moral judgments, in spite of the peculiarity of their form as practical judgments, are established by familiar patterns of argument, has been under-emphasised by post-Kantian moral philosophers as a consequence of three connected logical doctrines: *(a)* the doctrine that so-called value judgments cannot be derived from factual judgments: *(b)* the doctrine that, although we deliberate and argue about the facts of moral situations, for example, about the probable consequences of various possible actions), no further argument is possible when once the facts of the situation have been determined; we are thus left in every case of practical deliberation with *(c)* an ultimate moral judgment, which cannot be replaced by any statement of fact, or by an empirical statement of any kind, and which cannot itself be defended by further argument. From no consideration of facts, or accumulation of factual knowledge, can we ever deduce a moral judgment of the form "this ought to be done" or "this is the right action in these circumstances." Therefore all appeal to the procedure of deliberation is irrelevant to the real problem, which is the analysis or characterisation of these *ultimate* moral judgments.

The fallacy in this position, as I have stated it, emerges in the words "derive" and "deduce." It is only in limiting cases that, in describing the logic of any class of sentences of ordinary discourse, one can reasonably expect to find another class of sentences from which the problem-sentences are logically deducible. Statements about physical things cannot be deduced, or logically derived, from statements about sensations; statements about people's character or dispositions cannot be deduced, or logically derived, from statements about their behaviour; yet in both cases the truth of the first kind of statement is established exclusively by reference to the second kind. In general, one kind of sentence may be established and defended exclusively by reference to another kind, without the first kind being deducible, or logically derivable, from the second. When as philosophers we ask how a particular kind of sentence is to be categorised or described, we are asking ourselves by what sort of arguments it is established and how we justify its use if it is disputed; to explain its logic and meaning is generally to describe and illustrate by examples the kind of sentences which are conventionally accepted as sufficient grounds for its assertion or rejection. So we may properly elucidate moral or practical judgments by saying that they are established and supported by arguments consisting of factual judgments of a particular range, while admitting that they are never strictly deducible, or in this sense logically derivable, from any set of factual judgments.

Certainly no practical judgment is logically deducible from any set of statements of fact; for if practical judgments were so deducible, they would be redundant; we could confine ourselves simply to factual or theoretical judgments; this is in effect what strict Utilitarians, such as Bentham, proposed that we should do. Bentham recommended the removal of distinctively moral terms from the language, so that moral problems would be replaced by technical problems, or problems of applied science. He made this proposal quite self-consciously and deliberately, wishing to introduce a science of morals, in which all moral problems would be experimentally decidable as technical problems. The distinctive form in which moral problems are posed and moral conclusions expressed disappears in his usage, precisely because he makes arguments about matters of fact *logically conclusive* in settling moral problems; and it is precisely to this *replacement* of moral terms that critics of strict Utilitarians have always objected, (for example, Professor G. E. Moore in *Principia Ethica*); they have argued that Utilitarians confuse the reasons on which moral judgments may be based with those judgments themselves; and this confusion arises from supposing that the reasons must be logically conclusive reasons, so that to accept the empirical premises and to deny the moral conclusion is self-contradictory. But it does not follow from the fact that moral or practical judgments are not in their normal use so deducible that they must be described as ultimate, mysterious, and removed from the sphere of rational discussion. All argument is not deduction, and giving reasons in support of a judgment or statement is not necessarily, or even generally, giving logically conclusive reasons.

Once this assumption is removed, it is possible to reconsider, without philosophical prejudice, what is the difference and the relation between ordinary empirical statements and moral judgments as we actually use them when we are arguing with ourselves, or with others, about what we ought to do. It is important to consider examples of practical or moral problems which are neither trivial in themselves nor abstractly described; for it is only by reflecting on our procedure when confronted with what would ordinarily be called a genuine moral problem that the characteristic types of argument can be seen clearly deployed. A simplified variant of the situation presented in a recent novel[4] may serve the purpose. Suppose that I am convinced that if I continue to live, I cannot avoid inflicting great and indefinitely prolonged unhappiness on one or both of two people and at the same time on myself; by committing suicide without detection I can avoid this accumulation of unhappiness; I therefore decide, after careful deliberation, that the right or best thing to do is to commit suicide. This is a moral judgment of the primary kind. (Having reached this conclusion, I may of course in any particular case fail to act in accordance with it; as Aristotle points out, deciding that x is the best thing to do and deciding *to* do x are both distinguishable and separable.) Suppose that in this case the moral judgment, which is the conclusion of my deliberation, is challenged by someone who at the same time agrees with me in my assessment of all the facts of the situation; that is, he agrees with me about the probable consequences of all the possible courses of action, but does not agree with my conclusion that it is right to commit suicide. An argument develops; we each give our reasons for saying that suicide under these circumstances is right or wrong. However the argument may develop in detail, it will generally exhibit the following features. (1) Although it is assumed that my disputant agrees with me about the facts of this particular situation (probable consequences of various actions etc.), he will in his argument appeal to other facts or beliefs about the world, which are not strictly describable as beliefs about the facts of this particular situation. For instance, we might both recognise as relevant a dispute, partly empirical and partly logical, about whether there is life after death, and whether the Christian dogmas on this subject are true or significant; or we may become involved in a largely historical argument about the social effects of suicide; and it would be recognised as pertinent to produce psychological arguments to the effect that intense unhappiness is often preferred to mere loneliness and *therefore* (and this "therefore" is not the sign of an entailment) it would be better not to desert the other two people involved. *The point is that it does not follow from the fact that two people are in agreement about the facts of a particular situation, but disagree in their moral judgment, that their disagreement is ultimate and admits of no further rational argument;* hence (2) our disagreement about the facts of the particular situation, is nevertheless, a disagreement to which empirical arguments, beliefs about an indefinitely wide range of matters of fact, are recognised to be relevant. If we are deliberating or arguing about whether suicide is right or wrong in these particular circumstances (or in any circumstances), then our psychological, historical and religious beliefs are always taken to be relevant parts of the argument. By representing so-called value judgments as ultimate and logically divorced from ordinary factual judgments, philosophers have implicitly or explicitly suggested that such sentences as "suicide is always wrong" or "suicide is wrong in these circumstances" cannot be defended or refuted by appeals to facts or to the empirical sciences. This paradox is a legacy of Kant's anxiety to underline as strongly as possible the difference between practical problems which are moral problems and those which are purely technical problems. Almost all previous philosophers—and most people without Kantian or other philosophical prejudices—have assumed accumulating knowledge, or changing beliefs arising out of the study of history, psychology, anthropology and other empirical sciences, to be relevant to their moral judgments; to be relevant, not in the sense that the falsity of moral judgments previously accepted as true can be *deduced* from some empirical propositions of history, psychology or any natural science, but in the sense in which (for example) propositions about somebody's conduct are relevant to propositions about his character; that is, previous moral judgments are shown to be groundless, the empirical propositions on which they were based having been contradicted as scientific or historical knowledge increases. The conflicting moral conclusions of a Marxist and a Christian Fundamentalist, or the differences which may arise even between two contemporary and similarly educated liberal unbelievers, will generally (but not always or necessarily) be shown in argument to rest on different empirical or at least corrigible beliefs about the constitution of the universe. Whenever we argue about any moral question which is not trivial, our beliefs and assumptions, however rudimentary and half-formulated, about psychological, sociological and probably theological questions are recognised as relevant, as logically involved in the nature of the dispute.

The result of the supposed argument about my judgment that suicide is the right policy in this particular circumstance might be that I am convinced that my judgment was wrong, and am persuaded that suicide is not the right policy. I might be persuaded to withdraw my original judgment, either because I have been made to recognise a fault in the logic of my previous argument, or because I have been persuaded to abandon admittedly relevant beliefs about matters of fact, or because my attention has been directed to new facts as being relevant to the decision, facts which I had known but the relevance of which I had previously overlooked. To direct attention to further known facts as relevant to a judgment is perhaps the most important effect and function of moral arguments or practical deliberation (for example, of giving practical advice). It is misleading to speak of "the facts of a situation" in such a way as to suggest that there must be a closed set of propositions which, once established, precisely determine the situation.[5] The situations in which we must act or abstain from acting, are "open" in the sense that they cannot be uniquely described and finally circumscribed. Situations do not present themselves with their labels attached to them; if they did, practical problems would be conclusively soluble theoretical problems, the philosopher's dream; but ἐν τῇ αἰσθήσει ἡ κρίσις—the crux is in the labelling, or the decision depends on how we see the situation.

For these reasons the logical divorce between so-called judgments of value and factual judgments is misleading; for arguments about practical conclusions are arguments about facts. Our moral or practical judgments—"x is the right or best course of action (in these or in all circumstances)"—are corrigible by experience and observation; we feel certain about some, and very doubtful about others.

4. Certainly there may (logically) be cases in which we cannot attribute conflicting solutions of practical moral problems to conflicting beliefs about matters of fact; that is, two disputants, in giving their reasons for conflicting moral judgments, may be unable to find among their reasons any empirical proposition which is accepted by one of them and rejected by the other. It is logically possible that A and B should agree entirely, for example, about the effects of capital punishment, and furthermore should find no relevant differences in their general psychological or sociological or other beliefs, and yet disagree as to whether capital punishment should or should not now be abolished. However rare such situations may be (and I believe them to be much more rare than is commonly allowed) such so-called ultimate moral differences may occur. Both A and B, if they can claim to be making a moral judgment and not merely expressing their own feelings about, or attitudes towards, capital punishment, will be able to give the reasons which seem to them sufficient to justify their conclusion; but what is accepted by A as a sufficient reason for a practical conclusion is not accepted by B as a sufficient reason and vice versa. They may then argue further to ensure that each does recognise the reason which he is claiming to be sufficient in this case as sufficient in other cases; but, when this consistency of use is once established, the argument must terminate. How is such an "ultimate" or irresoluble difference about a moral judgment properly described?

Compare this ultimate difference about the practical judgment with a similar ultimate difference about a theoretical judgment: if A and B were to disagree about whether somebody is intelligent, and yet find that they did not disagree about the facts (actual behaviour) or probabilities (how he is likely to behave under hypothetical conditions) on which their judgment is based, they would describe their difference as a difference in the use of the word "intelligent"; they would say "you use a different criterion of intelligence, and so do not mean by 'intelligent' exactly what I mean."[6] Similarly when it has been shown that A and B generally apply wholly or largely different tests in deciding whether something ought or ought not to be done, they might properly describe their so-called ultimate difference by saying that they do not both mean the same, or exactly the same, thing when they say that something ought or ought not to be done; and in most such cases of ultimate or irresoluble moral differences this is in fact what we do say—that different societies (and even different individuals within the same society) may have more or less different moral terminologies, which are not mutually translatable. But of practical judgments one cannot say that differences which are in principle irresoluble are *simply* terminological misunderstandings and in *no* sense genuine contradictions; for it is the distinguishing characteristic of practical judgments that they have a prescriptive or quasi-imperative force as part of their meaning. There is therefore one sense in which, when A says that capital punishment ought to be abolished and B says that it ought not, they are contradicting each other; their judgments contradict each other in the sense in which two conflicting commands or recommendations may be said to contradict each other. They can only argue about which of their prescriptions is right if they can agree on some common criteria of rightness. A, following the practice of all reforming moralists and many moral philosophers, may try to influence B's actions by giving moral reasons for preferring his own criteria of use to B's use; but in his advocacy of his own use of moral terms, he will be using his moral terms in his own way. The argument might have shown B that his conclusion was wrong in A's sense of "wrong" or even in his own sense of "wrong"; but no argument can show that B *must* use the criteria which A uses and so must attach the same meaning (in this sense) to moral terms as A. Between two consistently applied terminologies, whether in theoretical science or in moral decision, ultimately we must simply choose; we can give reasons for our choice, but not reasons for reasons for . . . *ad infinitum.*

5. We may find that many people do not deliberate and so can scarcely be said to make moral judgments, but simply act as they have been conditioned to act, and, when challenged, repeat the moral sentences which they have been taught to repeat or merely state or express personal feelings or attitudes. A second, and much smaller class, act generally, and even wholly, on impulse, in the sense that they do not propose practical problems to themselves or choose policies, but simply do whatever they feel inclined to do—and such people are to be distinguished from those who have *decided that* to act on impulse, or to do what one feels inclined to do, is the right policy; for this is to make a moral judgment. But the great majority of people for some part of their lives are thinking about what is the best thing to do, sometimes reaching a conclusion and failing to act on it, sometimes reaching a conclusion which, in the light of corrections of their empirical beliefs or their logic, they later recognise to have been a wrong conclusion, and sometimes reaching a conclusion which they are prepared to defend by argument and acting in accordance with it.

"Thinking what is the best thing to do" describes a procedure which it is unprofitable, if not impossible, to analyse, or find a paraphrase for, in general terms without constant reference to specific cases. Aristotle begins by describing it as calculating means to a vaguely conceived end (happiness or well-doing), the nature of the end being more precisely determined by the means chosen as involved in its realisation. But he progressively qualifies and complicates this schematic account in such a way as to suggest that to make a moral decision is not to choose means to an already decided end, but to choose a policy of means-to-end which is judged right or wrong as a whole. Practical problems are (as Kant emphasised and over-emphasised) sub-divisible into moral and purely technical problems; the choice of the most efficient means to an already determined end is not called a moral choice. It is the defining characteristic of a moral problem, that it requires an unconditional decision, the choice of an action or policy as a whole.

6. There is another and related logical fallacy, often implicitly assumed and not explicitly stated, which has led philosophers to describe moral or practical judgments as expressions or reports of feeling or as established by *a priori* intuitions, and to neglect their normal occurrence as the corrigible conclusions of arguments involving the facts of a particular situation and our general beliefs about the world; this is the fallacy of assuming that all literally

significant sentences must correspond to something, or describe
something. As ordinary empirical statements were said to correspond to facts, so some philosophers have introduced the word
"values" in order that there should be something to which moral
(and aesthetic) judgments can be said to correspond; we are said to
"intuit" or to "apprehend" these values, these words being used to
suggest an analogy with sense-perception. Other philosophers,
wishing to define the world as the totality of facts, or as the objects
of sense and introspection, have inferred that, as moral judgments
cannot be said to correspond to anything in the external world, they
must either correspond to something in the internal world, (that is,
to feelings) or, failing that, that they cannot be admitted to be
literally significant. The question "what do moral judgments correspond to?" or "what do they describe?" suggests itself particularly
to those who are preoccupied with the critical use of these
judgments as expressions of retrospective praise or blame; in so far
as we relate them to practical deliberations and decisions, we come
to recognise them as not descriptions of, but prescriptions for, actions. Practical judgments, no less than theoretical or descriptive
statements, are in the natural sense of the words, literally significant, although they do not in the normal sense describe. If I say
"this is (or would have been) the right action in these circumstances,"
this judgment can be significantly denied; but, as it is not a descriptive statement or statement of fact, the denial is not normally expressed in the form "it is *false* that this is the best action in these
circumstances"; "true" and "false" are more naturally used with
theoretical judgments and statements of fact.[7] Of course this
distinction between true or false descriptive statements and right or
wrong practical judgments is not absolute and clear; many
sentences are partly descriptive and are partly expressions of practical judgments. But there is a distinction which emerges clearly in
simple cases of pure moral judgments and purely descriptive
statements. One *can* describe somebody's behavior or character
without making any moral judgment, (that is, prescription), even if
in fact prescriptions and descriptions are often almost inextricably
combined.

7. There is (I think) a widespread impression that the concentration of academic moral philosophers on the attempt to *define* ethical
expressions—"good," "right," "ought," etc.,—as being the principal problem of moral philosophy has tended to make the subject
sterile and unenlightening. One is inclined to say that it does not

matter whether "right," as ordinarily used, is definable in terms of "good" or not. There is the feeling that the clarifications which one expects from the moral philosopher cannot be answered by verbal definitions or the discovery of paraphrases. And I think this apparently philistine impatience with the search for verbal definitions or equivalences has good logical grounds. If we wish to clarify our own or somebody else's use of moral terms, the discovery of verbal equivalences or paraphrases among these terms is not an answer, but, at the most, a preliminary step towards an answer. I can become clear about what somebody means by saying "this is the right action in these circumstances" only by finding out under what conditions he makes this judgment, and what reasons (and there may be many) he regards as sufficient to justify it. What we want to know, in clarifications of differences in our use of moral (or aesthetic) terms, is—What makes me (in the logical, not the causal sense) decide that this is the right action? There is no reason to expect a simple answer in terms of a single formula, for example, "it is likely to increase happiness." But to search only for definitions or verbal equivalences is to assume that there must be a single sufficient reason from which I always and necessarily derive my judgment. This is another expression of the fundamental fallacy of thinking of analysis or clarification of the standard use of words or sentences as necessarily a matter of exhibiting deducibilities or entailments. If I am asked what I mean by saying of someone that he is intelligent, I explain my use of the word by describing specimens of the type of behaviour to which I apply the word; I give some specimens of the types of statements about his behaviour which would be taken as sufficient grounds for asserting or denying that he is intelligent. Similarly, one can only clarify the use of the principal moral (or aesthetic) terms—"good," "right," "ought," etc.—by describing specimens of conduct to which they are applied, that is, by quoting the different characteristics of actions which are normally and generally taken to be sufficient grounds for deciding that they are the right actions. The type of analysis which consists in defining, or finding synonyms for the moral terms of a particular language cannot illuminate the nature of moral decisions or practical problems; it is no more than local dictionary-making, or the elimination of redundant terms, which is useful only as a preliminary to the study of typical moral arguments. An informative treatise on ethics—or on the ethics of a particular society or person—would contain an accumulation of examples selected to illustrate the kind of decisions which are said to be right in various circumstances, and the reasons given and the arguments used in concluding that they are right. An uninformative treatise on ethics consists of specimens of moral sentences, separated from actual or imaginable contexts of argument about particular practical problems, and treated as texts for the definition of moral terms; and many academic text-books follow this pattern.

Summary—The four logically related fallacies underlying the typical post-Kantian approach to moral philosophy are *(a)* The assimilation of moral or practical judgments to descriptive statements, which is associated with concentration on the use or moral terms in sentences expressing a spectator's praise or blame; *(b)* the inference from the fact that moral or practical judgment cannot be logically derived from statements of fact that they cannot be based on, or established exclusively by reference to, beliefs about matters of fact; hence theories that moral judgments must be ultimate and irrational, that they are established by intuition or are not literally significant; *(c)* the assumption that all literally significant sentences must correspond to or describe something; moral decisions do not correspond to or describe anything, but they may, nevertheless, be said to be rational or irrational, right or wrong.[8] *(d)* The confusion between clarifying the use of ethical terms with discovering definitions of, or verbal equivalences between, these terms; the search for definitions is another expression of the old obsession of philosophers with entailment and deducibility as the only admissible relation between sentences in rational argument. To interpret "rational argument" so narrowly is, although misleading, not in itself fallacious; but if, on the basis of this arbitrary restriction, moral judgments are relegated to a logical limbo, labelled "emotive," the study of the characteristic logic of these sentences, and of the types of argument in which they occur, is obscured and suppressed.

NOTES

1. Hume never denied that our moral judgments are based on arguments about matters of fact; he only showed that these arguments are not logically conclusive or deductive arguments.
2. Insofar as we now distinguish between the creative artist and the mere craftsman, a work of art by definition is not the answer to any problem; the artist is only said to have problems when conceived as a craftsman, that is, as having technical problems of devising means towards a given or

presumed end. Where there is no problem posed, there can be no question of a right or wrong solution of it. Therefore the critic of poetry cannot be expected to show how the poem should be rewritten; he describes, but he does not prescribe or make a practical judgment, as does the critic of conduct or technique. So the aesthetic analogy misleads in at least this respect; the valued critic of art excels in description and classification; he is not the artist's adviser, while moral or technical criticism is necessarily the giving of practical advice.

3. To pose the problem of ethics as the problem of "ethical predicates" or "non-natural characteristics," is at the outset to suggest that moral judgments are to be interpreted as a peculiar kind of descriptive statement.

4. *The Heart of the Matter,* by Graham Greene.

5. The word "fact," here as always, is treacherous, involving the old confusion between the actual situation and the description of it; the situation is given, but not "the facts of the situation"; to state the facts is to analyse and interpret the situation. And just this is the characteristic difficulty of actual practical decisions, which disappears in the textbook cases, where the "relevant facts" are pre-selected. So the determining arguments are cut out of the textbook, and the gap is filled by "intuition" or feeling.

6. "What do you mean by saying that he is intelligent?" is ordinarily interpreted as the same question as "what are your reasons for saying, or why do you say, that he is intelligent?" Similarly, "What do you mean by saying that that was a wrong decision?" is the same question as "*Why* do you say that that was a wrong decision?" To find the different reasons in different cases is to find the meaning of "wrong," although no *one* set of reasons is *the* meaning.

7. Although we can speak of believing that this is the right action we cannot speak of evidence that it is right. "Evidence" is tied to statements which are true or false.

8. "I decided that *x* was the right thing to do" is a descriptive statement, true or false; but "*x* was the right thing to do" is a practical or moral judgment, right or wrong.

5

On "God" and "Good"

Iris Murdoch

To do philosophy is to explore one's own temperament, and yet at the same time to attempt to discover the truth. It seems to me that there is a void in present-day moral philosophy. Areas peripheral to philosophy expand (psychology, political and social theory) or collapse (religion) without philosophy being able in the one case to encounter, and in the other case to rescue, the values involved. A working philosophical psychology is needed which can at least attempt to connect modern psychological terminology with a terminology concerned with virtue. We need a moral philosophy which can speak significantly of Freud and Marx, and out of which aesthetic and political views can be generated. We need a moral philosophy in which the concept of love, so rarely mentioned now by philosophers, can once again be made central.

It will be said, we have got a working philosophy, and one which is the proper heir to the past of European philosophy: existentialism. This philosophy does so far pervade the scene that philosophers, many linguistic analysts for instance, who would not claim the name, do in fact work with existentialist concepts. I shall argue that existentialism is not, and cannot by tinkering be made, the philosophy we need. Although it is indeed the heir of the past, it is (it seems to me) an unrealistic and over-optimistic doctrine and the purveyor of certain false values. This is more obviously true of flimsier creeds, such as "humanism," with which people might now attempt to fill the philosophical void.

The great merit of existentialism is that it at least professes and tries to be a philosophy one could live by. Kierkegaard described the

This essay from *The Anatomy of Knowledge*, ed. Marjorie Grene, copyright © by Marjorie Grene for the Study Group (University of Massachusetts Press, Amherst, 1969 and Routledge and Kegan Paul Ltd) is reprinted by permission.

Hegelian system as a grand palace set up by someone who then lived in a hovel or at best in the porter's lodge. A moral philosophy should be inhabited. Existentialism has shown itself capable of becoming a popular philosophy and of getting into the minds of those (e.g., Oxford philosophers) who have not sought it and may even be unconscious of its presence. However, although it can certainly inspire action, it seems to me to do so by a sort of romantic provocation rather than by its truth; and its pointers are often pointing in the wrong direction. Wittgenstein claimed that he brought the Cartesian era in philosophy to an end. Moral philosophy of an existentialist type is still Cartesian and egocentric. Briefly put, our picture of ourselves has become too grand, we have isolated, and identified ourselves with, an unrealistic conception of will, we have lost the vision of a reality separate from ourselves, and we have no adequate conception of original sin. Kierkegaard rightly observed that "an ethic which ignores sin is an altogether useless science," although he also added, "but if it recognizes sin it is *eo ipso* beyond its sphere."

Kant believed in Reason and Hegel believed in History, and for both this was a form of a belief in an external reality. Modern thinkers who believe in neither, but who remain within the tradition, are left with a denuded self whose only virtues are freedom, or at best sincerity, or, in the case of the British philosophers, an everyday reasonableness. Philosophy, on its other fronts, has been busy dismantling the old substantial picture of the "self," and ethics has not proved able to rethink this concept for moral purposes. The moral agent then is pictured as an isolated principle of will, or burrowing pinpoint of consciousness, inside, or beside, a lump of being which has been handed over to other disciplines, such as psychology or sociology. On the one hand a Luciferian philosophy of adventures of the will, and on the other natural science. Moral philosophy, and indeed morals, are thus undefended against an irresponsible and undirected self-assertion which goes easily hand in hand with some brand of pseudo-scientific determinism. An unexamined sense of the strength of the machine is combined with an illusion of leaping out of it. The younger Sartre, and many British moral philosophers, represent this last dry distilment of Kant's views of the world. The study of motivation is surrendered to empirical science: will takes the place of the complex of motives and also of the complex of virtues.

The history of British philosophy since Moore represents intensively in miniature the special dilemmas of modern ethics. Empiricism, especially in the form given to it by Russell, and later by

Wittgenstein, thrust ethics almost out of philosophy. Moral judgments were not factual, or truthful, and had no place in the world of the *Tractatus*. Moore, although he himself held a curious metaphysic of "moral facts," set the tone when he told us that we must carefully distinguish the question "What things are good?" from the question "What does 'good' mean?" The answer to the latter question concerned the will. Good was indefinable (naturalism was a fallacy) because any offered good could be scrutinized by any individual by a "stepping back" movement. This form of Kantianism still retains its appeal. Wittgenstein had attacked the idea of the Cartesian ego or substantial self and Ryle and others had developed the attack. A study of "ordinary language" claimed (often rightly) to solve piecemeal problems in epistemology which had formerly been discussed in terms of the activities or faculties of a "self." (See John Austin's book on certain problems of perception, *Sense and Sensibilia*.)

Ethics took its place in this scene. After puerile attempts to classify moral statements as exclamations or expressions of emotion, a more sophisticated neo-Kantianism with a utilitarian atmosphere has been developed. The idea of the agent as a privileged centre of will (for ever capable of "stepping back") is retained, but, since the old-fashioned "self" no longer clothes him he appears as an isolated will operating with the concepts of "ordinary language," so far as the field of morals is concerned. (It is interesting that although Wittgenstein's work has suggested this picture to others, he himself never used it.) Thus the will, and the psyche as an object of science, are isolated from each other and from the rest of philosophy. The cult of ordinary language goes with the claim to be neutral. Previous moral philosophers told us what we ought to do, that is they tried to answer both of Moore's questions. Linguistic analysis claims simply to give a philosophical description of the human phenomenon of morality, without making any moral judgments. In fact the resulting picture of human conduct has a clear moral bias. The merits of linguistic analytical man are freedom (in the sense of detachment, rationality), responsibility, self-awareness, sincerity, and a lot of utilitarian common sense. There is of course no mention of sin, and no mention of love. Marxism is ignored, and there is on the whole no attempt at a *rapprochement* with psychology, although Professor Hampshire does try to develop the idea of self-awareness towards an ideal end-point by conceiving of "the perfect psychoanalysis" which would make us perfectly self-aware and so perfectly detached and free.

Linguistic analysis of course poses for ethics the question of its relation with metaphysics. Can ethics be a form of empiricism? Many philosophers in the Oxford and Cambridge tradition would say yes. It is certainly a great merit of this tradition, and one which I would not wish to lose sight of, that it attacks every form of spurious unity. It is the traditional inspiration of the philosopher, but also his traditional vice, to believe that all is one. Wittgenstein says "Let's see." Sometimes problems turn out to be quite unconnected with each other, and demand types of solution which are not themselves closely related in any system. Perhaps it is a matter of temperament whether or not one is convinced that all is one. (My own temperament inclines to monism.) But let us postpone the question of whether, if we reject the relaxed empirical ethics of the British tradition (a cheerful amalgam of Hume, Kant and Mill), and if we reject, too, the more formal existentialist systems, we wish to replace these with something which would have to be called a metaphysical theory. Let me now simply suggest ways in which I take the prevalent and popular picture to be unrealistic. In doing this my debt to Simone Weil will become evident.

Much of contemporary moral philosophy appears both unambitious and optimistic. Unambitious optimism is of course part of the Anglo-Saxon tradition; and it is also not surprising that a philosophy which analyses moral concepts on the basis of ordinary language should present a relaxed picture of a mediocre achievement. I think the charge is also true, though contrary to some appearances, of existentialism. An authentic mode of existence is presented as attainable by intelligence and force of will. The atmosphere is invigorating and tends to produce self-satisfaction in the reader, who feels himself to be a member of the élite, addressed by another one. Contempt for the ordinary human condition, together with a conviction of personal salvation, saves the writer from real pessimism. His gloom is superficial and conceals elation. (I think this to be true in different ways of both Sartre and Heidegger, though I am never too sure of having understood the latter.) Such attitudes contrast with the vanishing images of Christian theology which represented goodness as almost impossibly difficult, and sin as almost insuperable and certainly as a universal condition.

Yet modern psychology has provided us with what might be called a doctrine of original sin, a doctrine which most philosophers either deny (Sartre), ignore (Oxford and Cambridge), or attempt to render innocuous (Hampshire). When I speak in this context of modern psychology I mean primarily the work of Freud. I am not a "Freudian" and the truth of this or that particular view of Freud does not here concern me, but it seems clear that Freud made an important discovery about the human mind and that he remains still the greatest scientist in the field which he opened. One may say that what he presents us with is a realistic and detailed picture of the fallen man. If we take the general outline of this picture seriously, and at the same time wish to do moral philosophy, we shall have to revise the current conceptions of will and motive very considerably. What seems to me, for these purposes, true and important in Freudian theory is as follows. Freud takes a thoroughly pessimistic view of human nature. He sees the psyche as an egocentric system of quasi-mechanical energy, largely determined by its own individual history, whose natural attachments are sexual, ambiguous, and hard for the subject to understand or control. Introspection reveals only the deep tissue of ambivalent motive, and fantasy is a stronger force than reason. Objectivity and unselfishness are not natural to human beings.

Of course Freud is saying these things in the context of a scientific therapy which aims not at making people good but at making them workable. If a moral philosopher says such things he must justify them not with scientific arguments but with arguments appropriate to philosophy; and in fact if he does say such things he will not be saying anything very new, since partially similar views have been expressed before in philosophy, as far back as Plato. It is important to look at Freud and his successors because they can give us more information about a mechanism the general nature of which we may discern without the help of science; and also because the ignoring of psychology may be a source of confusion. Some philosophers (e.g., Sartre) regard traditional psychoanalytical theory as a form of determinism and are prepared to deny it at all levels, and philosophers who ignore it often do so as part of an easy surrender to science of aspects of the mind which ought to interest them. But determinism as a total philosophical theory is not the enemy. Determinism as a philosophical theory is quite unproven, and it can be argued that it is not possible in principle to translate propositions about men making decisions and formulating viewpoints into the neutral languages of natural science. (See Hampshire's brief discussion of this point in the last chapter of his book *The Freedom of the Individual.*) The problem is to accommodate inside moral philosophy, and suggest methods of dealing with the fact that so much of human conduct is moved by mechanical energy of an egocentric kind. In the moral life the enemy is the fat relentless ego. Moral philosophy is properly, and in the past has sometimes been, the discussion of this ego and of the techniques (if any) for its defeat. In this respect moral philosophy has shared some aims with religion. To say this is of course also to deny that moral philosophy should aim at being neutral.

What is a good man like? How can we make ourselves morally better? *Can* we make ourselves morally better? These are questions the philosopher should try to answer. We realize on reflection that we know little about good men. There are men in history who are traditionally thought of as having been good (Christ, Socrates, certain saints), but if we try to contemplate these men we find that the information about them in scanty and vague, and that, their great moments apart, it is the simplicity and directness of their diction which chiefly colours our conception of them as good. And if we consider contemporary candidates for goodness, if we know of any, we are likely to find them obscure, or else on closer inspection full of frailty. Goodness appears to be both rare and hard to picture. It is perhaps most convincingly met with in simple people—inarticulate, unselfish mothers of large families—but these cases are also the least illuminating.

It is significant that the idea of goodness (and of virtue) has been largely superseded in Western moral philosophy by the idea of rightness, supported perhaps by some conception of sincerity. This is to some extent a natural outcome of the disappearance of a permanent background to human activity: a permanent background, whether provided by Good, by Reason, by History, or by the self. The agent, thin as a needle, appears in the quick flash of the choosing will. Yet existentialism itself, certainly in its French and Anglo-Saxon varieties, has, with a certain honesty, made evident the paradoxes of its own assumptions. Sartre tells us that when we deliberate the die is already cast, and Oxford philosophy has developed no serious theory of motivation. The agent's freedom, indeed his moral quality, resides in his choices, and yet we are not told what prepares him for the choices. Sartre can admit, with bravado, that we choose out of some sort of pre-existent condition, which he also confusingly calls a choice, and Richard Hare holds that the identification of mental data, such as "intentions," is philosophically difficult and we had better say that a man is morally the set of his actual choices. That visible motives do not necessitate acts is taken by Sartre as a cue for asserting an irresponsible freedom as an obscure postulate; that motives do not readily yield to "introspection" is taken by many British philosophers as an excuse for forgetting them and talking about "reasons" instead. These views seem both unhelpful to the moral pilgrim and also profoundly unrealistic. Moral choice is often a mysterious matter. Kant thought so, and he pictured the mystery in terms of an indiscernible balance between a pure rational agent and an impersonal mechanism, neither of which represented what we normally think of as personality; much existentialist philosophy is in this respect, though often covertly, Kantian. But should not the mystery of choice be conceived of in some other way?

We have learned from Freud to picture "the mechanism" as something highly individual and personal, which is at the same time very powerful and not easily understood by its owner. The self of psychoanalysis is certainly substantial enough. The existentialist picture of choice, whether it be surrealist or rational, seems unrealistic, over-optimistic, romantic, because it ignores what appears at least to be a sort of continuous background with a life of its own; and it is surely in the tissue of that life that the secrets of good and evil are to be found. Here neither the inspiring ideas of freedom, sincerity and fiats of will, nor the plain wholesome concept of a rational discernment of duty, seem complex enough to do justice to what we really are. What we really are seems much more like an obscure system of energy out of which choices and visible acts of will emerge at intervals in ways which are often unclear and often dependent on the condition of the system in between the moments of choice.

If this is so, one of the main problems of moral philosophy might be formulated thus: are there any techniques for the purification and reorientation of an energy which is naturally selfish, in such a way that when moments of choice arrive we shall be sure of acting rightly? We shall also have to ask whether, if there are such techniques, they should be simply described, in quasi-psychological terms, perhaps in psychological terms, or whether they can be spoken of in a more systematic philosophical way. I have already suggested that a pessimistic view which claims that goodness is the almost impossible countering of a powerful egocentric mechanism already exists in traditional philosophy and in theology. The technique which Plato thought appropriate to this situation I shall discuss later. Much closer and more familiar to us are the techniques of religion, of which the most widely practised is prayer. What becomes of such a technique in a world without God, and can it be transformed to supply at least part of the answer to our central question?

Prayer is properly not petition, but simply an attention to God which is a form of love. With it goes the idea of grace, of a super-natural assistance to human endeavour which overcomes empirical limitations of personality. What is this attention like, and can those who are not religious believers still conceive of profiting by such an activity? Let us pursue the matter by considering what the tradi-tional object of this attention was like and by what means it af-fected its worshippers. I shall suggest that God was (or is) *a single perfect transcendent non-representable and necessarily real object of attention;* and I shall go on to suggest that moral philosophy should attempt to retain a central concept which has all these characteristics. I shall consider them one by one, although to a large extent they interpenetrate and overlap.

Let us take first the notion of an object of attention. The religious believer, especially if his God is conceived of as a person, is in the fortunate position of being able to focus his thought upon something which is a source of energy. Such focusing, with such results, is natural to human beings. Consider being in love. Consider too the attempt to check being in love, and the need in such a case of another object to attend to. Where strong emotions of sexual love, or of hatred, resentment, or jealousy are concerned, "pure will" can usually achieve little. It is small use telling oneself "Stop being in love, stop feeling resentment, be just." What is needed is a reorien-tation which will provide an energy of a different kind, from a dif-ferent source. Notice the metaphors of orientation and of looking. The neo-Kantian existentialist "will" is a principle of pure move-ment. But how ill this describes what it is like for us to alter. Deliberately falling out of love is not a jump of the will, it is the ac-quiring of new objects of attention and thus of new energies as a result of refocusing. The metaphor of orientation may indeed also cover moments when recognizable "efforts of will" are made, but ex-plicit efforts of will are only a part of the whole situation. That God, attended to, is a powerful source of (often good) energy is a psychological fact. It is also a psychological fact, and one of impor-tance in moral philosophy, that we can all receive moral help by focusing our attention upon things which are valuable: virtuous peo-ple, great art, perhaps (I will discuss this later) the idea of goodness itself. Human beings are naturally "attached" and when an attach-ment seems painful or bad it is most readily displaced by another at-tachment, which an attempt at attention can encourage. There is nothing odd or mystical about this, nor about the fact that our ability to act well "when the time comes" depends partly, perhaps largely, upon the quality of our habitual objects of attention. "Whatsoever things are true, whatsoever things are honest, whatsoever things are just, whatsoever things are pure, whatsoever things are lovely, whatsoever things of good report; if there be any virtue, and if there be any praise, think on these things."

The notion that value should be in some sense *unitary*, or even that there should be a single supreme value concept, may seem, if one surrenders the idea of God, far from obvious. Why should there not be many different kinds of independent moral values? Why should all be one here? The madhouses of the world are filled with people who are convinced that all is one. It might be said that "all is one" is a dangerous falsehood at any level except the highest; and can that be discerned at all? That a belief in the unity, and also in the hierarchical order, of the moral world has a psychological importance is fairly evident. The notion that "it all somehow must make sense," or "there is a best decision here," preserves from despair: the difficulty is how to entertain this consoling notion in a way which is not false. As soon as any idea is a consolation the tendency to falsify it becomes strong: hence the traditional problem of preventing the idea of God from degenerating in the believer's mind. It is true that the intellect naturally seeks unity; and in the sciences, for instance, the assumption of unity consistently rewards the seeker. But how can this dangerous idea be used in morals? It is useless to ask "ordinary language" for a judgment, since we are dealing with concepts which are not on display in ordinary language or unambiguously tied up to ordinary words. Ordinary language is not a philosopher.

We might, however, set out from an ordinary language situation by reflecting upon the virtues. The concepts of the virtues, and the familiar words which name them, are important since they help to make certain potentially nebulous areas of experience more open to inspection. If we reflect upon the nature of the virtues we are constantly led to consider their relation to each other. The idea of an "order" of virtues suggests itself, although it might of course be difficult to state this in any systematic form. For instance, if we reflect upon courage and ask why we think it to be a virtue, what kind of courage is the highest, what distinguishes courage from rashness, ferocity, self-assertion, and so on, we are bound, in our explanation, to use the names of other virtues. The best kind of courage (that which would make a man act unselfishly in a concentration camp) is steadfast, calm, temperate, intelligent, loving. . . . This may not in fact be exactly the right description, but it is the right sort of description. Whether there is a single supreme principle in the united world of the virtues, and whether the name of that principle is love, is something which I shall discuss below. All I suggest here is that reflection rightly tends to unify the moral world, and that increasing moral sophistication reveals increasing unity. What is it like to be just? We come to understand this as we come to understand the relationship between justice and the other virtues. Such a reflection requires and generates a rich and diversified vocabulary for naming aspects of goodness. It is a shortcoming of much contemporary moral philosophy that it eschews discussion of the separate virtues, preferring to proceed directly to some sovereign concept such as sincerity, or authenticity, or freedom, thereby imposing, it seems to me, an unexamined and empty idea of unity, and impoverishing our moral language in an important area.

We have spoken of an "object of attention" and of an unavoidable sense of "unity." Let us now go on to consider, thirdly, the much more difficult idea of "transcendence." All that has been said so far could be said without benefit of metaphysics. But now it may be asked: are you speaking of a transcendent authority or of a psychological device? It seems to me that the idea of the transcendent, in some form or other, belongs to morality: but it is not easy to interpret. As with so many of these large elusive ideas, it readily takes on forms which are false ones. There is a false transcendence, as there is a false unity, which is generated by modern empiricism: a transcendence which is in effect simply an exclusion, a relegation of the moral to a shadowy existence in terms of emotive language, imperatives, behaviour patterns, attitudes. "Value" does not belong inside the world of truth functions, the world of science and factual propositions. So it must live somewhere else. It is then attached somehow to the human will, a shadow clinging to a shadow. The result is the sort of dreary moral solipsism which so many so-called books on ethics purvey. An instrument for criticizing the false transcendence, in many of its forms, has been given to us by Marx in the concept of alienation. Is there, however, any true transcendence, or is this idea always a consoling dream projected by human need on to an empty sky?

It is difficult to be exact here. One might start from the assertion that morality, goodness, is a form of realism. The idea of a really good man living in a private dream world seems unacceptable. Of course a good man may be infinitely eccentric, but he must know certain things about his surroundings, most obviously the existence

of other people and their claims. The chief enemy of excellence in
morality (and also in art) is personal fantasy: the tissue of self-
aggrandizing and consoling wishes and dreams which prevents one
from seeing what is there outside one. Rilke said of Cézanne that he
did not paint "I like it," he painted "There it is." This is not easy,
and requires, in art or morals, a discipline. One might say here that
art is an excellent analogy of morals, or indeed that it is in this
respect a case of morals. We cease to be in order to attend to the existence of something else, a natural object, a person in need. We can
see in mediocre art, where perhaps it is even more clearly seen than
in mediocre conduct, the intrusion of fantasy, the assertion of self,
the dimming of any reflection of the real world.

It may be agreed that the direction of attention should properly
be outward, away from self, but it will be said that it is a long step
from the idea of realism to the idea of transcendence. I think,
however, that these two ideas are related, and one can see their relation particularly in the case of our apprehension of beauty. The link
here is the concept of indestructibility or incorruptibility. What is
truly beautiful is "inaccessible" and cannot be possessed or
destroyed. The statue is broken, the flower fades, the experience
ceases, but something has not suffered from decay and mortality.
Almost anything that consoles us is a fake, and it is not easy to prevent this idea from degenerating into a vague Shelleyan mysticism.
In the case of the idea of a transcendent personal God the degeneration of the idea seems scarcely avoidable: theologians are busy at
their desks at this very moment trying to undo the results of this
degeneration. In the case of beauty, whether in art or in nature, the
sense of separateness from the temporal process is connected
perhaps with concepts of perfection of form and "authority" which
are not easy to transfer into the field of morals. Here I am not sure if
this is an analogy or an instance. It is as if we can see beauty itself
in a way in which we cannot see goodness itself. (Plato says this at
Phaedrus 250 E.) I can *experience* the transcendence of the
beautiful, but (I think) not the transcendence of the good. Beautiful
things contain beauty in a way in which good acts do not exactly
contain good, because beauty is partly a matter of the senses. So if
we speak of good as transcendent we are speaking of something
rather more complicated and which cannot be experienced, even
when we see the unselfish man in the concentration camp. One
might be tempted to use the word "faith" here if it could be purged
of its religious associations. "What is truly good is incorruptible
and indestructible." "Goodness is not in this world." These sound

like highly metaphysical statements. Can we give them any clear meaning or are they just things one "feels inclined to say"?

I think the idea of transcendence here connects with two separate ideas, both of which I will be further concerned with below: *perfection* and *certainty*. Are we not certain that there is a "true direction" towards better conduct, that goodness "really matters," and does not that certainty about a standard suggest an idea of permanence which cannot be reduced to psychological or any other set of empirical terms? It is true, and this connects with considerations already put forward under the heading of "attention," that there is a psychological power which derives from the mere idea of a transcendent object, and one might say further from a transcendent object which is to some extent mysterious. But a reductive analysis in, for instance, Freudian terms, or Marxist terms, seems properly to apply here only to a degenerate form of a conception about which one remains certain that a higher and invulnerable form must exist. The idea admittedly remains very difficult. How is one to connect the realism which must involve a clear-eyed contemplation of the misery and evil of the world with a sense of an uncorrupted good without the latter idea becoming the merest consolatory dream? (I think this puts a central problem in moral philosophy.) Also, what is it for someone, who is not a religious believer and not some sort of mystic, to apprehend some separate "form" of goodness behind the multifarious cases of good behaviour? Should not this idea be reduced to the much more intelligible notion of the interrelation of the virtues, plus a purely subjective sense of the certainty of judgments?

At this point the hope of answering these questions might lead us on to consider the next, and closely related "attributes": *perfection* (absolute good) and *necessary existence*. These attributes are indeed so closely connected that from some points of view they are the same. (Ontological proof.) It may seem curious to wonder whether the idea of perfection (as opposed to the idea of merit or improvement) is really an important one, and what sort of role it can play. Well, is it important to measure and compare things and know just how good they are? In any field which interests or concerns us I think we would say yes. A deep understanding of any field of human activity (painting, for instance) involves an increasing revelation of degrees of excellence and often a revelation of there being in fact little that is very good and nothing that is perfect. Increasing understanding of human conduct operates in a similar way. We come to perceive scales, distances, standards, and may incline to see as less than excellent what previously we were prepared to "let by."

(This need not of course hinder the operation of the virtue of tolerance: tolerance can be, indeed ought to be, clear-sighted.) The idea of perfection works thus within a field of study, producing an increasing sense of direction. To say this is not perhaps to say anything very startling; and a reductionist might argue that an increasingly refined ability to compare need not imply anything beyond itself. The idea of perfection might be, as it were, empty.

Let us consider the case of conduct. What of the command "Be ye therefore perfect?" Would it not be more sensible to say "Be ye therefore slightly improved?" Some psychologists warn us that if our standards are too high we shall become neurotic. It seems to me that the idea of love arises necessarily in this context. The idea of perfection moves, and possibly changes, us (as artist, worker, agent) because it inspires love in the part of us that is most worthy. One cannot feel unmixed love for a mediocre moral standard any more than one can for the work of a mediocre artist. The idea of perfection is also a natural producer of order. In its *light* we come to see that A, which superficially resembles B, is really better than B. And this can occur, indeed must occur, without our having the sovereign idea in any sense "taped." In fact it is in its nature that we cannot get it taped. This is the true sense of the "indefinability" of the good, which was given a vulgar sense by Moore and his followers. It lies always beyond, and it is from this beyond that it exercises its *authority*. Here again the word seems naturally in place, and it is in the work of artists that we see the operation most clearly. The true artist is obedient to a conception of perfection to which his work is constantly related and re-related in what seems an external manner. One may of course try to "incarnate" the idea of perfection by saying to oneself "I want to write like Shakespeare" or "I want to paint like Piero." But of course one knows that Shakespeare and Piero, though almost gods, are not gods, and that one has got to do the thing oneself alone and differently, and that beyond the details of craft and criticism there is only the magnetic non-representable idea of the good which remains not "empty" so much as mysterious. And thus too in the sphere of human conduct.

It will be said perhaps: are these not simply empirical generalizations about the psychology of effort or improvement, or what status do you wish them to have? Is it just a matter of "this works" or "it is as if this were so"? Let us consider what, if our subject of discussion were not Good but God, the reply might be. God exists *necessarily*. Everything else which exists exists contingently. What can this mean? I am assuming that there is no plausible "proof" of the existence of God except some form of the ontological proof, a "proof" incidentally which must now take on an increased importance in theology as a result of the recent "de-mythologizing." If considered carefully, however, the ontological proof is seen to be not exactly a proof but rather a clear assertion of faith (it is often admitted to be appropriate only for those already convinced), which could only confidently be made on the basis of a certain amount of experience. This assertion could be put in various ways. The desire for God is certain to receive a response. My conception of God contains the certainty of its own reality. God is an object of love which uniquely excludes doubt and relativism. Such obscure statements would of course receive little sympathy from analytical philosophers, who would divide their content between psychological fact and metaphysical nonsense, and who might remark that one might just as well take "I *know* that my Redeemer liveth," as asserted by Handel, as a philosophical argument. Whether they are right about "God" I leave aside: but what about the fate of "Good"? The difficulties seem similar. What status can we give to the idea of certainty which does seem to attach itself to the idea of good? Or to the notion that we must receive a return when good is sincerely desired? (The concept of grace can be readily secularized.) What is formulated here seems unlike an "as if" or a "it works." Of course one must avoid here, as in the case of God, any heavy material connotation of the misleading word "exist." Equally, however, a purely subjective conviction of certainty, which could receive a ready psychological explanation, seems less than enough. Could the problem really be subdivided without residue by a careful linguistic analyst into parts which he would deem innocuous?

A little light may be thrown on the matter if we return now, after the intervening discussion, to the idea of *"realism"* which was used earlier in a normative sense: that is, it was assumed that it was better to know what was real than to be in a state of fantasy or illusion. It is true that human beings cannot bear much reality; and a consideration of what the effort to face reality is like, and what are its techniques, may serve both to illuminate the necessity or certainty which seems to attach to "the Good"; and also to lead on to a reinterpretation of "will" and "freedom" in relation to the concept of love. Here again it seems to me that art is the clue. Art presents the most comprehensible examples of the almost irresistible human tendency to seek consolation in fantasy and also of the effort to resist this and the vision of reality which comes with success. Success in fact is rare. Almost all art is a form of fantasy-consolation and few artists achieve the vision of the real. The talent of the artist can be readily, and is naturally, employed to produce a picture whose purpose is the consolation and aggrandizement of its author and the projection of his personal obsessions and wishes. To silence and expel self, to contemplate and delineate nature with a clear eye, is not easy and demands a moral discipline. A great artist is, in respect of his work, a good man, and, in the true sense, a free man. The consumer of art has an analogous task to its producer: to be disciplined enough to see as much reality in the work as the artist has succeeded in putting into it, and not to "use it as magic." The appreciation of beauty in art or nature is not only (for all its difficulties) the easiest available spiritual exercise; it is also a completely adequate entry into (and not just analogy of) the good life, since it *is* the checking of selfishness in the interest of seeing the real. Of course great artists are "personalities" and have special styles; even Shakespeare occasionally, though very occasionally, reveals a personal obsession. But the greatest art is "impersonal" because it shows us the world, our world and not another one, with a clarity which startles and delights us simply because we are not used to looking at the real world at all. Of course, too, artists are pattern-makers. The claims of form and the question of "how much form" to elicit constitutes one of the chief problems of art. But it is when form is used to isolate, to explore, to display something which is true that we are most highly moved and enlightened. Plato says (*Republic*, VII, 532) that the *technai* have the power to lead the best part of the soul to the view of what is most excellent in reality. This well describes the role of great art as an educator and revealer. Consider what we learn from contemplating the characters of Shakespeare or Tolstoy or the paintings of Velasquez or Titian. What is learnt here is something about the real quality of human nature, when it is envisaged, in the artist's just and compassionate vision, with a clarity which does not belong to the self-centred rush of ordinary life.

It is important too that great art teaches us how real things can be looked at and loved without being seized and used, without being appropriated into the greedy organism of the self. This exercise of *detachment* is difficult and valuable whether the thing contemplated is a human being or the root of a tree or the vibration of a colour or a sound. Unsentimental contemplation of nature exhibits the same quality of detachment: selfish concerns vanish, nothing exists except the things which are seen. Beauty is that which attracts this particular sort of unselfish attention. It is obvious here what is the role, for the artist or spectator, of exactness and good vision: unsentimental, detached, unselfish, objective attention. It is also clear that in moral situations a similar exactness is called for. I would suggest that the authority of the Good seems to us something necessary because the realism (ability to perceive reality) required for goodness is a kind of intellectual ability to perceive what is true, which is automatically at the same time a suppression of self. *The necessity of the good is then an aspect of the kind of necessity involved in any technique for exhibiting fact.* In thus treating realism, whether of artist or of agent, as a moral achievement, there is of course a further assumption to be made in the fields of morals: that true vision occasions right conduct. This could be uttered simply as an enlightening tautology: but I think it can in fact be supported by appeals to experience. The more the separateness and differentness of other people is realized, and the fact seen that another man has needs and wishes as demanding as one's own, the harder it becomes to treat a person as a thing. That it is realism which makes great art great remains too as a kind of proof.

If, still led by the clue of art, we ask further questions about the faculty which is supposed to relate us to what is real and thus bring us to what is good, the idea of compassion or love will be naturally suggested. It is not simply that suppression of self is required before accurate vision can be obtained. The great artist sees his objects (and this is true whether they are sad, absurd, repulsive or even evil) in a light of justice and mercy. The direction of attention is, contrary to nature, outward, away from self which reduces all to a false unity, towards the great surprising variety of the world, and the ability so to direct attention is love.

One might at this point pause and consider the picture of human personality, or the soul, which has been emerging. It is in the capacity to love, that is to *see*, that the liberation of the soul from fantasy consists. The freedom which is a proper human goal is the freedom from fantasy, that is the realism of compassion. What I have called fantasy, the proliferation of blinding self-centred aims and images, is itself a powerful system of energy, and most of what is often called "will" or "willing" belongs to this system. What counteracts the system is attention to reality inspired by, consisting of, love. In the case of art and nature such attention is immediately rewarded by the enjoyment of beauty. In the case of morality, although there are sometimes rewards, the idea of a reward is out of place. Freedom is not strictly the exercise of the will, but rather the experience of accurate vision which, when this becomes appropriate, occasions action. It is what lies behind and in between actions and prompts them that is important, and it is this area which should be purified. By the time the moment of choice has arrived the quality of attention has probably determined the nature of the act. This fact produces that curious separation between consciously rehearsed motives and action which is sometimes wrongly taken as an experience of freedom. (*Angst.*) Of course this is not to say that good "efforts of will" are always useless or always fakes. Explicit and immediate "willing" can play some part, especially as an inhibiting factor. (The daemon of Socrates only told him what not to do.)

In such a picture sincerity and self-knowledge, those popular merits, seem less important. It is an attachment to what lies outside the fantasy mechanism, and not a scrutiny of the mechanism itself, that liberates. Close scrutiny of the mechanism often merely strengthens its power. "Self-knowledge," in the sense of a minute understanding of one's own machinery, seems to me, except at a fairly simple level, usually a delusion. A sense of such self-knowledge may of course be induced in analysis for therapeutic reasons, but "the cure" does not prove the alleged knowledge genuine. Self is as hard to see justly as other things, and when clear vision has been achieved, self is a correspondingly smaller and less interesting object. A chief enemy to such clarity of vision, whether in art or morals, is the system to which the technical name of sado-masochism has been given. It is the peculiar subtlety of this system that, while constantly leading attention and energy back into the self, it can produce, almost all the way as it were to the summit, plausible imitations of what is good. Refined sado-masochism can ruin art which is too good to be ruined by the cruder vulgarities of self-indulgence. One's self is interesting, so one's motives are interesting, and the unworthiness of one's motives is interesting. Fascinating too is the alleged relation of master to slave, of the good self to the bad self which, oddly enough, ends in such curious compromises. (Kafka's struggle with the devil which ends up in bed.) The bad self is prepared to suffer but not to obey until the two selves are friends and obedience has become reasonably easy or at least amusing. In reality the good self is very small indeed, and most of what appears good is not. The truly good is not a friendly tyrant to the bad, it is its deadly foe. Even suffering itself can play a demonic role here, and the ideas of guilt and punishment can be the most subtle tool of the ingenious self. The idea of suffering confuses the mind and in certain contexts (the context of "sincere self-examination" for instance) can masquerade as a purification. It is rarely this, for unless it is very intense indeed it is far too interesting. Plato does not say that philosophy is the study of suffering, he says it is the study of death (*Phaedo* 64A), and these ideas are totally dissimilar. That moral improvement involves suffering is usually true; but the suffering is the by-product of a new orientation and not in any sense an end in itself.

I have spoken of the real which is the proper object of love, and of knowledge which is freedom. The word "good" which has been moving about in the discussion should now be more explicitly considered. Can good itself be in any sense "an object of attention"? And how does this problem relate to "love of the real"? Is there, as it were, a substitute for prayer, that most profound and effective of religious techniques? If the energy and violence of will, exerted on occasions of choice, seem less important than the quality of attention which determines our real attachments, how do we alter and purify that attention and make it more realistic? Is the *via negativa* of the will, its occasional ability to stop a bad move, the only or most considerable conscious power that we can exert? I think there is something analogous to prayer, though it is something difficult to describe, and which the higher subtleties of the self can often falsify; I am not here thinking of any quasi-religious meditative technique, but of something which belongs to the moral life of the ordinary person. The idea of contemplation is hard to understand and maintain in a world increasingly without sacraments and ritual and in which philosophy has (in many respects rightly) destroyed the old substantial conception of the self. A sacrament provides an external visible place for an internal invisible act of the spirit. Perhaps one needs too an analogy of the concept of the sacrament, though this must be treated with great caution. Behaviouristic ethics denies the importance, because it questions the identity, of anything prior to or apart from action which decisively occurs, "in the mind." The apprehension of beauty, in art or in nature, often in fact seems to us like a temporally located spiritual experience which is a source of good energy. It is not easy, however, to extend the idea of such an influential experience to occasions of thinking about people or action, since clarity of thought and purity of attention become harder and more ambiguous when the object of attention is something moral.

It is here that it seems to me to be important to retain the idea of Good as a central point of reflection, and here too we may see the significance of its indefinable and non-representable character.

Good, not will, is transcendent. Will is the natural energy of the psyche which is sometimes employable for a worthy purpose. Good is the focus of attention when an intent to be virtuous coexists (as perhaps it almost always does) with some unclarity of vision. Here, as I have said earlier, beauty appears as the visible and accessible aspect of the Good. The Good itself is not visible. Plato pictured the good man as eventually able to look at the sun. I have never been sure what to make of this part of the myth. While it seems proper to represent the Good as a centre or focus of attention, yet it cannot quite be thought of as a "visible" one in that it cannot be experienced or represented or defined. We can certainly know more or less where the sun is; it is not so easy to imagine what it would be like to look at it. Perhaps indeed only the good man knows what this is like; or perhaps to look at the sun is to be gloriously dazzled and to see nothing. What does seem to make perfect sense in the Platonic myth is the idea of the Good as the source of light which reveals to us all things as they really are. All just vision, even in the strictest problems of the intellect, and *a fortiori* when suffering or wickedness have to be perceived, is a moral matter. The same virtues, in the end the same virtue (love), are required throughout, and fantasy (self) can prevent us from seeing a blade of grass just as it can prevent us from seeing another person. An increasing awareness of "goods" and the attempt (usually only partially successful) to attend to them purely, without self, brings with it an increasing awareness of the unity and interdependence of the moral world. One-seeking intelligence is the image of "faith." Consider what it is like to increase one's understanding of a great work of art.

  I think it is more than a verbal point to say that what should be aimed at is goodness, and not freedom or right action, although right action, and freedom in the sense of humility, are the natural products of attention to the Good. Of course right action is important in itself, with an importance which is not difficult to understand. But it should provide the starting-point of reflection and not its conclusion. Right action, together with the steady extension of the area of strict obligation, is a proper criterion of virtue. Action also tends to confirm, for better or worse, the background of attachment from which it issues. Action is an occasion for grace, or for its opposite. However, the aim of morality cannot be simply action. Without some more positive conception of the soul as a substantial and continually developing mechanism of attachments, the purification and reorientation of which must be the task of morals, "freedom" is readily corrupted into self-assertion and "right action" into some sort of *ad hoc* utilitarianism. If a scientifically minded empiricism is not to swallow up the study of ethics completely, philosophers must try to invent a terminology which shows how our natural psychology can be altered by conceptions which lie beyond its range. It seems to me that the Platonic metaphor of the idea of the Good provides a suitable picture here. With this picture must of course be joined a realistic conception of natural psychology (about which almost all philosophers seem to me to have been too optimistic) and also an acceptance of the utter lack of finality in human life. The Good has nothing to do with purpose, indeed it excludes the idea of purpose. "All is vanity" is the beginning and the end of ethics. The only genuine way to be good is to be good "for nothing" in the midst of a scene where every "natural" thing, including one's own mind, is subject to chance, that is, to necessity. That "for nothing" is indeed the experienced correlate of the invisibility of nonrepresentable blankness of the idea of Good itself.

I have suggested that moral philosophy needs a new and, to my mind, more realistic, less romantic, terminology if it is to rescue thought about human destiny from a scientifically minded empiricism which is not equipped to deal with the real problems. Linguistic philosophy has already begun to join hands with such an empiricism, and most existentialist thinking seems to me either optimistic romancing or else something positively Luciferian. (Possibly Heidegger is Lucifer in person.) However, at this point someone might say, all this is very well, the only difficulty is that none of it is true. Perhaps indeed all is vanity, *all* is vanity, and there is no respectable intellectual way of protecting people from despair. The world just is hopelessly evil and should you, who speak of realism, not go all the way towards being realistic about this? To speak of Good in this portentous manner is simply to speak of the old concept of God in a thin disguise. But at least "God" could play a real consoling and encouraging role. It makes sense to speak of loving God, a person, but very little sense to speak of loving Good, a concept. "Good" even as a fiction is not likely to inspire, or even be comprehensible to, more than a small number of mystically minded people who, being reluctant to surrender "God," fake up "Good" in his image, so as to preserve some kind of hope. The picture is not only purely imaginary, it is not even likely to be effective. It is very much better to rely on simple popular utilitarian and existentialist ideas, together with a little empirical psychology, and perhaps some doctored Marxism, to keep the human race going. Day-to-day empirical common sense must have the last word. All specialized ethical vocabularies are false. The old serious metaphysical quest had better now be let go, together with the out-dated concept of God the Father.

I am often more than half persuaded to think in these terms myself. It is frequently difficult in philosophy to tell whether one is saying something reasonably public and objective, or whether one is merely erecting a barrier, special to one's own temperament, against one's own personal fears. (It is always a significant question to ask about any philosopher: what is he afraid of?) Of course one is afraid that the attempt to be good may turn out to be meaningless, or at best something vague and not very important, or turn out to be as Nietzsche described it, or that the greatness of great art may be an ephemeral illusion. Of the "status" of my arguments I will speak briefly below. That a glance at the scene prompts despair is certainly the case. The difficulty indeed is to look at all. If one does not believe in a personal God there is no "problem" of evil, but there is the almost insuperable difficulty of looking properly at evil and human suffering. It is very difficult to concentrate attention upon suffering and sin, in others or in oneself, without falsifying the picture in some way while making it bearable. (For instance, by the sado-masochistic devices I mentioned earlier.) Only the very greatest art can manage it, and that is the only public evidence that it can be done at all. Kant's notion of the sublime, though extremely interesting, possibly even more interesting than Kant realized, is a kind of romanticism. The spectacle of huge and appalling things can indeed exhilarate, but usually in a way that is less than excellent. Much existentialist thought relies upon such a "thinking reed" reaction which is nothing more than a form of romantic self-assertion. It is not this which will lead a man on to unselfish behaviour in the concentration camp. There is, however, something in the serious attempt to look compassionately at human things which automatically suggests that "there is more than this." The "there is more than this," if it is not to be corrupted by some sort of quasi-theological finality, must remain a very tiny spark of insight, something with, as it were, a metaphysical position but no metaphysical form. But it seems to me that the spark is real, and that great art is evidence of its reality. Art indeed, so far from being a playful diversion of the human race, is the place of its most fundamental insight, and the centre to which the more uncertain steps of metaphysics must constantly return.

As for the élite of the mystics, I would say no to the term "élite." Of course philosophy has its own terminology, but what it attempts to describe need not be, and I think is not in this case, removed from ordinary life. Morality has always been connected with religion and religion with mysticism. The disappearance of the middle term leaves morality in a situation which is certainly more difficult but essentially the same. The background to morals is properly some sort of mysticism, if by this is meant a nondogmatic essentially unformulated faith in the reality of the Good, occasionally connected with experience. The virtuous peasant knows, and I believe he will go on knowing, in spite of the removal or modification of the theological apparatus, although what he knows he might be at a loss to say. This view is of course not amenable even to a persuasive philosophical proof and can easily be challenged on all sorts of empirical grounds. However, I do not think that the virtuous peasant will be without resources. Traditional Christian superstition has been compatible with every sort of conduct from bad to good. There will doubtless be new superstitions; and it will remain the case that some people will manage effectively to love their neighbours. I think the "machinery of salvation" (if it exists) is essentially the same for all. There is no complicated secret doctrine. We are all capable of criticizing, modifying and extending the area of strict obligation which we have inherited. Good is nonrepresentable and indefinable. We are all mortal and equally at the mercy of necessity and chance. These are the true aspects in which all men are brothers.

On the status of the argument there is perhaps little, or else too much, to say. In so far as there is an argument it has already, in a compressed way, occurred. Philosophical argument is almost always inconclusive, and this one is not of the most rigorous kind. This is not a sort of pragmatism or a philosophy of "as if." If someone says, "Do you then believe that the Idea of the Good exists?" I reply, "No, not as people used to think that God existed." All one can do is to appeal to certain areas of experience, pointing out certain features, and using suitable metaphors and inventing suitable concepts where necessary to make these features visible. No more, and no less, than this is done by the most empirically minded of linguistic philosophers. As there is no philosophical or scientific proof of total determinism the notion is at least allowable that there is a part of the soul which is free from the mechanism of empirical psychology. I would wish to combine the assertion of such a freedom with a strict and largely empirical view of the mechanism itself. Of the very small area of "freedom," that in us which attends to the real and is attracted by the good, I would wish to give an equally rigorous and perhaps pessimistic account.

I have not spoken of the role of love in its everyday manifestations. If one is going to speak of great art as "evidence," is not ordinary human love an even more striking evidence of a transcendent principle of good? Plato was prepared to take it as a starting-point. (There are several starting-points.) One cannot but agree that in some sense this is the most important thing of all; and yet human love is normally too profoundly possessive and also too "mechanical" to be a place of vision. There is a paradox here about the nature of love itself. That the highest love is in some sense impersonal is something which we can indeed see in art, but which I think we cannot see clearly, except in a very piecemeal manner, in the relationships of human beings. Once again the place of art is unique. The image of the Good as a transcendent magnetic centre seems to me the least corruptible and most realistic picture for us to use in our reflections upon the moral life. Here the philosophical "proof," if there is one, is the same as the moral "proof." I would rely especially upon arguments from experience concerned with the realism which we perceive to be connected with goodness, and with the love and detachment which is exhibited in great art.

I have throughout this paper assumed that "there is no God" and that the influence of religion is waning rapidly. Both these assumptions may be challenged. What seems beyond doubt is that moral philosophy is daunted and confused, and in many quarters discredited and regarded as unnecessary. The vanishing of the philosophical self, together with the confident filling in of the scientific self, has led in ethics to an inflated and yet empty conception of the will, and it is this that I have been chiefly attacking. I am not sure how far my positive suggestions make sense. The search for unity is deeply natural, but like so many things which are deeply natural may be capable of producing nothing but a variety of illusions. What I feel sure of is the inadequacy, indeed the inaccuracy, of utilitarianism, linguistic behaviourism, and current existentialism in any of the forms with which I am familiar. I also feel sure that moral philosophy ought to be defended and kept in existence as a pure activity, or fertile area, analogous in importance to unapplied mathematics or pure "useless" historical research. Ethical theory has affected society, and has reached as far as to the ordinary man, in the past, and there is no good reason to think that it cannot do so in the future. For both the collective and the individual salvation of the human race, art is doubtless more important than philosophy, and literature most important of all. But there can be no substitute

for pure, disciplined, professional speculation: and it is from these
two areas, art and ethics, that we must hope to generate concepts
worthy, and also able, to guide and check the increasing power of
science.

6

Quandary Ethics

Edmund Pincoffs

Ethics is everybody's concern.... Everyone ... is faced
with moral problems—problems about which, after more
or less reflection, a decision must be reached.
S. E. Toulmin, Reason in Ethics, p. 1.

I ask the reader to start by supposing that someone (himself perhaps) is faced with a serious moral problem....
R. M. Hare, Freedom and Reason, p. 1.

What is ethical theory about? Someone might propose as
an answer: "Everyone knows what an ethical problem is;
ethical theory must be about the solutions to such problems." ... But do we really know precisely what an "ethical problem" is?
R. M. Brandt, Ethical Theory, p. 1.

My ultimate aim is to determine ... how moral judgments
can rationally be supported, how moral perplexities can be
resolved, and how moral disputes can rationally be settled.
M. G. Singer, Generalization in Ethics, p. 6.

Only when he has linked these parts together in well-
tempered harmony and has made himself one man instead
of many, will he be ready to go about whatever he may
have to do, whether it be making money and satisfying
bodily wants, or business transactions, or the affairs of
state. In all these fields when he speaks of just and
honorable conduct, he will mean the behavior that helps to
produce and preserve this habit of mind. ... Any action
which tends to break down this habit will be unjust; and
the notions governing it he will call ignorance and folly.
Plato, The Republic

This essay from *Mind* 80 (1971): 552-71 is reprinted by permission.

There is a consensus concerning the subject-matter of ethics so general that it would be tedious to document it. It is that the business of ethics is with "problems," that is, situations in which it is difficult to know what one should do; that the ultimate beneficiary of ethical analysis is the person who, in one of these situations, seeks rational ground for the decision he must make; that ethics is therefore primarily concerned to find such grounds, often conceived of as moral rules and the principles from which they can be derived; and that meta-ethics consists in the analysis of the terms, claims, and arguments which come into play in moral disputation, deliberation, and justification in problematic contexts. It is my purpose in this paper to raise some questions about this conception of ethics, which I shall refer to, for convenience and disparagement, as Quandary Ethics.

I

Before proceeding to more philosophical matters it may be well to attend to rhetorical ones: to present considerations which might at least cause the reader to hesitate before replying, "Of course ethics is concerned to resolve problems on rational grounds! With what else would it be concerned? To abandon the search for rationally defensible rules and principles is to abandon moral philosophy," etc.

The first and most obvious rhetorical point is that Quandary Ethics is a newcomer: that the quandarist is fighting a very long tradition with which he is at odds. Plato, Aristotle, the Epicureans, the Stoics, Augustine, Aquinas, Shaftesbury, Hume, and Hegel do not conceive of ethics as the quandarists do. If they are read for their "theories," that is, for the grounds they give for making particular difficult moral decisions, their teachings are inevitably distorted. To give such grounds, such justifications of particular difficult choices, was not their objective. They were, by and large, not so much concerned with problematic situations as with moral enlightenment, education, and the good for man. Again, the shift in emphasis is too patent to require documentation, but we may illustrate the point by means of a brief glance at the ethics of Aristotle.

He, as is well known, thought of ethics as a branch of politics, which in turn he thought of as a very wide-ranging subject having to do generally with the planning of human life so that it could be lived as well as possible. In the *Politics* the question concerns the best political arrangements, and a large and important preliminary is the comparative study of constitutions so that one will know what kind of arrangements there are, with their advantages and disadvantages, so that a choice may be made. Similarly in ethics the leading question concerns the best kind of individual life, and the qualities of character exhibited by the man who leads it. And again, a necessary preliminary is the study of types of men, of characters, as possible exemplars of the sort of life to be pursued or avoided. This study occupies a large part of the Nicomachean Ethics. Moral problems are given their due but are by no means stage-centre. The question is not so much how we should resolve perplexities as how we should live. Both the "we" and the "perplexity" or "quandary" must be carefully qualified. The "we" in question is not a mere place-holder, but refers to those of us who were well brought up, who have had some experience of life, who know something of the way in which the social order operates, who have some control over the direction of our lives in that we are capable of living according to a pattern and are not washed about by emotional tides or pulled hither and yon by capricious whim. So that if Aristotle is presented with a moral quandary he has a right to presuppose a great deal concerning the upbringing, knowledge, and self-control of the persons concerned. But the notion of presenting Aristotle with a quandary is not really clear if looked at through our spectacles. The kind of problems Aristotle's qualified agents typically have concern not so much what is to be done by anyone, qualified or not, in certain sorts of circumstances, as how not to fall into the traps which seize the unwary and convert them into one or another kind of undesirable character. When Aristotle discusses moral deliberation it is not so much in the interest of finding grounds for the solution of puzzles as of determining when we may assign responsibility, not when deliberation was impossible, or of determining what it is that sets off practical from scientific reasoning.

But if Aristotle does not present us with quandaries into which the individual may fall, and which he must puzzle and pry his way out of, this may be just because Aristotle does not value the qualities that allow or require a man to become bogged down in a marsh of indecision. There is, after all, the question when we should and should not be involved in perplexities, when to avoid, as we often should, the *occasion* of perplexity. Men can be perplexed because they are sensitive and conscientious people; because they do not have the sense to avoid perplexity; or because they are pathologically immobilized by moral questions. A well-founded ethics would encourage the development of moral sensitivity, but discourage the entertainment of moral quandaries which arise out of moral ineptness or pathological fixation. The quandarists do not insist upon these distinctions, yet they are as important and obvious as the distinction between preventive and curative medicine. That the moral philosopher can be thought of as prescribing a regimen for a healthy moral life rather than a cure for particular moral illnesses would surely not be news to Aristotle.

The second rhetorical point to be made is that even though there may be philosophers who have thought through their reasons for accepting the present posture of ethics, very little argument can be found in defence of it. In fact it rests, so far as I can tell, on unexamined assumptions which are perpetuated more by scholarly convention than by reasoned agreement. This posture, it may be well to emphasize, is not that of the casuist but one in which the ultimate objective of ethics is conceived to be the resolution of quandaries. It may be felt indeed that the nature of the times dictates what ethics must be, and that therefore no critical examination of the role of ethics is in order. It may be believed that the era in which we live, beset by problems if men ever were, somehow militates in itself against any form of ethics but a problem-oriented one; that in this respect our time differs from all previous less problem-plagued ones; that these problems are loosed upon us by technological and social change; and that since change is so rapid and unpredictable the best we can do for ourselves is to learn how to make decisions as they come along, discover the form of a good decision; and the best we can do for our children is to teach them how to go about making decisions in the tight places into which they are sure to be crowded. This means that the tools for decision-making must be put into their hands: the very general, and quite empty, principles from which rules appropriate to the occasion, whatever it is, may be derived. It may be felt, also, that the kaleidoscopic character of the times rules out an ethics focused, as in most of the long tradition, on qualities of character and their development, since the inculcation of traits presupposes precisely the social stability which we do not have, because if we cannot count on social stability we cannot know what character traits will be appropriate to the times in which our children will live.

This argument, which I have heard but not read, fails for two reasons, either of which is conclusive. The first is that it rests on a premise which is historically false. Character Ethics has flourished

in times of change comparable in their kaleidoscopic quality to our
own. The Stoic ethic was taught and practised over five hundred
years, during which there were periods of violent change in the ancient world. These changes were often of such scope as to make individual citizens uncertain what kind of world their children were
likely to inhabit. Athens, the original home of the movement, flut-
tered about in the surgings and wanings of empires, now moving
forward with a democratic form of government now languishing
under tyrants supported by armies of occupation. The form that
Stoicism took in Rome during the early empire, with its emphasis on
the individual's control of his own soul no matter what the external
circumstances might be like, is ample testimony to the insecurity
even of the privileged classes in a time of tyranny and corruption.

The second reason is that the argument, even if it were sound,
would militate as effectively against Quandary Ethics as against
Character Ethics. Quandary Ethics must, according to the argument, provide some stable means of arriving at decisions, no matter
how circumstances may change. This is usually interpreted as requiring that rules and principles (or anyway "good reasons") of
universal application should be provided. But it is not at all clear
why rules and principles will transcend change when qualities of
character will not. If there are principles which would seem to apply
in any conceivable world, why should there not be qualities of
character equally universal in scope? If there are character traits of
narrower application, then there are principles which would be applicable in some circumstances but not in others. Indeed it would be
hard to imagine a world in which we should not make it a principle
not to do to others what we would not want them to do to us; but it
would be equally hard to imagine a world in which the quality of
justice was without relevance. If there could be a world in which
there was no place for justice, might there not also be a world in
which there was no place for the Silver Rule? The argument works
not so much to demonstrate the advantages of principles and rules
in an uncertain world as to point up the limits of any form of moral
education in times of change.

The rhetorical points, then, are that Quandary Ethics diverges
from the main lines of discussion followed through most of the
history of ethics; and that there seems to be little offered in
justification of this change of orientation, and that little not convincing. Of course, it may well be that there are excellent reasons
why ethics should now be focused on disputation, deliberation, and
justification to the exclusion of questions of moral character. At

best, the rhetorical arguments can challenge the defender of the contemporary trend to produce those reasons.

II

But there are philosophical questions as well, questions which at least have the advantage that they point up some of the presuppositions of Quandary Ethics, and at most reveal that indefensible distortions of ethics result from the contemporary fixation on problems and their resolution. Quandary Ethics, remember, supposes that the ultimate relevance of ethics is to the resolution of the problematic situations into which we fall. The problems in question are, of course, practical and not philosophical. Moral philosophers, like other philosophers, must deal with philosophical quandaries; and these are not escaped, although they may be emphasized or deemphasized, by changing the focus of ethics. For example, questions about the logical status of "moral assertions" will present as much of a problem for the non-quandarist as for the quandarist. But the assertions in question are as likely to be about ideal standards as about the duties and obligations that are incumbent upon everyone.

The questions I want to raise are: What is a problematic situation? and Who are "we" who find ourselves in these situations? But discussion of these questions will require that I rehearse briefly some time-honoured distinctions.

The quandarist typically thinks of the problem-question as: What is the right thing to do? or What would be a good thing to do? or What ought I to do? But these questions are, as is recognized, ambiguous at least in the sense that they fail to distinguish between queries concerning what is the morally *correct* (rule-required, expected, proper, appropriate, fitting) thing to do; and queries concerning the morally *useful* (fruitful, helpful, practical, optimum) thing to do. The questions concerning the rightness, goodness, and oughtness can be questions about correctness, or usefulness, or both. The discussion of these questions is likely to be informed by general theories concerning correctness and usefulness: in particular the theory that the correct thing to do is the thing that it would be correct for any person in similar circumstances to do, and the theory that the useful thing to do is the thing that will, directly or indirectly, increase the happiness and decrease the misery of everyone concerned as much as possible.

Now if we ask the quandarist what a moral problem is, and who "we" are, who are enmeshed in the problem, certain difficulties arise for the quandarist conception of ethics. The quandarist might hold that a moral problem concerns what it is correct, or what it is useful to do, or both. Whether he holds that correctness entails usefulness, or *vice versa* need not concern us. Let us consider the correctness-question, through examination of a typical quandary.

I have made a promise, one of these promises encountered so frequently in the literature and so infrequently in life. It is to meet a friend to attend a concert. That is to say, I have solemnly averred, using the words, "I promise," that this time I will not disappoint him, as I did the last time; and that I will indeed be on hand at eight at the theatre. Meantime (back at the ranch) a neighbour calls to remind me of my agreement to attend an eight o'clock school board meeting to argue that a proposed desegregation plan is inadequate. What is the correct thing to do? How shall I decide? What is and is not relevant in my deliberations? Roughly: what is supposedly relevant is the agreements I have made; and what is supposedly not relevant is any personal wants or desires or characteristics I may have. The question is whether a promise of this and this sort may be violated so that I may keep an agreement of that and that sort: whether anyone should violate the promise to keep the agreement, whether there is an exception to the rule that one should keep promises, or another more stringent rule which would justify my keeping the agreement and not the promise.

The analogy with the law is never far beneath the surface. A case in which I must decide whether or not to keep a promise is regarded as analogous to a case in which I must decide whether or not I have the right-of-way at an intersection. I have the right-of-way if I am approaching from the right. I must keep the promise if it has been made. There are, however, appropriate exceptions in both cases. I do not have the right-of-way, even though approaching from the right, if I have a "yield" sign against me. I need not keep the promise, even though made, if to do so would result in my failure to keep an even more binding promise. For example, I need not keep a promise made in passing on a trivial matter, if to do so would result in my violating a promise made in great solemnity on a matter of real importance. In both the moral and the legal case what counts is the rule and its exceptions (or, understood differently, the rule and other rules with which it can conflict). What counts as relevant is differences in the situation; what does not count as relevant is differences in the personal descriptions of the persons involved. In a court of law it is irrelevant to the question whether I have the right-of-way that I am in a hurry to get home. It is irrelevant to the question whether I should keep the promise to attend the concert that I am very fond of music. What is relevant must have nothing to do with *me*, but only with the situation: a situation in which anyone could find himself. What is right for me must be right for anyone.

On the courtroom board the model cars are moved through the diagrammed intersection to represent the movement of the cars which collided. What is relevant is direction, signals given, signs, lighting conditions. Similarly we rehearse promise-breaking. What is relevant is the nature of the emergency, the conflict of agreements, the likelihood of injury or damage if the promise is kept. These are relevant matters in that a general rule can be formulated governing any one of them. For example, it is a general rule that if a promise is a trivial one, and serious injury is likely to result from its being kept, then it need not be kept.

The analogy with law, with respect to the impersonality of the decision whether an action is or is not correct is, I believe, widely accepted. It informs the quandarist conception of what a problematic situation is. According to this conception, it is irrelevant who the person is who is in the situation. It is relevant, at most, what tacit or explicit agreements he has made, and what role, for example, father, employer, judge, he finds himself playing. The conflicts of rules, or conflicts of duties, are conflicts into which anyone can fall; and the resolution of the conflicts must be such as to be right for anyone who falls into them. This consensus seems to me to hide a confusion.

There is, in fact, an important disanalogy between moral and legal correctness-decisions. There are considerations which are in a sense personal, which would be irrelevant in legal cases, but which are relevant in moral ones. They have to do with what the agent will allow himself to do and suffer in accordance with the conception that he has of his own moral character. The quandarist cannot, I think, ignore these considerations; but to give them their due is to shift the focus of ethics away from problematics toward character: away from Hobbes and toward Aristotle.

The moral question, inevitably, is: What would it be correct for me to do? It may be, indeed, that I cannot both keep my promise to my friend and my agreement with my neighbour. So I will have to decide. Say I decide to keep the agreement. How can I justify this decision to my friend? If I can do so at all, I must make use of principles I set for myself but not necessarily for other people, and of moral ideals I have, but do not necessarily attribute to other people. I must justify myself to him for what I have done. I cannot do this by talking only about what anyone should have done in the circumstances. Indeed, if what I did would have been wrong for anyone in the same circumstances to do, then it would have been wrong for me. If there had been no conflicting agreement, and I simply broke the promise to avoid the perturbation of my soul likely to be caused by rushing to be on time, then I decided incorrectly. But *it does not follow that because my decision would have been right for anyone in the same circumstances it would have been right for me.* It follows only that almost no one could rightly blame me for what I did: that what I did was permissible. But I can blame myself. Those persons close enough to me to understand and share my special moral ideals can blame me, too.

Suppose that I have devoted my life to the cause of desegregation: that all of my spare time and energy and means are devoted to it. Suppose that I have taken a particular interest in the development of school policy in my town. Suppose that it is simply a part of my self-conception and a part of the conception that others have of me, that I could not miss an opportunity to press the cause of desegregation: that if I did so I would have to question my own integrity as a person. Suppose that I know that this particular meeting of the school board is a crucial one: one at which the final decision on a plan will be made. Suppose that I am recognized as the chief spokesman for the cause of meaningful desegregation. Suppose that I have built a deserved reputation with others and with myself for persistence and courage in the face of obstacles, for being a man of principle, for sensitivity to the needs of others. Then what would be right for anyone in a situation in which a solemnly given promise conflicts with an agreement to attend a meeting might well not be right for me. If my personal ideals and my conception of myself as a moral person are to be excluded from consideration as merely personal; if nothing is to remain but considerations which have to do with the situation as it would appear to anyone regardless of his former character; then the decision-process has been distorted in the interest of a mistaken conception of ethics. The legal analogy has been taken too seriously.

It is easy to be misunderstood here. I am not glorifying the prig, nor do I intend to offer him comfort. I am not suggesting that the person who takes into account his ideals of character should agonize in public over them, nor that he should be pointedly or even obnoxiously rigid in his adherence to his standards. In fact, his ideals of character may rule out priggishness, too. Nevertheless, even though he should not take his ideals inappropriately into account, he should take them into account.

But suppose the quandarist is quite willing to allow all of the sorts of considerations I have mentioned in the previous paragraph. Suppose he insists that there is nothing inherent in his conception of ethics as focused upon the resolution of moral difficulties which prevents him from taking these matters into account. Well, fine! That is all that I am arguing for. Then ethics must take seriously the formation of character, and the role of personal ideals. And these matters must be discussed at length before decision-making is discussed. Moral decision-making will no longer appear in the literature as an exercise in a special form of reasoning by agents of undefined character. But the quandarist might take a different tack, arguing that the distinction between considerations having to do with the situation and considerations having to do with the character of the agent breaks down. "Why should not my formed character be a part of the situation?" he might ask. My response must be a qualified one. In courts of law such a distinction is maintained, even though it may not always be clear what is and is not relevant to the issue of guilt (that is one reason we must have judges). In the "court of morals" we maintain it fairly well, although there is a wide twilight zone between the two. But, again, this is an objection which works more in my direction than in his. To whatever extent it is impossible to maintain the distinction, to that extent we must pay more attention in ethics to character and its formation.

The general point I have made is that what would be right for anyone in the same circumstances (understanding "circumstances" to refer to what in law would be the "collision situation" only: and not to refer to what is "merely personal") is not necessarily right for me. Because what I have to take into account as well as the situation is the question what is worthy of me: What may I permit myself to do or suffer in the light of the conception I have of my own so far formed, and still forming, moral character?

It may be useful in expanding this point to return for a time to the concept of rules. It is here that the legal analogy has the strongest grip on the imagination. We say to ourselves: If I want to know what is the correct thing to do, then I must know whether there is a rule that covers this situation, or two rules, or a rule and an exception. But even if, as I would deny, we are tied by some kind of logical necessity to the concept of rule-abiding in thinking what is and is not correct, we would still have to let in considerations of character by the back door. Let me explain.

To do so, it is necessary to distinguish between different ways in which a rule may come to bear upon an agent. An analogous distinction could be made for prescriptions. In the armed services, as I remember dimly from an ancient war, it is customary to distinguish between orders and commands. A command tells us what to do or refrain from doing in such explicit terms that there is no, or very little, room for variation in the way in which it is obeyed or disobeyed. An order, on the other hand, does not so much specifically tell us what to do as what to accomplish, or at what we should aim. "Report at 10.00" is a command; "Provide protective screen for the convoy" is an order. There can, of course, be general and standing orders and commands. A general command would be, "All hands report at 10.00 tomorrow morning," and a general standing command would require all hands to report every morning at 10.00. "Exercise extreme caution when in enemy waters" can serve as a general standing order. General commands and orders apply to everyone; standing orders and commands apply to recurrent situations. Rules may be like general standing commands or like general standing orders; analogously they may be like general standing specific and non-specific prescriptions. They may allow no leeway in compliance, or they may allow a great deal.[1]

Some moral rules are more like general standing orders than like general standing commands, for example, "Love thy neighbour" or "Do not cause suffering." They say what is wanted, but not what to do. If, however, we concentrate upon moral rules that are like commands, such as "Do not kill" or "Never break promises," we are likely to think of moral rules much like criminal laws, in that they will consist, for us, largely of specific injunctions and directions. But if we recognize that they can also be like orders, we will be more aware of the discretion they sometimes allow. They do not tell us exactly what to do so much as indicate what we should struggle toward in our own way. But, since we are already moral beings with characters formed, the way in which I will abide by an order-rule is not the same as the way in which you will. In fact, I have to decide not just what the rule is which governs the case, but how to go about honouring it. In deciding this, it is inevitable that I will not approach the problem in a vacuum, as any anonymous agent would, but in the light of my conception of what is and is not worthy of me. So considerations of character, of my own character, do enter in by the back door, even if, as I have assumed for the sake of argument, the notion is that being moral is nothing but following a set of moral rules.

Personal considerations, then, in moral decisions, as opposed to legal decisions, need not be merely personal. It is often not irrelevant to the correctness of my moral decision that I take into account what I am: the conception that I have of myself as a moral being. In fact, the recognition of these considerations of worthiness leads us away from the typical examples of Quandary Ethics. We may now also consider examples in which the individual is not so much faced with a quandary concerning what he should do, as one in which he is reacting as an admirable moral character would to a situation which might call forth less admirable responses on the part of another. He turns the other cheek, walks the second mile, storms the impossible bastion, exhibits his finely tuned sense of justice by his decision, refrains from pleasurable recreation until the last job of his work is done. He exhibits his character in doing these things: shows forth the kind of man that he is.

Now it might be said, in weary professional tones, that I have simply insisted upon a distinction which is quite familiar to the contemporary moral philosopher: the distinction, with us at least since Aristotle, between the rightness of the act and the praiseworthiness of the agent. The act, it will be said, may be right even though the agent is not praiseworthy for having done it. Or it will be said that I have failed to distinguish between obligation and supererogation: that what a man is obliged to do is one thing, but that if he is a saint or a hero he may of course exceed the demands of duty and be accorded a halo or garland as the case may be.

In response, I want to say that both of these distinctions, while in other ways useful, may lead us to miss the point I want to make. Consider first the distinction between the rightness of the act and the praiseworthiness of the agent. I want to insist that the question whether the act is right may only with care be severed from the question whether the agent is praiseworthy. The agent earns praise by doing what in his lights is only right, by doing what he could not conceive of himself as not doing. In considering whether the action is right he brings in considerations beyond those of the generalizability of a rule. He wants to know not merely whether anyone may do it, but whether he may. Indeed we would not blame him for failing to go the second mile, but from his standpoint he is convinced that this is what it was right for him to do. He in fact exhibits himself as the moral character that he is by the demands that he makes upon himself, and by his taking it for granted that these demands must be met.

Now take the distinction between obligation and supererogation. Again: it does not follow that, since a man has more guide-rails than the rules that in his opinion should apply to everyone, that he is either a saint or a hero: that he is morally extraordinary. In fact a man's character is likely to exhibit itself in his making obligatory for himself what he would not hold others obliged to do. A man does not attain moral stature by what he demands of others but by what he demands of himself; and that he demands more of himself than others is not something in itself admirable, but is what is to be expected if he is to have a distinct moral character. The question whether an act would be right for anyone in the same circumstances can show only that it would be permissible for everyone, or that it would be mandatory for everyone. What is permissible or mandatory for everyone is so for the moral man, but, even leaving aside the question of leeway discussed above, he may not consider it right for him to do what would be permissible for anyone, or he may regard it as mandatory for him to go the second mile rather than merely the first which is mandatory for everyone. The question what is right for anyone in the same circumstances therefore provides the agent with but the beginnings of an answer to the question what he should do.

The special requirements I place upon myself in virtue of the conception I have of what is and is not worthy of me must not be confused, either, with the special requirements incumbent upon me in virtue of "my station and its duties." These requirements deal with duties I have as a father, a judge, a village lamplighter, a sergeant-at-arms, or what have you. These are again in the realm of the minimal requirements which should be met by anyone: anyone, this time, who falls into the same role as I do.

Quandary ethics, then, conceives of a quandary which arises because I fall into a certain situation. The situation is such that it can be described in perfectly general terms, without any reference to me as an individual, including my personal conceptions of what are and are not worthy deeds and attitudes and feelings: worthy of me. I may, according to this conception, fall into the situation in virtue of my falling under a rule which would apply to any person, or in virtue of my falling under a rule which would apply to any person playing a particular role. The general situation is what gives rise to the quandary; and it is only by reference to the features of the situation that I may deliberate concerning what I should do, or justify my action. Just as I may refer only to the position of my automobile at the intersection and not to my personal standards or ideals, so I may refer only to the promising and to the nature of the emergency which caused its violation: with no reference to my standards or ideals. But, I contend, reference to my standards and ideals is an essential, not an accidental feature of my moral deliberation. An act is or is not right from my standpoint, which is where I stand when I deliberate, not merely as it meets or fails to meet the requirements of an ideal universal legislation, but also as it meets or fails to meet the standards I set for myself. I am not judged morally by the extent to which I abide by the rules (those which are like general standing commands) which set the minimal limits anyone should observe in his conduct, even though it may be a necessary condition of my having any degree of moral worth that I should abide by such rules.

The man who is concerned in non-stupid and non-pathological ways over what he should and should not do is, to that extent, a conscientious man. Quandary Ethics is addressed to the conscientious man. He is its ultimate customer. But two things should be said here: that the truly conscientious man is concerned not just with what anyone should do but with what he should do, this I have discussed; and that conscientiousness is but one feature of moral character. Loyalty, generosity, courage, and a great many other qualities may figure as well. We cannot identify morality with conscientiousness. This, I charge, is what Quandary Ethics does. By starting from problems and their resolution, and by confining the description of problematic situations to those features of which a general description can be given, the whole of the question of morality of character is restricted to judgments concerning the conscientiousness of the agent. Since it may be somehow possible to reduce being moral to being conscientious, we should examine the plausibility of such a reductivist claim. But it is worth mentioning that the question what gives conscientiousness the sole claim to moral worth is not so much as recognized as such by the quandarists. It is worth repeating that in speaking of conscientiousness we do not speak of those degenerate forms, seldom recognized by the quandarist, in which there is mere moral dithering (the Buridan's Ass

Complex) or in which there is a seeking out of occasions for moral puzzlement when there is no real ground for such puzzlement (pathological conscientiousness).

Why is it, then, that conscientiousness gets the nod from contemporary moral philosophers over such qualities as loyalty, integrity, and kindness? Why would not honesty have equal claim to consideration? Or sensitivity to suffering? The answer may be obvious to others, but it is not so to me. I suspect that the best answer would take the form of an historico-sociological disquisition upon the increasing complexity of the social order, the increase in the possibilities of breakdown and disorder, the resultant need for more and more complex rules, and, finally, the consequent demand for the kind of individual who will not only be rule-abiding but also "rule-responsible": in that he does not flap, panic, or throw up his hands when—as is inevitable—the rules conflict in a given situation in which he may find himself. He should be rule-responsible also in that where there is no rule to govern a given choice he will create a rule consistent with the other rules which he accepts; and in that he has at heart the attainment of a community governed by a set of rules which is ideal; and that he evinces this interest in the legislation for himself of rules which would be consistent with the rules governing such a community. Such a man would have an intense regard for rules: for their enactment, interpretation, and application. This regard would extend not only to "public" rules: rules which govern everyone's action in recurrent situations, but to "private" rules as well: rules which result from particular relationships with other persons into which he voluntarily enters. These rules, which might be distinguished from others by being called "obligations," resting on tacit or explicit commitment to do or refrain, require constant interpretation, since the implications of our commitments in future contingencies is often far from clear at the time that we make them ("Love, honour, and obey," ". . . help you get started").

Surely the disquisition need extend farther. It could easily be expanded into a convincing case for the importance of rule-responsibility in our culture. But it would show at best that one desirable, even socially necessary, quality in men is rule-responsibility or conscientiousness. It does not have the consequence that we must confine our assessments of moral character to judgments of the extent to which the individual is rule-responsible.

Suppose that a man wants to know what he should do about the moral education of his children. What will he learn from the quandarists? He will learn, as might be expected, that he should teach them how to make decisions: that is, according to one popular version, he will impart to his children as stable a set of principles as is possible in the changing circumstances in which he lives; but he will also give them the idea that they must learn to make their own decisions of principle when the occasion arises, even though he cannot teach them how to do so. We later learn that the principles in question must be universalizable prescriptions applicable to any persons similarly situated. But is moral education best understood as the teaching of children how to make moral decisions? One might almost reply that the problem of moral education is not so much teaching children how to make moral decisions as giving them the background out of which the demands that decisions be made arise. The focus of moral education might well be not so much decisions as the inculcation of excellences of character. The adult of good moral character must indeed be able to handle difficult situations as they arise, and to reason about problems unforeseeable by his parents; but to reason well he must already be an adult of good moral character: loyal, just, honest, sensitive to suffering, and the rest. Everything is not up for grabs! Unless he has these qualities, moral dilemmas will not arise for him. Unless he has a well-formed character his prescriptions for himself and others are not likely to be morally acceptable. It is, as Aristotle notes, the prescriptions of qualified moral agents to which we should bend our ears.

An aim of moral education, likely to be overlooked by quandarists, is the development of the sense of the moral self as the product of continuous cultivation. It is as a formed and still forming self that one confronts, or properly avoids, moral problems. There are no moral problems for the child whose character is yet to be formed. For the quandarist, problems may arise for anyone at whatever stage of development he may be, when there is a conflict of rules or principles. What is socially essential is that there should be a workable and working set of rules and that there should be principles which serve as arbitrators between them. The argument that there is a need for such rules and principles is inevitably a Hobbesian one. But it was precisely the source of the discomfort with Hobbes that he approached ethics from this administrative point of view. He abandoned the cultivated moral self and insisted on reducing ethics to a code of minimal standards of behaviour: standards which cannot be ignored without social disaster.

There is very close to the surface in Quandary Ethics the presupposition that there is an essence of morality: that being

Moral can be reduced to being rule-responsible. But there is no more reason to believe that there is an essence of morality than that there is an essence of beauty. The suspect notion that there is an essence of morality is confused with the defensible idea that some moral rules are socially essential. However men may conceive their moral characters, whatever moral education they may have had, whatever moral models they may hold dear, whatever may be their religious beliefs, whatever virtues they may consider paramount—it is socially essential that they should be rule-responsible. But to grant that rule-responsibility is socially essential is not to grant that it is the essence of morality, in that all other moral character traits can be reduced to or derived from some form of this one. We may, even if we hold to the administrative point of view, expand our list of socially necessary character traits beyond rule-responsibility. Chaos also threatens in the absence of tolerance, temperance and justice, for example. These too are socially essential virtues.

To say that they are socially essential is of course to speak elliptically. What is essential is that everyone should exhibit some virtues to a certain degree, and that some persons should exhibit others to a certain degree. It is not essential that all be as honest as Lincoln, nor is it essential that any but judges or others who have something to distribute should be just in any degree, since the opportunity for justice or injustice does not otherwise arise. It is clearly socially essential that all should be rule-responsible to a degree commensurate with the complexity of the society; and it is socially desirable that all should be rule-responsible to as high a degree as possible, and that moral models or prophets should show the way. But it does not follow from any of this that morality can be reduced to rule-responsibility. The attempt to reduce moral character to any given trait by philosophical fiat is open to suspicion. Individuals may, and perhaps should, give focus to their moral lives by centring them around some particular virtues, for example sensitivity to suffering, or honesty. But to contend that morality is nothing but sensitivity to suffering or honesty is to attempt to legislate for everyone what cannot be legislated. We may encourage children and ourselves in the development of certain virtues, but the form which each person's character assumes will inevitably be the result of his own selective cultivation and his own conception of what is and is not worthy of himself. It is, once we move beyond the minimal needs of society, his problem, peculiar to him, his training, and his ideals. To insist otherwise is to espouse the cause of the moral Leveller.

The remark that certain virtues are socially essential is ellip-
tical, also, in that it fails to distinguish between virtues which are
essential, to a certain degree, in all or some men, to the very existence of any social order, and those which are essential to the continued existence of a particular social order. The distinction is, as
Hobbes recognized, a crucial one. "Gentility," as that term was
understood in the pre–Civil War South was necessary to the existence of the social order created by white landholders. When the
non-gentile Snopeses appeared, that social order collapsed. It may
be that men are so attached to a particular social order, or so averse
to another, that they are willing to entertain the possibility of the
absence of any social order rather than see the one collapse or the
other prevail. This is social nihilism, but it does not entail moral
nihilism. The individual may prize non-socially-essential virtues
over socially essential ones. In the interest of the continued existence of society, we cannot allow such moralities to prevail.

III

Earlier I distinguished between questions of correctness and
questions of usefulness. I have confined my discussion to the former
sort of question, but it could be extended with little difficulty to the
latter. Suppose that the conception of decision-making is that it has
to do with the best way to use the circumstances, to take advantage
of the situation, to maximize the happiness of everyone concerned.
Again, the question will be not, What should I—in the light of my
moral character and ideals—do? but What might anyone who finds
himself in this situation most usefully do? It is a question about
means to ends; not a question about how I might be most useful in
the circumstances, but about how anyone might increase happiness.
Conceived this way, and supposing the goal of happiness to be one
that we all understand in the same way, then the question what I
should do is not a moral question at all; but one that could best be
answered by a social engineer familiar with the circumstances. Even
if the question what would be most useful does not trail behind it a
general theory to the effect that there is only one kind of thing
which is ultimately useful, and if the possibility that there are a
great many useful kinds of things that one may do is left open, as it
should be, there is still a tendency to regard the question what
"one" may do which is most useful in a given "situation" as if it

could be answered without regard to the moral character of the agent. Again: granting that the promotion of a given state of affairs would be useful, and that a given line of action would promote that state of affairs, it might seem to follow that I should undertake that line of action. It does not. All that follows is that it would be generally desirable if I, or anyone, should. But, in the light of the commitments, interests and tendencies which I have already developed, it might seem a great deal more desirable that I should follow some alternative course of action. It might be generally desirable that I, and others, should join in a general demonstration against a war; but it might be more desirable that I should follow my already developed moral commitment to the abolition of capital punishment. I cannot decide what would be most useful without taking into account my own conception of myself as a committed moral agent who has already for some time been active in the world.

Hegel suggests that an approach to understanding a philosophical view may be to find out what, on that view, are the chief obstacles to overcome. The chief obstacle for the quandarist faced with a moral perplexity is, I think, the void. It is the nightmare realm in which we can find no ground as heavier and disconcertingly heavier burdens descend upon us. The chief problem is how to find footing. The existentialists create it: harden thin air. The naturalists and intuitionists claim to discover it where intelligent men had somehow missed it before. The subjectivists fashion it out of their own approval. None of this is very plausible. We must ask, not how we find ground in the void, but why we think that we are in one. Who are "we" who are supposed to be in a void? Are we not concerned to find answers to our repeated demands for ground? We are not then morally featureless, but we have concerns. The intuitions are ours, the discoveries ours, the introspection ours. We are not disembodied, historyless, featureless creatures. We are beings who have developed to a point, have even cultivated ourselves. The problems which we face must qualify as problems for us, be our problems: it makes a difference who we are. We cannot describe the problem by describing an anonymous collision situation. Aristotle did not give open lectures; St. Paul did not write open letters. When they used the word "we," they spoke from within a community of expectations and ideals: a community within which character was cultivated.

In part, the problem of the featureless "we" arises out of the sense that somehow a universal ethic must be created. The "must" is, of course, a Hobbesian one: it is socially essential. But if we create a universal ethic it must, it seems, be for abstract, general man: the man who has no special features, moral or otherwise. But of course it does not follow that an ethic which is for the man who has no special features is for the man who has none. It is precisely these special features which are likely to give form to the perplexities which arise. They arise for us, not in a void.

It might seem as if they could arise in a void, in which considerations of our own character-defined possibilities and impossibilities are irrelevant, if we fix our gaze on quasi-legal, collision-situation paradigms: on what seem to be moral general standing commands, "Keep promises," "Don't kill." But even if these bare rules be admitted as moral, one could hardly give an acceptable account of moral quandaries by reference to them alone. For, in the first place, there are also general standing moral orders, which give us vast scope in application; and, secondly, there are the perplexities which arise quite outside of the supposedly rule-governed realm of morals: perplexities which come about because of the conflict of commitments and ideals that I as a moral agent have.

To take the resolution of problems as central, and to conceive of problems on the collision-model is indefensibly reductivist. It reduces the topic of moral character to the topic of conscientiousness or rule-responsibility. But it gives no account of the role of the character as a whole in moral deliberation; and it excludes questions of character which are not directly concerned with the resolution of problems.

It may be useful, in closing, to mention some things that I am not claiming. My position is not the subjectivist one that whatever seems right to me is right. Universalizability does provide a test for the rightness of my action, but it sets only minimal requirements, and these often in such fashion as to leave me a range of ways in which I can meet them. I am not claiming that an interest in finding grounds for the resolution of moral problems is the wrong door through which to enter ethics. But there can be more than one door; and the house is a larger one than the quandarists would lead us to believe. I am not insisting that every moral agent must be a saint or a hero, or some combination of both; but only that his moral character cannot be defined solely by reference to his conscientiousness in finding the appropriate rules-of-the-road, or the appropriate means to a common end. I do not contend that all that should count in moral deliberation is whether the proposed action would be acceptable to me in the light of the moral conception that I have of myself. I must first ask what would, in this or any similar situation, be mandatory or permissible for anyone. But this is not all that I must ask. To hold, or presuppose, that it is, is to adopt an indefensibly narrow conception of the subject of ethics.

NOTE

1. The distinction is very similar to Kant's distinction between perfect and imperfect duties. I have avoided making it in Kant's terms because of the possibilities for confusion inherent in Kant's association of the former with one form of ethics "the doctrine of right," and the latter with another.

7

Moral Knowledge and
Moral Principles

J. B. Schneewind

What is the function of moral principles within the body of
moral knowledge? And what must be the nature of moral principles
in order for them to carry out this function? A specific set of
answers to these questions is widely accepted among moral
philosophers—so widely accepted as almost to constitute a sort of
orthodoxy. The answers embody a view of the place of principles
within the body of morality which crosses the lines between
cognitivism and non-cognitivism. Though I have put the question in
cognitivist terms and shall discuss it in those terms, I think a
similar question and a more or less parallel discussion could be
given in non-cognitivist terms. Perhaps the time-honoured debate
between the two positions can be suspended, at least temporarily,
while we examine, not the nature of morality, but its structure.

The generally accepted view of moral principles consists of four
main points. First, moral principles must possess a high degree of
substantial generality. Generality of logical form is not sufficient;
moral rules have this type of generality, but principles must in addition be applicable to a wide variety of cases and circumstances.
They must, I shall say, be relatively context-free; unlike "One ought
to help old ladies crossing busy streets," which is relevant only to a
fairly limited set of situations, "One ought to help people in need" is
applicable to an indefinitely large number of kinds of case, and can,
so far, be a principle. Second, these moral principles must allow of
no exceptions, nor can they rightly be overridden. Unlike moral
rules, such as the one telling us to keep our promises, which may
rightly be broken or suspended in certain circumstances, the principles of morality must always hold and always be binding. Third,

This essay from *Knowledge and Necessity*, Royal Institute of
Philosophy Lectures, vol. 3, 1968–69, pp. 249–62 is reprinted by permission.

moral principles must be substantive and not merely formal. It must, that is, be possible to derive answers to specific and detailed moral questions from a moral principle by applying it to the facts giving rise to the questions. This is the feature which critics of Kant's ethics have frequently said is missing in his formulation of the moral law; its absence is fatal to its claims to be the principle of morality. These three features mark what, for convenience, I shall call a classical moral principle. When we add a fourth feature to these three—relative context-freedom, unexceptionability, substantiality—we have what I shall call a classical first principle. The fourth feature is that the principle must be foundational or basic. Other principles, rules, or particular judgements may derive their validity from a first principle, but it must be an originating source of the authority of lower-order parts of morality and must not in turn depend on other moral judgements or principles for its own binding power. It must possess prior basic validity or authority or truth, not derived or dependent power.

This view of moral principles rests—at least in part—on the claim that if there is to be such a thing as genuine moral knowledge, then there must be at least some true classical first principles. It is this claim which I propose to examine. There are a number of interrelated arguments in its favour. The first, which is tied to the three features making a principle a classical moral principle, is that there must be such principles if any reasons for or against particular moral judgements, or less context-free rules, are to be sound. There must be classical moral principles, that is, according to the first argument, if it is to be possible to reason about moral problems. Building on this position, two further arguments are used to show that these principles must be first principles. One is an attempt to show that first principles must exist if morality is to constitute a rational and coherent system; the other is an attempt to show that first principles must exist if morality is to be more than a merely hypothetical or possible system—if it is to be genuine knowledge, then, the argument goes, we must know the truth of at least one classical first principle. I shall sketch these arguments briefly and indicate why they seem to me to be unsuccessful in establishing their conclusions.

The attempt to show that there must be classical moral principles if reasoning is to be possible about moral matters proceeds on the assumption that the reasoning needed in morality is purely deductive. Now if the only generalities available as premises for such reasoning were rules to which exceptions could be made, or which could be overridden, then one could never be certain that a particular case to which a rule applies is not one of the anomalous ones. Then it would always be possible to assert the general premiss—the rule—and the fact-stating minor premises, and yet deny the conclusion. But then no reason at all would have been given, on this view, for the particular moral judgement asserted in the conclusion. Hence, if it is to be possible to give reasons for moral judgements, there must be some exceptionless principles.

An explanation can of course be given along these lines of the reasoning involved in applying rules or practical principles to the cases where they are relevant, and similar explanations can be given of the many other ways in which we actually think about moral problems—drawing comparisons with similar cases, using analogies, considering what some ideal or admired person would do. Our procedures may, however, be given another interpretation, according to which to adduce a principle may be to give a good reason for doing a certain act, and to apply a principle may be to subsume a case under it in deductive fashion, even if the principle allows of exceptions. For in morality, it may be argued, as frequently in law, we have to do with rebuttable subsumptions. When a relevant and acceptable principle has been adduced, a reason has been given for doing the act it dictates in the circumstances. The burden of proof has thereby been shifted to anyone who thinks that the act ought not to be done. It is open to an objector to give reasons for thinking the case in question to be exceptional; but if no such reasons are given, then the act dictated by the principle remains the act that ought to be done, since it is the act for doing which the best reason has been given. In the absence of definite grounds for thinking the particular case exceptional it would be foolish to take the logical possibility of its being exceptional as a serious reason for doubting that it ought to be done. Similarly it would be foolish to take the bare logical possibility that I might be hallucinating now as a serious reason for thinking that I am not now perceiving my surroundings correctly. We are, therefore, not compelled to interpret the procedures we use in thinking about moral problems as aiming at the production of logically conclusive reasons for or against moral assertions; and so the argument to show that there must be classical moral principles if there is to be reasoning on moral matters collapses.

The next step in the argument is an attempt to show that there must be classical *first* principles if morality is to be rational and coherent (and rationality and coherence are clearly necessary if morality is to be essentially a body of knowledge). The line of thought I shall consider is in fact used to prove an even stronger claim: it is used to prove that there must be one and only one first principle. It is a simple argument. No rational, coherent system can contain contradictions. But if there are a multiplicity of rules and principles, they are liable to become involved in conflicts over particular cases. These conflicts are the equivalents of contradictions among assertions, and it cannot, therefore, be admitted that they are the final truth about morality. It follows that there must be a method of resolving them. There must, then, be a principle in terms of which any conflicts arising between or among relatively context-bound principles can be resolved. There can be only one such principle, for if there were more than one the same sort of conflict could arise again. This principle must be completely context-free, since it must be capable of being applied to any kind of situation. And, finally, it must be supreme in authority, for it may be called upon to adjudicate disputes involving any other principles within the morality over which it reigns. Hence, it must be able to override any other principle and no other principle must be able to override it. And this being so, the authority of other principles must depend on their being allowed to dictate by what is plainly the first principle.

This line of thought—if I may make an historical comment—is of great importance in classical utilitarianism. It enabled Bentham and J. S. Mill to give reasoned support to the utilitarian principle as the one candidate that could fill the requirements for being the classical first principle, without relying on any premises drawn from the content of the accepted morality. The line of argument they invoked is epistemological, yet, if sound, it establishes a principle which can be used to override any common-sense rule or principle, even if no conflict of principles has arisen. For the argument establishes the total supremacy of the conflict-resolving principle and therefore justifies its use in any context.

Yet I think the argument is not sound, for two reasons. First, to say that there are conflicts of rules and principles in specific cases is not to say that there are contradictions in morality which destroy its coherence. Just as there may be good reasons for believing each of two incompatible factual assertions, so there may be good reasons for doing each of two incompatible actions. We may be in a position in which we are unable to tell which of the two assertions—if either of them—is really true and we may similarly be unable to tell for which of the two actions—if either—there are ultimately better reasons. It might in such cases be *morally* desirable to have a principle which would always resolve such conflicts, but even if it were this would not show that the existence of such a principle is a necessity for the cognitive status of morality. Second, even if there were some conflict-resolving principle (or perhaps I should say, even if there is one), it would not follow that such a principle must be the first principle of morals, in the desired sense. From the fact that a given principle is supreme in resolving conflicts it does not follow that it must be supreme in every context. To suppose that it does follow would be like supposing that every decision and rule agreed upon by a happily married couple depends on the authority of the divorce court, since that court has the final word in settling all their affairs if they cannot settle them by themselves. An authority to settle difficulties may conceivably be restricted to doing just that, and its interference in normal cases, where no other conflict of principles or rules is involved, may be totally unwarranted. Any principle established with the help of this argument might simply be as it were a moral ambulance, not for everyday use, having the right of precedence only in emergencies and not in the ordinary run of events. I do not say that this is the correct view: I mention it only as an alternative possibility which militates against this particular argument.

The last set of considerations to be examined leads to the conclusion that there must be some classical first principles, but does not allow the conclusion that there can be only one. It embodies an argument that frequently leads to intuitionism or "Cartesianism" in ethics, and though it is extremely old it has a perennial appeal, appearing even in the thought of those who do not intend to draw intuitionist conclusions from it. Thus Professor D. H. Monro, a defender of naturalism, writes that "we settle moral questions by appealing implicitly to some general principle," and this principle serves as a major premiss to enable us to deduce from a minor, factual, premiss a particular moral judgement. "There does not seem to be any way of testing this [major premiss]," he continues, "except by an appeal to some further principle about what is right or what ought to be the case."[1] This is the way the argument usually begins. It continues with the threat of an infinite, and vicious, regress of moral principles, each one used to support the one to which we have just appealed. The conclusion is that there must be some principle which can be known to be authoritative or true without needing further moral support, and which can give support to the lower-order principles which have been adduced to prove the particular judgement. But such a principle answers to the description of a classical first principle.

This argument presupposes the strict deductive model of giving reasons, which we have already touched on. More interestingly, it presupposes that there is a context-free order of dependence among moral propositions, so that if a particular judgement or a rule or principle ever depends on another then it always does. Since it seems undeniable that we frequently settle particular moral questions by appeal to general principles, and support these by showing that they follow from still more general principles, the conclusion of the argument follows quite obviously. Yet the assumption that there is a context-free order of dependence, though rarely discussed by moral philosophers, is to say the least doubtful. It has been attacked, in rather different ways, by C. S. Peirce and other pragmatists, and more recently by J. L. Austin. They have argued that the distinction between knowledge which depends on being inferred and knowledge which is independent of inference is not one which can be drawn simply in terms of the content or the degree of generality of the knowledge. It is a context-bound distinction. What is for me dependent on some other information need not be so for you: that your name is Jones may be known by me through a complicated inference, and if so my knowledge depends on the premises of the inference, but presumably the knowledge of your name is not thus dependent for you. Similarly, time can make a difference: presumably after years of friendship my knowledge of your name is not dependent on the premises from which I first inferred it. In fact I might now adduce my knowledge of your name as evidence that those premises themselves were true. This point applies as well to moral as to factual knowledge. What is a matter of moral perplexity for one person need not be so for another, and hence a moral assertion which is in need of support, and is dependent for its authority on a further principle, need not be in this position for everyone alike. I may change my mind about a particular class of cases under the influence of a principle I have always accepted; but I may later come to see that this class of cases also falls under a different principle which I have not previously accepted, and may come to accept the principle as showing more clearly the justification for my judgement of the class of cases. Moral philosophers, whatever their theoretical programmes, have in practice always recognised that allegedly basic moral principles depend no less on fairly specific moral propositions than on the other sorts of grounds that have been offered for them; a principle that led to the conclusion that truth-telling was usually wrong, and torturing children normally permissible would be rejected, no matter what kind of proof it might have. But if general principles may sometimes depend on particular moral judgements, and particular judgements sometimes on general principles, then there is no impersonal, necessary order of dependence within the realm of moral knowledge, and we are not compelled to conclude that there must be classical first principles.

So far we have discussed arguments to show that there *must* be classical first principles. Could it simply be that there just *are* such principles? There seem to be two difficulties with this. One is the problem of finding any candidates which fit the requirements for being a classical moral principle. The principles that operate in daily life seem generally to allow of exceptions or of being overridden, and the candidates proposed by philosophers fail, either—like Bentham's version of the utilitarian principle—for the same reason, or—like Kant's formulation of the moral law—because they are only formal. But even if some such principle were to be found, there would remain the problem of whether it would be a *first* principle in the required sense. And here the difficulty seems to be insurmountable. For it is a defining characteristic of moral directives, as contrasted with those of law, tradition, custom, or manners, that none of them can be always relieved of the need to be justified. If particular moral assertions need at times to be justified, so too do moral principles. The facts seem to be that we give reasons for particular judgements in terms of principles, and also that we justify principles in terms of particular judgements. If in different types of situation and in response to different problems we use both procedures to justify moral directives, then it cannot be claimed that in fact there just are principles which never receive support and always give it. To say that there must be some acceptable classical first principles is to insist on forcing the facts to fit a theoretical model.

The epistemological arguments we have considered do not force us, then, to adopt the view that there must be classical first principles if there is to be moral knowledge. There may well be other important arguments to show that there must be principles of this sort if a given morality is to be viable, and it would be interesting to discuss the question of the extent to which, and the ways in which, the above arguments could be rephrased to fit a non-cognitivist view of morality (how can moral attitudes guide conduct if they are not coherent? and how can they be coherent if they are not ultimately based on one fundamental attitude?). Yet as one of the considerations leading to the belief in classical first principles is that there is no other model for understanding moral knowledge than the one which involves commitment to them, I should like to devote the remainder of this essay to a very rough sketch of a different way of viewing it, one which does not involve this commitment.

The model of knowledge which I shall use for discussing morality is the scientific model. It is almost inevitable that a cognitivist view of morality should stress the resemblances between science and ethics; yet to do so is not necessarily to escape from a demand for classical first principles. The ideal of reasoning, and the correlated ideal of knowledge, behind the belief in classical first principles, is a geometric and deductive ideal, and frequently leads to intuitionistic positions. But it can also lead to certain varieties of "scientific" morality. Thus, Herbert Spencer's moral theory is essentially a deductive system based on a single classical first principle. What is supposed to be distinctively "scientific" about it is that the principle is allegedly derived wholly from the discoveries of the positive sciences. J. S. Mill's version of utilitarianism is less wholeheartedly scientific than Spencer's view: Mill does not think that the single basic principle of morality can be scientifically proven. But every moral problem and every other rule of morality can, under the supervision of the utilitarian principle, be given purely scientific treatment (or will be susceptible of it, when the social sciences have matured). Still, one need not fall back on classical first principles when one attempts to show that morality can be understood along the lines of a science. There is at least one other way in which science can serve as a model, a way pointed out in certain of its aspects by John Dewey. It may be argued that what is scientific about morality is neither some basic principle or principles on which it rests, nor its reliance on special sciences for most of the premises on which moral reasoning proceeds, but the general structure of its contents and its methods. Moral beliefs show the same kind of susceptibility to systematisation, criticism, revision, and re-systematisation that factual beliefs show. There are analogues to theory and data among our moral beliefs, and these can be understood as related in ways like those in which theory and data are related in the sciences. If we can show that this way of understanding morality is feasible, we shall have undercut the argument claiming that the model which commits us to classical first principles is the only possible one.

Principles of morality function in some ways like the formulations of laws which scientists propose. There are, at any given time, a number of specific judgements, rules and ideals, the correctness of which we have no hesitation in affirming. Formulations of moral principles serve to systematise and generalise these beliefs, and in doing so they articulate what may be called the spirit of our morality. They pick out the aspects of our less general beliefs which are not tied to specific circumstances and which would remain constant in a variety of situations. This enables them to express the point or rationale of specific moral convictions. And this in turn enables us to carry out a critical and explicit projection of our moral beliefs to new kinds of problem and new combinations of circumstances. The formulation of a principle to cover classes of cases where we know the rights and wrongs, and the application of the principle thus formed to the solution of difficulties which arise where we have no firm convictions, are analogous, in a rough but fairly clear way, to the formulation of a law to cover a set of well-established data and its use to predict results of new combinations of causal factors.

We must avoid taking too simple a view of this procedure, either in science or in morality. Recent work in the philosophy of science shows that it is misleading to think of each formulation of a scientific law as operating in isolation from every other formulation. Laws are expressed in the context of general theories, and they, as well as many of the concepts involved in assembling the data of the science, must be understood within that context. Similar points hold of morality. I do not mean to suggest that philosophical theories of ethics occupy the position of general theories in the sciences. What occupies the analogous position is rather the general world outlook—typically a religious outlook, or a non-religious world-view still conscious of its non-religiousness—in which a morality is embedded. A large part of the terms and beliefs of these general metaphysical views of life and the world are inseparably intertwined with what we tend to think of as distinctively moral beliefs. The very concepts by which we pick out subjects for moral predication may be rooted in religious or metaphysical propositions, and these in turn may be unintelligible without their evaluative and moral implications. Thus it will take a whole set of moral principles, understood against a metaphysical background, to articulate our moral beliefs adequately and to provide an intelligible and applicable projection of them to new problems. These complex interconnections give rise in morality to a phenomenon comparable to the use in scientific practice of "theory-laden" observation terms. Many terms employed in the description of particular things and events carry strong theoretical implications, so that in using them we are committed to accepting certain scientific laws. Similarly, many of the terms used for describing our commonest actions and social relations have moral implications built into them. Those who use them are by that fact committed to at least the prima facie acceptance of certain moral directives: to say, e.g., that I am "married to" so-and-so is to imply my acceptance of a directive against having sexual relations with anyone else. The moral implications of terms like this have been called "practice-defining rules," and contrasted with "summary rules." It is not necessary that a comparison of moral principles with scientific laws should force us to accept the view that all moral principles are of the latter type. But it must equally be borne in mind that the vocabulary embodying practice-defining rules is itself open to alteration and in this respect like the theory-laden terms used in scientific observation.

If the relations between fact and theory in science are complex, so is the way in which the acceptability of a theory depends on the data it organises and the predictions it warrants. Laws that unify a large body of well-established facts and empirical generalisations, that enable us to make successful predictions over a wide range, and that suggest numerous points for further fruitful experiment and theory-construction, are not easily abandoned. A well-founded theory cannot be overthrown by the negative results of a single "crucial experiment." Logically speaking, it is always possible to defend a formulation of law from a counter-instance by explaining the instance in terms of an *ad hoc* hypothesis, or by treating it as due to faulty instruments, bad observation, freakish accident, etc. In terms of the economy and strategy of research this is not always a bad move to make. It is only when the amount of evidence that must be avoided instead of absorbed grows fairly large, when the original theory becomes cumbrous and difficult to use because of the qualifications and adjustments needed to make it fit the evidence, that serious exploration of alternative theories takes place; and the existence of some viable alternative theory is needed before an accepted view will be abandoned. A new theory, if it is of the most attractive kind, will explain the evidence which told in favour of the older view—perhaps recasting it in a new terminology—and it will explain as well what was anomalous or required special hypotheses from the older standpoint. It will enable new areas of investigation to be developed and new types of prediction to be successfully made. It will, in short, perform the same functions as the replaced theory, but better.

If the study of the history of science is still at a comparatively early stage of development, the study of the history of moral systems has hardly even begun. At this point it can only be proposing a hypothesis to say that the pattern of thought revealed in studies of "scientific revolutions" may be useful as a guide in investigating the development of norms and values. Still, even a rudimentary knowledge of history may allow us to see how this pattern could be relevant. Moral systems are used, not to predict, but to direct and evaluate conduct. They can fail to operate in any number of ways, as scientific theories can fail. Yet accepted systems have a definite value in virtue of the fact that they are widely accepted: they give shape and coherence and predictability to large segments of life, and they are therefore not lightly to be abandoned. Hence no single failure is likely to suffice to overthrow an accepted morality. As in the case of reasonably good theories, it is likely to take an accumulation of difficulties before serious investigation of alternatives occurs. These difficulties may arise from a number of causes. There can, for instance, be failure of relevance to prevalent problems. A morality developed within one type of social or economic situation may be carried over while technological or financial changes occur which effectively alter the nature of the society in which people accept it; and in the new situation the old directives may simply fail to cover recurring problems generally felt to be important. In such circumstances a morality also may fail by giving guidance which is not specific enough, or which it is not feasible to expect people to follow. R. H. Tawney's well-known discussion of the failure of the medieval church to provide an adequate set of precepts for action in a developing capitalist economy gives illustrations of these points. Either the types of monetary transaction vital to a capitalist economy were not covered by any of the standard directives or else they were covered by directives involved in concepts like that of usury and just price which it was no longer feasible to apply. People simply could not live in accordance with the dictates implied by those terms, and were forced to find new ways of organising their actions. Another kind of difficulty with a moral code arises when a change of circumstances transforms a once coherent set of practical demands into directives that repeatedly require incompatible or self-defeating actions. This is the sort of situation involved in what R. K. Merton calls "anomie," where (roughly) socially acceptable goals can only be reached by breaking socially acceptable rules; and there are other types as well. Still another kind of difficulty with a moral system arises when the religious or metaphysical outlook with which it is involved ceases to be widely accepted: its categories may then cease to seem relevant to the daily problems people face, and therefore its judgements may be increasingly wide of the mark.

Complaints of these kinds about an accepted morality have often been answered by its defenders with the claim that the fault lies not in the moral code but in the social system which is changing in immoral directions, or in the weakness of men, which makes them less willing than usual to expend the effort needed to live up to moral demands, or in the faithlessness of men, which leads them to abandon the revealed truth, or in any of an innumerable variety of factors which allow one to admit the failure of the system to give useful guidance but to cling to the system nonetheless. As in similar cases where counter-evidence to a well-based scientific law is presented, this procedure has a definite justification. But in morality, as in science, it is not always used. There are times when abandoning a moral principle seems more reasonable than continuing to claim that it is true despite the numerous exceptions and qualifications it requires. And the abandonment of one principle is likely to involve repercussions in other parts of the system: the controversy over the morality of birth-control may be mentioned in illustration, touching as it does on the nature of the family, the function of sexual relations and the permissibility of pleasure, the place of women, the authority of various institutions, etc. In this connection it would be interesting to investigate the part played, in basic moral change, by the availability of some alternative system of morality, which would incorporate what is still held to be true in the old view while advancing to new insights on the points of difficulty in that view.

These brief comments may indicate some of the ways in which the structure of morality is like the structure of science, and may point towards an interpretation of moral principles and moral knowledge which does not force us to a belief in what I have called classical first principles. It may help to clarify the hypothesis being suggested if I add one or two further remarks.

The claim that morality is "cognitive" and that we now have some moral knowledge is not the claim that all our moral convictions as they now stand are true or justifiable. We do not think any such implication to be involved in the claim that we have knowledge of geology or physics or mathematics. We are aware that many of the particular opinions and theories we now hold in these disciplines will eventually be discarded as mistaken, but we have no hesitation in claiming knowledge within these fields nonetheless. The situation is the same as regards morality. I have suggested that moral principles can be supported by showing that they provide adequate articulation of less general moral beliefs which are at a given time held without doubt. I do not mean to imply, however, that the beliefs to which we are at this moment committed are beyond criticism—far from it. Our morality has been derived from many sources and shaped by many influences. It is moreover deeply involved with our factual and religious or metaphysical beliefs. There is no guarantee that it is free from inconsistency, error, or superstition, either on the purely moral plane or in its non-moral involvements. Though it is bound to be our main starting-point in thinking about practical matters, we must assume that progress and improvement in moral knowledge are possible. This is no more, and no less, than we must assume in every area of thought where truth is an aim. Most moral philosophers, however, have thought of moral progress chiefly as the progressive improvement of the human race—as a slow growth in the degree to which men live up to the demands of morality. Few have considered the possibility that moral progress may consist primarily in the growth of moral knowledge. One reason for this may have been their acceptance of the presuppositions that lead to a demand for classical first principles. For on that view, if we do not now know at least the first principles of morality, we cannot really know anything of morality (though of course our opinions may be true). But if we already know the first principles of morality then whatever progress is to be made in our knowledge of the subject (discounting that which will result solely from the improvement of scientific knowledge) must be comparatively minor. The view being put forward here in opposition to this places no such block in the way of contemplating the improvement of even our most general or most cherished principles.

Does this view leave open the possibility that moral knowledge might be, or become, esoteric, the possession of a small group of experts? This did happen to scientific knowledge, yet we do not wish to grant that it could occur with respect to morality. Nor, indeed, are we required to grant it. Any claim to know something must be open to assessment by the relevant group of those qualified to judge. In the case of morality this group consists of those who are able and willing to live their lives—to the usual extent—under the guidance of moral directives understood as such, and not taken simply as customs or taboos or religious commands or positive laws. It is a necessary, if not a sufficient, condition of the justifiability of any claim to knowledge that those who are competent to judge should come to agree with the claim when they investigate it in the proper manner. Moral claims are no exception, and the disagreement of informed and thoughtful moral agents with our own moral assertions gives us a reason for being less confident of them. Still, disagreement, even when the reasons for it are given, is not refutation, and one defense of controversial opinions which must be admitted does leave an opening for the charge of esotericism. It must, I think, be granted that some people really are more insightful and sensitive, morally speaking, than others, and that these people may possibly be ahead of the majority in their grasp of the morality of a particular kind of action. But the distinction between insight and delusion—between wisdom and charlatanry—is no less real than that between science and quackery, and it involves the same basic point: eventually the community of competent judges will come to accept the one and reject the other, if it looks into the matter with sufficient care.

Our moral principles, then, must articulate our unshakable convictions and provide us with adequate guidance for future decisions. In addition they must be capable of calling forth agreement in a potentially unlimited community of moral agents. How can we be sure enough of any principles, under such stringent conditions, to claim that we know they are correct? Well, of course, our scientific theories and hypotheses must survive similar tests, and we manage to make this claim about some of them. And after all the quest for moral knowledge did not begin yesterday. The moral principles most of us accept have had to survive a fair amount of testing and sifting in the course of time. There is therefore a fair amount of evidence to show that they can give acceptable guidance and can form the nucleus of a moral community. To say that we *know* some of them to be correct is to express our reasoned confidence that they, or something very close to them, will, of those available for consideration, come out best in relation to all the evidence, future as well as past. It is also to express our decision, at least for the present, to hold to these principles despite any objections to or difficulties with them. This decision need be no more irrational than similar decisions made by scientists. The principles that we decide, in this fashion, to maintain are the ones we consider basic. The theory of classical first principles involves mistaking this kind of decision for a discovery that certain principles are basic because of their own inherent nature.

NOTE

1. D. H. Monro, *Empiricism and Ethics* (Cambridge, 1967), p. 8.

8

The Experience of Values

Frithjof Bergmann

I. THE WORLD IS NOT "NEUTRAL"

The world is not an object that confronts me. It does not "present itself"; it is not something that faces me from the other side of a distance and submissively waits for my appraisal. It is not a separated tame thing. It is not neutral. It is not a field indifferently strewn with indifferent facts. It almost never is simply *the case*. It is not just there. It acts on me in ten thousand different ways. It invites and rejects, excites and charms, threatens and overwhelms me. It horrifies and disappoints me but fills me in the next minute with exhilaration. Occasionally it wounds me, but it also soothes and calms.

I am not at all sure that all these complex interactions can be reduced to a matter of "positive" and "negative" value, to a single parameter that points only in two directions. And yet most contemporary theories of ethics seem at least to give the *impression* that this can be done. Part of this is due to the very frequently employed distinction between values and facts. When the factual, descriptive content of judgments is separated from the evaluative component or force, all the variety and concreteness is usually treated as part of the description, and the evaluative aspect is reduced to a quite general endorsement or to a rejection. One does, of course, distinguish the degree or the manner of this positive or negative judgment. There are judgments supported by reasons, recommendations, commands, and merely emotive expressions of approval and of disfavor. But that is not my point. My concern at the moment is not with degrees, or even with degrees of support, but with the varieties among different values. One is apt to think that words like "rotten," "awful," "filthy," "horrible," "disgusting," and "dirty" have quite different descriptive contents but that the evaluative

This essay from *Inquiry* 16 (1973): 247–79 is reprinted by permission.

part of their meaning is simply "negative" yet of one and the same kind. One imagines, in other words, that the meanings of words like "horrible" and "disgusting" and "rotten" can each be divided into two parts. One of these is descriptive. It refers to a complex occurrence of features, to a set of "neutral," "objective" facts. The other part is thought to contain the evaluation, and it is thought of primarily in terms of degrees. It is imagined as a kind of minus-sign or as a head-shake which can be big or little, hesitant or emphatic, but which is otherwise dumb. Eventually I will argue that this view is quite implausible—if one considers words like "awful" and "dirty" it seems to me fairly obvious even on superficial inspection that this framework is somehow mistaken, that the evaluative components are different in kind and not only in degree—but first some clarification is needed.

The most important part of this can be put briefly. I do not maintain that the view that the evaluative content is of one kind is logically or otherwise entailed by the fact/value distinction. Obviously one can make that distinction and hold at the same time that the evaluative content of words is very diverse (one could even hold that it is *sui generis* for each word). Also I do not want to raise the question whether three or seven important philosophers have explicitly defended this view. This would be quite contrary to my picture of this situation. To my mind the notion that the evaluative force could be charted on a single or at least on very few scales (say the moral, the aesthetic, and the prudential) is a hidden assumption, or one might also say an unintended and unacknowledged result. It underlies most discussions in the theory of value, but it is not itself contested or brought out into the open. This, in fact, is precisely one of the things I mean to accomplish. An enormous amount of attention has been lavished on the question concerning the degree of the evaluative force, on what reasons can be used to support it, and on the nature of the support that these reasons give. This concern has been so paramount that the various ethical theories that currently contend with each other are all essentially different answers to this principal question. This is the issue that names and divides them: are the reasons merely persuasive or are they of a stricter logical nature? I want to claim only that philosophers often *sound* as if the evaluative component, once its degree and the reasons for it have been considered, is no more than a pro or a con, and that the fact/value distinction has helped to produce that *impression*, since the evaluative component is often so treated when it is employed. If someone protested that this is decidedly no more than an impression; that it is but an unfortunate misunderstanding produced by the accidental professional preoccupation with this rather than with other, less interesting questions; that one of course never meant to deny that the evaluative components may be extraordinarily various, since surely "horrible" and "disgusting" could not be analyzed into two different descriptive contents plus two essentially similar evaluations—both simply "negative" though perhaps to different degrees—if one so protested, I would be pleased. An occasional agreement among philosophers does not mean that we are done for. Things may still become interesting later. But I would go on to say that this—in such a case unintended impression—is not only given by the non-cognitivist or non-descriptivist theories of value but is also created by the other theories, even by those who do not make a radical fact/value distinction but think of ethical judgments as making certain assertions of fact. It may receive more power from emotivism than from anywhere else, since the reduction to a pro- and con-attitude is there most explicitly present, but it is fed by all theories that are currently discussed in ethics and may even be the one thing they all have in common.

What I have in mind in the case of cognitivism is, for example, the fact that intuitionists usually speak only of very few non-natural properties, those denoted by the words "right," "good," or "ought." (Sidgwick, "ought"; Moore, "good"; Ross, both "good" and "ought.") An intuitionist may of course be prepared to introduce additional "non-natural" properties. But it is a fact that intuitionists have not usually done this, and that their theories give one the picture of a generally neutral and indifferent world in which one or two special properties gleam like nuggets of gold in a sandbox. These properties may be abundantly present, but there are only one or two against a uniform background. The situation is similar with the theories that have often been called "definist." R. B. Perry's definition of good as "being an object of favorable interest" and F. C. Sharp's which gives "desired upon reflection" as a translation of "good" both seem to me to reduce at least all *ethical* values to a matter of "desire," or respectively "interest."[1]

Telling me that I should think in terms of a simple positive or negative value, or in terms of "goodness" and "badness" is a little like asking me to go through a museum and telling me that I can only either shake my head or otherwise nod it. I could do that, of course, and I could shake or nod with more or less vigor, but it would be ludicrously confining, and I certainly could not communicate what I felt. Moreover—and this is the point—the situation would not change much if I had permission to use as many purely descriptive, valuationally neutral words as I liked and could shake or nod my head in addition. A painting might seem impressive, majestic, coy, timid, self-conscious, or sentimental; or it might be grotesque, clownish, boorish, or severe or ascetic. Each of these words would be normally regarded as having some evaluative ingredient; but if I were told to make the descriptive content explicit, to articulate that part and only that part of its meaning in words, I would not know how to do it. What is the strictly descriptive content of "grotesque" for example? I can think of words that are more or less close to it in meaning, like "ghoulish," "clumsy," "untoward," "fantastic," or "ugly," but these are, if anything, more evaluative and certainly not purely descriptive.

It still may seem as if my point depends on the relative strangeness of the words that I have picked for examples. But I do not think it does. We could take the modest and self-effacing word "pleasant" and I think we would find that all serious attempts to actually express its descriptive content in words—that is, all attempts actually to *do* this, where we no longer let ourselves off with the assumption that it must be possible somehow—would end in failure. (That the word "pleasant" can sometimes be used for a purely descriptive purpose—just like the still simpler word "good" is sometimes so used—does not affect my contention.) In fact, with the word "pleasant" one would not only find it impossible to complete this task; one would not even know how to begin. It would be as if somebody had asked one to specify the components of "red" or of some other primary color. That one here would not even know how to start shows, I think, that we are not only dealing with an accidental shortage of words. With the word "grotesque" we might have supposed this. One could have imagined that the components of "grotesque" can really be separated (in one's mind, as it were), and that the difficulty of articulating them was due simply to there not being any words for them in the English language, but that they perhaps could be expressed in a language that had more adjectives at its disposal. But if the difficulty is not of that sort with the word "pleasant," then this at least begins to suggest that the same may be true for the other examples we mentioned. (Of course I do not maintain that the descriptive content of words that also have evaluative meaning can *never* be expressed. Probably, on occasion, it can be. The word "cowardly" may be an instance.)

Earlier I spoke of the one-dimensional conceptualization of values and criticized it. This may have given the impression that I only wanted to substitute a larger number of parameters for the one, or the very few, that usually occur in such discussions. But this is not my intention. I am not only saying that something goes wrong if we add the same simple "negative" or "positive" value to the descriptive part of qualities that are so different, and that we should therefore conceive of quite various value-components that have to be added to the descriptive parts—one for grotesqueness and another different kind for the melancholic. This situation cannot be rectified through a diversification of values, for the trouble lies not only in the value-components. What I really mean to question is the more basic idea that these qualities can be divided, that they fundamentally should be understood on the model of "compounds."

This comes out more strongly, I think, if we turn from this analytic to a more phenomenological consideration and focus on the actual experience of these situations. What we notice is the stark and unqualified "givenness" of these qualities. They present themselves and they confront us. If we set aside all explanatory frameworks and assumptions, even those that are only hazy shadows and habits, and make the effort to see clearly nothing but the actual brute experience of them (and that is at least a large part of what Husserl meant by his "return to the facts") then we are struck by the simple "thereness" of them. We look and we *see* that this gesture is clumsy while that one is graceful. We listen and we *hear* the sadness of a little tune. In all of this we are spectators and the qualities do not act on us, do not even offer themselves to us, but they simply *are* in a stolid and assertive independence.

The purpose behind the hard look at these qualities is of course not to reject the fact/value distinction in general. Naturally there are contexts in which this categorization is useful. But that is not the issue. What I am saying is that this separation does not *work* for the qualities under discussion. Nor is this argument on its way to the conclusion that values and facts are so exquisitely blended that it is impossible to sort them apart. At stake is something completely different. It is this: The basic orientation, the kind of "stance" that one adopts toward the whole issue of values, and derivatively from that, toward the question of how one should live, is powerfully influenced by the subterranean conceptions that we have tried to bring to the surface. These ideas exist not only in philosophy but are pervasive. (Every time you are challenged to "stick to the facts" and not make value judgments you are in their presence.) Thus far, I have only made them explicit and set them into confrontation with a class of qualities that do not seem to fit into this framework. The eventual aim of this is not any one specific conclusion. The idea is rather to dissolve a conceptual pattern that has ordered the general approach to the theory of values, that has marked out the points that are regarded as problems and has defined what may count as their solution. In short: the aim is to achieve a new perception and a different orientation.

We can now move on to a second conception, though we will deal with it only quite briefly. It is again not a philosophical theory that is explicitly avowed and defended but another underlying view or image which has been fostered by much philosophical thinking, though it has numerous other and important sources. It differs in two respects from the first one. Its connection to technical philosophical claims is more tenuous and less transparent, and it is decidedly not intended. One rejects it as soon as it is openly stated.

I shall once more use the comparison to a museum, but now to make a quite different point. We sometimes talk as if life were a walk through a museum. We talk as if it were at a safe distance from us—a succession of objects, immobile and quiet—and we act as if living were an exercise in connoisseurship. To be blunter: we try to gainsay the fact that the world *acts* on us. We treat ourselves sometimes as if we were outside observers, as if we lived in a sacrosanct, extraterritorial bubble, from which we could safely and calmly survey not only the world but also everything that we imagine to occur inside us. In the process we misconstrue some of the ways in which the world affects us. We postulate a mitigating buffer that removes us from the external world. We make the effect that the world has on us less direct, and this, again, opens one road into the theory of values and bars others.

Take the experience of being tempted by a cigarette or a drink of whiskey. As soon as we begin to give a philosophical analysis of such a common situation a picture comes into play. Customarily it is only a tacit, shadowy backdrop but I will now bring it deliberately into relief. We imagine, or postulate, the cigarette as an essentially neutral object and think that it produces across the distance a sensation or a tickle of desire in us. So again we make a split, only this time we envision the parts in a sequence. The world "out there" is once more made neutral. It is a sheer causal agent. The element of value is separated off and relocated. It is internalized and vested in our own sensation. Thus we no longer confront value directly; there is a buffer, an almost temporary intermediary.

This way of seeing things may be a concretization of the more abstract idea that "nothing possesses value except in relation to the human." It may represent the transposition of that humanistic declaration into something of a story. If so, the extremes to which we have gone are amazing: to take from God the ultimate authority in moral matters we drained the whole world of value and placed all of it into man's sensations. In a sense we went even further. For this thinking postulates an inner Ego, a Subject, who observes these feelings, and ultimately even the sensations are still neutral, for in the end it is this inner Subject who values or rejects them, who exercises choices, and he therefore is the only real locus of all valuation.

That this inner observer does not actually exist becomes, I believe, obvious as soon as he is imagined vividly enough. But quite apart from him other questions must be raised against this bifurcation. Take a situation that is very threatening. Imagine a tree falling down in your direction. Does it really make sense to believe that we do not perceive the danger directly but that the "neutral" tree causes a sensation in us and that the whole response of our body is produced by it? But if not, then why should the experience of being charmed or tempted be metaphysically so different from that of terror? For that matter, what of other organisms? Are we to suppose that they too respond largely to their own sensations? If so, would this assumption not conflict with everything we know about awareness in the lower forms of life? Moreover, is this not in any case an inherently strange view of organisms? Is it not a needlessly complex theory of how organisms interact with their environment? Still further, what of Gestalt Psychology, or of Piaget's contention that infants perceive (in his terminology) "affective qualities" *before* they have either a concept of self, or of their own body? There are other, similar questions, but in the end some very simple points are stronger.

It is a matter of immediate experience. If we simply look and see (not in any special "bracketed" or Husserlian manner, but just with open eyes) we notice that this is plainly not what happens. In these situations there often is no sensation inside us. It may sound strange, but if one wanted to describe these experiences correctly one would have to say that it is the cigarette itself, or the drink itself that has the quality of "being-tempting." And the same is true for the falling, threatening tree, for a leaf that is luxurious, for a vulnerable face, or a voice that is revolting. The main pattern in all these situations is that of a presentation. One *confronts*. Just as earlier we noted that no seam separates fact from value, so we now contend that there is no duality of different, neutral stimulus and value-quality-endowed sensation. In direct experience these qualities are not by-products. On the contrary, they "come first," their assertion is immediate, and it is they who in turn evoke effects. They are of one piece with the "given" and are encountered as integral with it.

The imagery associated with the two-stage process completely falsifies the general structure of these situations. There is not a neutral world out there which causes sensations (pleasant or unpleasant) inside us to which we then in turn react. And there is no sacrosanct, unaffected "point of observation" from which these sensations are perceived. These qualities are outside, in the public world and they themselves affect us, and they do so not mediately but quite directly, very much as if they were forces. Their influence does not stop short before a "self" that surveys the scene from the calm of an "inner fortress." Nothing is a barrier to them. We are like bits of wood in their surf.

To say all this is not simply to propose an "alternative conceptual framework." It involves a different experience of oneself and of the world. There should be a powerful sense of displacement, of an outward shift; the discovery that much to which we had so far given only a doubtful, internal, flimsy existence is in fact real, and out there, and substantial.

Consider one further example. You enter a room and the silence inside is "oppressive." This is not a feeling imparted to you, it is *in* the room. Something has descended on the people sitting in their chairs, something holds them in place. But then the attention, first of one, then of the others, begins to turn to you. Sartre is fascinated by this experience of being looked at by another, and he describes it as a "restructuring of space." The lines of your world converge toward the other's eyes. "It is as if your world drained into the point from which his look originates," it feels like water flowing down a sink-hole. This too is something that happens outside, in the room. And in the next stage there might be the expectancy for you to speak. And it too originates outside you. It builds up as a pressure, comes closer, forms itself around you, and finally edges you over a brink. Suddenly you realize that you are speaking.

The main point at issue, of course, need not only be "seen." One is by no means forced to refer to nothing but "direct experience." Far from it. Perfectly conventional philosophic considerations can be adduced in its support. There is, for instance, the fact that we do not ordinarily either discover or verify the presence of these qualities through an act of introspection. What we observe is the object, and not a sensation inside us. If we are in doubt whether someone else is or is not angry, we look at *him* rather than inside ourself, and the same holds true for all the other examples that have been mentioned, from the gracefulness of a gesture to the bleakness of a landscape. This is philosophically telling, for if the objects we faced were indeed "neutral," and if they merely produced certain feelings in us, then we would be *compelled* to act otherwise; we would *have* to introspect to make these judgments.

Or, again, there are situations in which we do not realize that something does indeed tempt or attract us until we are already, so to say, in forward motion. We suddenly notice that we have begun to perform an action, and this first tells us that we were attracted. This, too, could not happen if the temptingness of the object were communicated to us via a sensation. (We would notice the sensation. That it is unconscious does not fit the account as given, and is in itself unlikely. Unconscious in what sense, and why?)

Other, similar considerations could be mentioned, but ultimately there is no need to list them, for my main thought has been all along to raise to daylight a set of assumptions that once exposed hardly call for slowly rehearsed refutations.

The result should be a sense of contrast: A certain kind of thinking is almost automatic to us ("The world, facts are *of course* neutral") and yet this seeming platitude rests on foundations that collapse if one inspects them. All the same these premises have had an almost uncontested hold on a domain of thinking. On their basis only some approaches seemed conceivable. With them gone it is like a new day.

We still have to look at a third division. To understand it properly one aspect of the so-called Mind/Body problem must be sketched. This quick delineation is of course not meant to address this problem in its own right. I only hope to trace some lines and to mark out a place from which the cut that runs into the theory of value can be sharply seen.

One root question which opens the Mind/Body problem is the doubt about the status of our perceptions. In the habits of our weekday thinking we live with the conviction that we perceive material objects, and that they exist quite independently of us. Their shapes and colors are real, are outside us, and are public and objective. This seems firm and stable and obvious, and yet, when we look again and only stumble along with the simplest kind of thinking, this stability begins to tilt. We only have to remember that our perceptions are of course communicated to us through sense-organs, that we really receive only a radiation of a certain wave-length, which our specific neural apparatus transforms into this shape or this green surface, but which might not look at all the same if our eyes were fashioned differently, and that security is lost. If we continue to think along these lines all manner of facts and general considerations drive us further. Facts like the occurrences of color-blindness, or the yellow that accompanies jaundice, facts like that shapes change when we press against our eyeballs, but also all we know from physics about light- and sound-waves, as e.g., the fact that there are many waves which our organs do *not* see—all this joins in, and soon the world begins to lose its substance. After some further steps along this path we may come to the conclusion that everything is mere appearance, is dependent on us and subjective, and finally we may end with the suspicion that everything perhaps exists but in the privacy of your or of my mind.

In this way we shift from one extreme to the other. Seen in a different perspective, we are in the presence of a paradox. There are two views which stand in radical conflict with each other. Yet both seem equally legitimate. On the one side, it seems perfectly obvious that we do perceive a public, objective, material world that is really out there, but it seems equally evident, on the other side, that this is not so, that our perceptions are a function of our sense-organs and hence subjective and private.

A large part of the history of philosophy since Descartes has consisted in attempts to resolve this main dilemma. One could think of the various philosophic positions as a set of proposals to draw the line between Mind and Matter, between the objective and subjective, the public and private, in different places. One might represent them as opting for points on a continuum between two extremes. Idealism and Materialism would be at the end poles, each following one side of the dilemma through to its conclusion while utterly denying the other. Locke's, Hume's and Kant's positions could be thought to make the claim for different places in between. Locke, for example, thinks of the primary qualities as outside and objective, and considers the secondary to be private and subjective.

I have already said that I am here only using this problem to mark out a point of perspective, and entirely to that end—not with any claim that they advance a solution. Two comments can now be made.

First: Whatever the center of this problem may be, one thing that certainly aggravates it is the tight interlocking of certain associations, the blending and coupling of several different and vague notions. We fuse the ideas of the "mental," of the "subjective," the "private," the "internal," the "illusory," and the "unreal" and form of them a single amalgam. This we constitute as a single, powerful pole on one side of this division. Similarly we join the notions of the "material," "objective," "external," and "real" again into one unit and set this on the other side. In this way we create the picture of a dichotomy. We make the world Manichean and divide it between an either and an or. If something is mental, we think of it also as somehow "subjective" and "unreal" and "internal" and "private." If not, then we tend to think of it under the ready-made juxtaposed configuration.

To single out some examples that illustrate this. The argument that our perceptions depend on our sense-organs is often believed to prove the conclusion that what we see is therefore illusory and not real. But this, clearly, is a confusion. The argument proves only what it says; namely, that our perceptions are functions of our sense-organs. Still we tend to link the notion of the "illusory" with that which is produced by our sense-organs, and that makes it easy to slide from one to the other. All the same it is an elementary error. And the same goes for the inference that the world must be "mental." The plain fact that our perceptions vary with our sense-organs simply does not carry us all the way to that startling conclusion. If we reach it then it is only because we first pretended that there was a gap, and then leapt from the side of the "either" all the way across to the side of the "or." An even more extreme case of the same sort occurs when the same argument brings people to suspect that the objects they see are not really outside them, but are really images inside their head. This is again the result of sliding via several associations from one of the terms we conglomerate in this amalgam to quite another. (Possibly from "mental" to "inside my head.") We again operate with a false either/or which occurs only because we illogically combine all these terms into two conglomerates that face each other. This allows us to think that because something has been shown to "depend on our sense-organs" it is therefore also "mental" and beyond that "in our heads."

Second: Wherever the real solution to the larger Mind/Body problem may lie, there can be no doubt that the careful and proper severing of these connections presents itself as a first task. The notions of the "mental," the "private," the "subjective," the "unreal," and the "inside us" must be cut apart from each other. In much of our common thinking, but in technical philosophy too, we still divide the world like Moses splitting the sea. We simplify our conceptual machinery and leave ourselves only a "here" and a "there": "there," the objective-material-external-and-real and "here," the subjective-mental-internal-unreal. In fact we not only reduce these multiple and different distinctions to the picture of two hostile "realms," we do not even keep the border between them in one single place. We shift and move the chasm between them, imagining it here at one time, and assuming it in other places at others.

Sometimes we imagine this break in a very peculiar place. This happens when we treat colors and shapes and sounds as objective, external and real but posit the main-line division between them and all the qualities we discussed: when we give to the sadness of a piece of music, to the gracefulness of a gesture, to the charm of a vase the modality of the subjective, internal and mental but imagine colors and sounds on the other, the far side of the split. It is this that establishes the connection between the general Mind/Body problem and everything we did before. By now it should be clear that the two earlier separations, those into descriptive and value component, and into neutral object and sensation represent embellishments and elaborations of this deeper division. The arguments against all three therefore flow together into one cumulative array; they reinforce each other and combine their weights.

This leads to the conclusion that the radical division suggested by the words "subjective" and "objective" does not apply. There are of course differences between the status of shapes and colors and the status of charm and grotesqueness, but they are differences of degree and of gradation. These naturally should be determined, yet it is clear even now that whatever they may turn out to be in the end they are not anything like the contrast between a brute given and a something that is created by the brain.

More exactly, at stake is a denial. Whatever the exact status of colors and of grotesqueness may be, I mean to deny that qualities like colors are on one side of this division while qualities like grotesqueness are on the other. The point is not that qualities like sadness or grotesqueness should be shifted from one side across to the other, that they are not subjective but objective instead. The upshot is rather that they are neither, that this bifurcation is a trapdoor into a blind alley.

In sum: I want to deny that the world is in any sense neutral. The sadness of a piece of music, the bleakness of a dried barren landscape, the melancholy of a weeping willow, the austerity of a building, the flamboyance of a leaf and even the attractiveness of a vase are qualities that are essentially on a par with the shapes and sizes and colors of things. This should challenge the tacit and silently assumed picture that many of us have of the world. The world of physics and of commonsense is not the "really real" world. The motions and dimensions and weights of things do not have privileged status. When things look somber or grotesque then they have these qualities in at least very nearly the same sense in which they have their weights and textures and colors. The world is therefore much richer and denser than we sometimes imagine. It is a proliferation and crowding; it is an excess.

I will still add four specific arguments in support of this general contention. First: One might object that our experience of the sadness of a piece of music, or our experience of the fact that it is majestic, is clearly a function of our sense-organs and of our cultural experience, that all we really receive are sound-waves, and that these are therefore not qualities which the music has but rather something that we "contribute," something that we make of the sound-waves. My reply to this would be that one can say exactly the same thing about colors. They, too, are dependent on the physiological equipment with which we perceive them, and experimental studies have shown that training and conditioning influence our perception of them to a surprising degree. But we nevertheless think of colors as qualities that objects have and think of them as external and as belonging to the real world. And to do this is proper, for to call them on that account "subjective," or to think of them as not really there would be to draw a conclusion that their dependence on our physiology does not warrant. This argument therefore cannot establish that there is a categorical difference between qualities like sadness on the one hand, and colors or shapes on the other. On the contrary, their dependence on our sense-organs is precisely a fact which they have in common. If anything it constitutes a similarity between them, but it certainly cannot demonstrate that they are radically different from each other.

Second: One might argue that the sadness or the majesty of a piece of music is "subjective," since there is much more disagreement in their case than in that of colors. My first reply to this would be that this, even if true, could never establish the *radical* difference that is at stake. What a leap of an inference! To move from the minor fact that the variations in the perception of one quality are statistically greater than they are in another to the conclusion that some are real, and independent of us, and out there, while others exist only in our minds. If these differences do exist then they should of course be exactly determined, but nothing about them either requires or justifies the postulation of two different worlds. (The same is true for similar arguments, like that we have laws about the objective qualities, but not about those that are subjective. This difference, even if true, also does not warrant anything like that juxtaposition.)

My second reply would be that the premise on which this argument rests is in any case very doubtful. There are empirical studies and also many examples from common experience, which show that at least very often the situation is, surprisingly enough, just the reverse. Particularly in the case of colors the perceptions of different people seem to vary greatly (think of the subtle distinctions that a good painter makes—two colors which look the same to us, may appear quite different to him), while the agreement on what is repulsive, or cheerful, or threatening or sad is surprisingly high. This is true even across very different cultures. If we look at a carved African mask, where the cultural background and the "conditioning" would be extraordinarily different, we still seem to see it as angry or peaceful. What is astonishing is therefore really not the amount of variation, but on the contrary, precisely the high uniformity. Surely there would not be much disagreement in the example of the falling tree. Who doesn't perceive it as dangerous?

My third reply would be that a great deal depends on the specificity of the words with which we make our descriptions. If one uses very precise color terms, disagreement increases, while it declines if one says that this is a red or a blue. The same applies to the description of music. Few people would disagree with the statement that the chorus in Beethoven's Ninth Symphony is somehow powerful or strong, while there might be argument over whether it is jubilant or majestic.

Third: The most important single consideration is that we experience these qualities not within us but as part of the world. Separating them off from the so-called "objective" or "factual" qualities and subsuming them under a juxtaposed classification tends to interpret this fundamental fact out of the picture. In our experience these qualities inhere in the objects or constitute them.

Their relationship to objects is not different from that of colors. If one were still to use the terms "objective" and "subjective," then there would at least be one very good reason for thinking of them as objective. They do confront us. They are something that is perceived; they obtrude on us and are experienced as given. They are received.

Fourth: If we approach the matter through language, then it seems clear that I do not mean that I feel sad or majestic when I predicate these qualities of a piece of music. Ordinary language makes the distinction between "being made to feel sad by a piece of music" and the music itself "being sad." We therefore could not claim that the statement "this piece of music is sad" really means that it produces in us a certain reaction. Language treats the sadness of music as something that is predicated of it.

Also, we often say such things as "the music really was very sad (or gay, or exciting) though I was unfortunately too tired to respond to it. I had no feelings at all during the concert." We simply could not say this if calling a piece of music sad were a circuitous way of reporting an introspection. When we say such things we obviously distinguish our own feelings from the sadness of the music itself. But that presupposes that the sadness of music is a real quality that has been perceived.

This brings us to a first way-station. The thoughts so far adduced were designed to lead us to one plain conclusion: the world does not consist of neutral objects which we disdain or value; the world is sad and alluring, horrible, magnificent and disgusting, attractive, splendid and mean in its own right.

II. SKETCH OF A THEORY

We perform the virtuosities of our surgical thinking in the dim light that falls through heavy and cracked metaphors. Above all we needed to *see* the new and different pattern that a less obstructed light reveals. If we now have this otherwise arranged perception, we can begin to trace the alterations engendered by it in the evolving structure of a theory.

As long as the world is seen as a gray collage of facts one problem stands unavoidably in the center: the question of how values are "justified." If the given is thought to be bare fact, and values are conceptualized as fundamentally different, the issue of their entrance, of their arrival in this strange domain, has to arise. From the outset, the discussion takes the form of a search: where in this great wall of facts is the chink through which values come in? And what gives them a creditable base? This is now radically changed. There is of course still a problem of "justification" but it no longer has the same meaning, or the same size. To say it first bluntly: there no longer is any question about how values "come in," or about the nature of their "derivation" from facts, for the plain reason that they are there from the beginning, and that they are not "secondary" to facts.

The psychologies of the two positions stand at opposite poles: the former is reminiscent of a Beckett landscape. An expanse of broken slate, dejected feet shuffling through stones, moving them, playing with hope to make hopeless time pass. The view to which we have come has its analogue in a sense of pressure. Now there is no question of looking for one thing that perhaps merits attachment, instead there is too much. Values clamor, crowd in, and exhaust us. One looks for a bench to find a rest from them.

But let us look at this contrast closely, and examine the workings of some details in the two schemes. On the traditional and customary view, we encounter this problem whenever a particular specific judgment is questioned, and we want to "justify" it in the face of this doubt. If we have condemned a given action as wrong, and someone intercedes with the question "Why do you think so?" we have to support our judgment. The question therefore centers on how we do this and in what the nature and quality of the mustered support consists.

The most prestigious and usual answer has been that we perform a deduction. In practical terms this means that we look for a generalization from which the particular judgment can be derived; i.e., we justify our judgment by referring the particular case to a more general rule, and by showing that it is an instance falling under the principle we have invoked.

Take an example: If a conversation started with my saying that it was rotten of you to lie, and you turned and asked "Why?" then the justification of my condemnation would move one level up to a more general rule—to something like "dishonesty is in general bad"—and from that my individual judgment on the lie could then be deduced. But if you were serious you very likely would not be ultimately satisfied with this answer. You would be apt to feel that this only shifts the place of the problem. So you might press further and ask what entitles me to such confidence in this rule, and how I propose to justify it. This would set off a repetition of the same procedure. To satisfy the renewed demand I would move up yet another level of generality, and invoke a still higher rule. But there is no reason why this process should come to a halt there. The second order, higher principle would have to be justified from a still higher rule. And of course that third principle could once more be doubted, and so forth and so on. It is easy to see that the repetition of this question and answer process would eventually drive us inevitably to a first, most general, and ultimate rule. Whether this would happen in very few steps or in a great many is quite unimportant (though it will be fewer than one often imagines), and the actual content of the highest principle also does not matter in our context. The crucial point is that this would occur, and that the highest principle, too, is subject to challenge. Now, however, there is a difference. If we really are dealing with the first and cardinal rule in our moral position, then there is, *ex hypothesi,* no more basic or encompassing principle from which it can be derived. (If there is one, we simply have not yet reached the first principle.) When this principle is called into question, we are therefore no longer in a position to give the answer that we have hitherto given. And it is this that has led many philosophers to the conviction that values are ultimately without justification.

The image which underlies many of these discussions is that of a hierarchy of principles and of values that ends with an impasse. It is like a pyramidical mobile that hangs in the air. The lower parts are always suspended from those which are higher up, but the pinnacle of the whole structure is without support. The whole, therefore, threatens to fall.

Continental philosophers commonly associate this picture with the "death of God," and the need for commitment. The idea is that God, before He absconded, served as an anchor that brought this unseemly regress to a halt, while it now has to be ended with a leap to commitment. The feeling is that on the final principles one is compelled to take a blind stand. They can only be clung to, but not rationally defended. And this, naturally, affects one's perception of the previous "justification." To what extent is it a foreground distraction designed to veil this stark and more basic fact? How much of its "rationality" is a self-deception, a game of postponement, an elegant minuet danced before the anguish of action?

This overall schematization of what in fact occurs, and of where the main problems lie, changes completely as soon as we replace the first premise of the "nothing-but factual world" with the axiom that things are sad and alluring, horrible, magnificent, and disgusting in their own right. If a specific, initial judgment is questioned, then the obvious way to support and justify it *in this new framework* is not by deduction. One does not turn upward to a general rule, but on the contrary to the object, as it were "downward." The slow systematic ascent hence does not even begin, and it therefore does not end in a blind shaft.

But we had better take one step at a time. The whole foregoing discussion was intended to lay the foundations on which we can now proceed to build. The upshot of it is in essence that the qualities whose status we examined at length constitute the base, the solid fundament, on which the theory and praxis of valuing rests. The judgments that ascribe these qualities to an object or an action are basic. They exist on the ground-level, and are the elementary particles from which the rest is built up. (There is an analogy here to the "report-sentences" of some Phenomenalists.) Their "justification," i.e., the kind of support that validates or establishes them, is quite simply that they are true, that they correspond, that the quality which they predicate is in fact there.

Involved in the actual making of these judgments is nothing more complicated than whatever is required for assertions like "this is red," or "this is green." If these statements presuppose the application of certain criteria and rules, then the same is true for our ability to say that something is sad or frightening or vulgar. But the crucial point is that it is *no more* than this, that only criteria of *that* sort, and *that* kind of use of them, are in play. Specifically, it is not a precondition that there be some more abstract or ultimate "standard," or a general measure or criterion of "goodness" or "value." In short, we need only the ability to recognize qualities and to use words.

There are of course instances of disagreement. But we have already seen that these are not nearly as common as one is apt to imagine, and that the metaphysical status of these qualities is in any case not radically affected by their occurrence. We can now add to this that we are not reduced to a dumb pointing when our judgment conflicts with that of others. How very far we are from this helpless silence comes into sharper focus if we distinguish the question of what gives legitimacy to a judgment—which in this case is the sheer "there-ness" of the quality—from the quite different question of how we conduct ourselves when there are disputes. Nothing could be more mistaken than the fear that we could only "agree to disagree" and then part. This specter haunts the discussion of values in the framework that we have discarded. For us it is the other way around. There is no end to what we could do, and the limits are set only by our patience. A complete psychoanalysis, for example, may help someone see that his mother is really "aggressive." And entire college curricula are meant to cultivate the ability to recognize some of these qualities in poems or plays. Just as painters spend a life-time learning how to see colors. So it is not at all as if there is "no more to be said" if I call it magnificent and you think it grotesque. We could talk about nothing else for the next ten years, if that is how we wanted to spend our lives. And this has theoretical importance: it means that we do not substitute innumerable little impasses on the ground for the single big impasse at the top.

The next logical question is, how do we ever come to formulate general rules from these beginnings, and what is it that finally makes something "bad" or "good"? Here we should not overlook the possibility that someone might decline to go on. There is nothing insane, or nihilistic in the position that only these particularistic judgments are to be made, and it would be utterly wrong to think that such a person "had no values." What he would not have are *principles*, but that is not the same thing.

Still, how could we move beyond these pointillistic judgments if that is what we wanted to do, and how is their justification to be conceived?

Into the framework of an otherwise neutral world the idea of goodness breaks with a sharp abruptness. There it appears as a *novum*, as *the* contrast, in short as "value" against a uniform backdrop of facts. This changes drastically once the full qualities have been restored to the outside that we confront. In the new framework, good or bad are not at all the value-terms *par excellence*. They do not have the central place assigned to them in most recent philosophical writings. The judgments close to the base that we have been discussing are all in all the more precise, the more discriminating, and the more informative evaluations. The strain is on, and our perceptivities are exerted, when we say of a dance, that it is "fluffy," or of a piece of music, that it "clowns." (And that is still only the surface. When we want to come closer, single words do not cut a sharp enough pattern. Then only images and metaphors draw a thin enough line.) Compared to that, "good" and "bad" only sort sheep from goats. In most circumstances these are precisely *not* the words that can be used for a genuine assessment. When that is asked for, we use another much more richly qualified language. This is the vocabulary that critics use. The discovery and articulation of these qualities *is* the critic's performance. One might say, that he uses the language of the myriad qualities when he is serious, when he is writing his book on Blake, or on Kafka or Yeats. And that is why a real appraisal often needs an entire book. It is only because there are other contexts, and because other purposes have to be served, that cruder and blunter judgments are also felled. Books must be reviewed—one doesn't want to waste one's investment—and for that a more abstract and loose-shanked set of terms will still do. Yet even there (in his newspaper column) the critic will still avoid "good" and "bad," or "ugly" and "beautiful." They are too slap-dash (and intellectually snubnosed) even for a morning-after review. They operate too much like the man in Hesse's parable who divided all things only into those he could eat and those he could not eat. This kind of yes/no judgment a critic might only make in exasperation, when his children have worn through the last thread of his patience: "No you can't go—because it is bad."

And is the critic's hierarchy of language so different from our own? What words do we use when in talking to a friend late at night the improbable is granted, and we say what we think? Do we ever judge a man, an action, or anything to be simply "bad" or "good" if we take the time to be precise?

Still, we need a rigorously formulated account of how a concept like good does function. (Even if it were only to understand *why* it is so blunt.) That there are many uses goes without saying. One, however, seems to be central. In that use the word "good" works in important ways like a generic term. It groups or orders the concrete, low-level qualities, and makes assertions in an abbreviated, shorthand fashion about whole sets or classes of them. If the subject were, for example, plays, then the lower, or intermediate level judgments might deal with qualities like the "clarity of structure," the "economy of style," the "deftness of characterization," the "intellectual substance," and so forth, while judgments concerning the "goodness" of a play would be quick summations that presuppose and *tally* these evaluations. The manner of this reduction to a single denominator is of course flexible and subject to change. A play, to be good, must not possess one set of qualities that all good plays have in common. If it lacks structure but is very witty it can still be good. So one might say that the idea of goodness is like a minimum that the sum-total of these qualities must reach on balance. And this is one of the principal reasons for the *essential* vagueness and uninformativeness of the word. It only conveys the *result* of a very general weighing. Everything else—which qualities were weighed and how they have been reduced—is omitted.

The fact that we can arrive at this kind of tallied judgment does *not* mean that there is after all a positive or a negative "value component" in each of these qualities. But the connection is important: the fact that this is *not* the case shows further how very gross the word "good" really is. It means that judgments which pronounce something "good" are not the outcome of a genuine adding or subtracting (give "six" for sensitivity, take away "three" for rashness), or of a fine-spun calculation. They *cannot* be, since the basic qualities are not sufficiently commensurate for that.

And here lies perhaps the crassest error of the theory of value. It is one thing for a theory to be exact. It is quite another thing if a theory makes the phenomena with which it deals more "geometric" than they actually are. Then the theory is wrong. The best theory of value is not the theory that reduces the activity of evaluating most nearly to a calculus, but the theory that comes closest to the truth.

Which qualities must be present in a given case, and to what degree, is to some extent fixed by convention. There is a rough consensus on what makes a fuse, a hammer, a painting, or a person "good." (This is no different from the understanding attached to other classifying terms.) It works rather like a check-list, and we perform a task similar to those which some workers execute on assembly lines. We simply know which properties are expected, very like a man who is testing radio tubes.

Of course this is not all. Often, though not always, another aspect comes into play, and that side is best understood on the analogy of a "special place" in a room, or garden, or to "the place of honor" at table. The fact that there is such a place is also, as it were, a social given. The aura with which it is invested, the distinction it confers, are relatively stable. They constitute a kind of instrument furnished by society and language—it is the use to which we put it that is more up to us.

Prose, for example, needed to have a measured and gracious elegance to be "good" in the early nineteenth century, but in a very gradual process the quality of elegance has been demoted. For the structural design of the theory of value it is important to understand that this sort of alteration results from a host of small-scaled reconsiderations, and even from shifts in perception: that the general thrust is *up* from the specific and concrete, and not *down*—via deduction—from general criteria and standards. The same is true on the more private plane. As we compare countless passages of prose, and become by slow degrees more aware of what elegance sometimes hides, and of the sacrifices it exacts—as we begin to see strength and economy where before we noticed only roughness—we gradually approach the point where we are ready to bring the cruder and more general level into line. We reach a decision and cross elegance from the list.

The genesis and justification of principles and rules follow essentially the same scheme. A rule, such as that prose should be lucid or transparent, has the same relationship to the more interesting, more perceptual judgments that the notion of "good" prose has to them. Again one has to tally the many qualities of many instances of prose and reduce them to one denomination. If many of the cases that were on balance "good," were also at the same time lucid or transparent, then one can tentatively postulate this general rule. But its force would be no greater than the examples on which it rests. In this case one could cite the prose of Tolstoy, of Heine, and of Lichtenberg to support this rule, while the works of Joyce or Faulkner could be adduced against it. This being so, one would not set great store by it. Instead one would introduce qualifications until some principle might be discovered, that conformed more closely to one's more concrete judgments.

The rules with which we judge our own and others' actions have the same foundation. The general proscription against lies has its actual final base only in the qualities of individual deceptions. It is a giant structure, but in the last analysis it rests on the loss of pride, or the isolation, in short on all the qualities produced in the great complexity of circumstances, by all manner of dishonesties. That measures the force to which this rule—or any other principle of conduct—is entitled. The rest, its authority beyond that, is insupportable excess.

This means that all valuational principles stand theoretically only until further notice. They all live by the grace of the more particular, concrete judgments that they entail. If there is conflict, then there may of course be reason for delay (considerations of consistency and so forth), but in the long run the concrete and perceptual judgments must prevail. The generalizations have to yield and are rejected or revised to suit the level of experience.

This Primacy of the Concrete is not at all put forward as a radical reversal. On the contrary, this is one place where our framework means only to produce a theory that is in line—and as intelligent—as parts of our practice already are. In the whole domain of art we have come to act on it, and there it is nearly banal. The testimonial that painters and composers violate old catechisms, and that their work succeeds precisely *because* of this, has been so faithfully repeated, that the mere crudity and fallibility of rules sounds by now like a middle-aged and mellow proposition that would be noddingly acknowledged. So, of course, would the idea that the rules of art are mere abstractions from the best art of the past, and that it is therefore the rules that must adjust themselves to art, and not the other way around.

But when it comes to conduct and to morality, then the situation is weirdly ambiguous and inconsistent. On the one hand we have begun to give priority to the concrete in actual practice. Especially when there is openly acknowledged conflict, in the debates over Capital Punishment or Birth Control, for instance, less and less weight is given to the high-flying arguments from the necessity of retribution, and gradually more and more is said about the concrete consequences. Single cases of prisoners in death-row, or of 16-year-old mothers are looked at closely, and we have moved some distance toward the idea that the laws and rules have to be changed until they conform to our individual judgments. This "turn to the concrete" may actually be the larger revolution. The other changes in our values and morality, compared to it, are small effects. Still, on the other hand, there remains the feeling that first principles must be adhered to, that they are somehow sacrosanct and sacred, and that morality could not survive without them.

It is this inconsistency that our framework allows us to eliminate, or that it compels us to abandon. There is no reason why what we already do in the sphere of art, and with conduct when it is controversial, should not be extended to the whole domain of values. The general status of the rules of conduct is not different from that of the precepts of art. Both derive from the same foundation and should be treated in accord with it.

This means of course that they are all subject to revision. But the loss of the presumption to infallibility (or *a priori*-ty, or even permanence) seems small compared to the gain of a solid basis. Yet there are other changes. Really one's whole relationship to the rules of conduct becomes different. It is no longer necessary to struggle for some deep and main foundation stone. The existence of values is quite secure; no leap of faith or any other act on our part is needed to prevent their metaphysical disintegration. Just as with art: rules are clumsy and make-shift things. Of course we need them: we could not possibly evaluate each situation fully; the effort of perception would exhaust us; a great deal must be filtered out and simplified to keep us sane. Still, that is all "principles" are: tools for crude, perfunctory estimations, which cannot serve us once we need to be precise. When we are not just flipping cards across a table but face a real decision, then all the rules are nothing but coy preparations. We have not begun until we face our situation in the same solitude in which we encounter books.

The categorical principles are no longer the main beams from which all other values hang. They are more like a grid that covers up and blocks out. Those who always follow them don't use their eyes.

All the same, we eventually do build a whole hierarchical structure of rules; and in this construction all levels are constantly in interaction with all other parts. Individual perceptions from the ground are pitted against high and ancient virtues; the most general rules are applied to everything that is subsumed beneath them and are yet at the same time revised and tested. All the intermediate levels are continuously matched against each other, and anything can be standard at one moment, and be on trial at the next. The whole system is thus in an unceasing flux. One never questions the whole body of rules and judgments at one and the same time. If one rule becomes problematic, other rules are still employed in the evaluation. Only gradually are all the rules held at one time replaced by others. It is possible to end up with a completely new system, but it happens as in a card game where one may get a totally new hand by exchanging two cards several times. The whole process moves slowly toward some coherence, but never reaches it; for long before all the rules conform to the concrete perceptions and particular judgments, these, influenced by the new rules, have themselves changed.

III. SOME IMPLICATIONS

We first moved the theory of value to a different beginning. The starting point was, for us, not a vast plain of facts on which values had somehow to descend. Values were always there: they inflict themselves on us. That premise, understandably, recast the problem of how values should be "justified," and gave it a quite different orientation. (A justification in a strong sense was simply no longer needed.) But the paths from these two separate origins continue to diverge and, in conclusion, some points of this evolving contrast can be marked out.

The main forms of intuitionism differ sharply from the position we have begun to sketch. Most patent is the conflict over the founding qualities. Intuitionism has mostly based itself on barely two or three ("goodness" or "rightness," for example), and these were always singled out and isolated—so much so that only a special, enigmatic power was capable of apprehending them. Disagreements, therefore, broke down almost at once into an exchange of charges—one was accused of moral blindness. In our framework, on the other hand, these qualities are panoramic and they are most emphatically mundane. Their perception is not the work of a special, "higher" faculty but takes place through the ordinary humdrum channels possessed even by lower organisms, and not just by man. In our case sporadic disagreements, therefore, do not begin to indicate the failure of a faculty. In fact an organism literally "blind" to the sum-total of all these qualities is almost inconceivable. (It certainly could not survive.) Someone who does not see vulgarity where others do is therefore still far from lacking the entire *faculty* for apprehending values.

But these contrasts lie relatively on the surface. The difference really runs much deeper, and is not seen until one has recognized that intuitionism presupposes precisely the gray and fact-made world, whose spell we mean to break. Only in a world in which most natural colors had long paled, in a world of dusk, already in half-sleep, eerie and too silent, would anyone insist that there are values *nonetheless*. Only such a world would prompt that tone of opposition, and only in a world so empty could anyone *insist* that values are only visible to an ethereal "intuition."

The relationship to emotivism follows the same pattern. No one would have paid much heed, if the emotivists had rested with the mild observation that *some* value judgments are also *sometimes* used to express emotions. (Even Kant could have agreed to that.) The position has only philosophic consequences if it maintains that no value judgments ever do more than this. But then it, too—though on the opposite extreme from intuitionism on the spectrum of contemporary philosophic ethics—assumes a world that has been drained of value. Thus the conflict, as in the case of intuitionism has again two levels: on the first we reject the "never more" pronouncement. There are value judgments that vent not only feelings but are genuine predications. But the deeper opposition concerns the underlying precondition. The idea that all value judgments express nothing but emotions (in effect, that they are not informative about the world) presupposes once more the neutral world view, i.e., the basic axiom which we have tried to undermine.

Following this contrast further to the blighted battleground of the "Ought vs. Is" discussion—two things stand out clearly from the more distant vantage point of the position proposed here: In the area of aesthetics this question basically asked whether "aesthetic properties" were "condition governed" by "natural properties," or, more roughly, whether any aesthetic qualities could be derived from natural properties.

That assumes, as far as I can see, that the natural properties are somehow prior, or more basic than the aesthetic ones. But just this presupposition the whole first part of this essay was again designed to question. There is no reason why aesthetic qualities like "exciting" *should be* derivable from natural properties like "curved." The aesthetic qualities are not ephemeral or brain-created. Nothing in the theory of perception, or in general knowledge of organisms makes them so secondary that their presence is merely a by-product of others.

Further—and this is the second point—this non-derivability in no way proves that aesthetics is "arbitrary," "non-cognitive," or "subjective." The debate was predicated on the misconception that the legitimacy of these qualities and judgments had to be demonstrated by descent; that only their relationship to natural qualities could give to the aesthetic their credentials. But this defense can be dispensed with: their own claim in their own right is good enough.

The same considerations run parallel for ethics. One has asked the same, equivalently malposed question there: do any facts, does anything that is the case ever imply a value? This again assumes that the neutral and factual has priority and is the case, and that the valuational is adrift unless it can be anchored there; and both these suppositions seem to me again unfounded. In the domain of conduct values are also not derivative, but this is again no embarrassment to them, for the implication is not that they are too insubstantial for the connection to obtain. On the contrary, the reverse is true: they cannot be derived because they are too basic.

The distance between our course and that of most contemporary philosophic ethics grows larger still if we narrow the focus from judging actions down to judging specifically their "morality." Concepts like "equality," or "justice," or "human rights" would be construed on the same overall interpretation that we have drawn throughout. They would not be regarded as firm first principles but would also be understood to rest on judgments and perceptions that are more specific. The concept of equality, for instance, arises on this account when some particular forms of degradation or suffering are experienced as so ghastly that a society decides that *no one* should be exposed to them. The basis of the concept is thus a compassion that lays down certain limits, certain *minima* below which it resolves not to let any human being fall. This reverses the usual direction, where first a seemingly complete and sweeping equality is proclaimed, which then, on second thought, however, is limited and curtailed until no one has much confidence in the remainder (from the equality of property and even brotherhood, down to mere equality before the law). Equality, on this interpretation, is not a starting point. Man is not somehow equal "to begin with." This idea signifies only the line to which *in*equality has been (or hopefully *will* be) forced back.

The same is true of justice, and of humanity, or for that matter of civil rights. In the present framework their origin would not be lofty. It would be understood that justice protects us only from some gross violations, and that it represents only a guarantee against a few selected injuries. The emblem of the balanced scale promises too much. The whole of what one man "deserves" cannot possibly be measured. The aim can therefore be no more than negative. The best that one can hope for is the prevention of some few *im*balances. (Not even a father can be fully [positively] just between two sons—even the fact of being first and second born creates differences that cannot be "equalized.") If a society resolves to give everyone a "correct" trial in courts of law, then this means only that some few outrages have been proscribed.[2]

Human rights again would be seen as the expression of a very frail attempt to set at least some limits to abuse and cruelty. The indignation at this violation would therefore come from the other side: one would cry out not because the highest and first principles, from which all else flows, had been transgressed. They too would be regarded as a bare minimum to which all are entitled. The anger provoked by their denial would therefore have a different force: one would demand them with the sense that at least this pittance, this bone from the table, cannot be refused.[3]

But these reinterpretations of specific concepts lie again on the surface. The deeper implication, that our framework would have for "morality" is yet to be brought out. It is this: a great quantity of philosophic writings conveys at least the *impression* that there are only two alternatives: either one lives one's life by genuine values, and that means by morality, or one is at once reduced either to mere selfish prudence (the alternative that English and American philosophy envisions) or to the "nothing matters"—to chaos and to nihilism (the death of morality as seen on the Continent). It is the appearance of this forced option, of this Either/Or that our framework means to dissolve. Throughout this essay we have tried to lift the sheets that cover the profusion—the excess of values. They surround us in abundance and "morality" represents only a singular and perhaps quite problematic handful of this whole. This places the assessment of morality in a different position. Now it appears as one distinctive institution, which has its sub-species, and which judges man with its own characteristic conceptual apparatus. In short, one could now begin to argue that what is distinctive of morality and sets it apart are several characteristic notions like "duty," and "responsibility," and "guilt." One could maintain that the use of these and of some other, similar terms indicates the occurrence of a genuinely "moral" judgment, while all other evaluations are something else.

On the base of this circumscription of the "moral" one could then take a further step. One could bear down on these concepts, and show perhaps that they lack an acceptable foundation; that they depend on assumptions which we no longer hold, not unlike the idea of "sin"—that they are chips from ancient tombs and should be in museums. One could study these relics of a past with the same curiosity that we give to magic: we could marvel at their power, and mourn the damage they have done. We might wonder how the idea of "guilt" was able to survive in a culture, which has also coined the concept "superstition." But in any case, we would be in a position to reject them *without* the fear that after that no up or down would still remain, that "nothing would make a difference, anymore."

I do not think of this as an at all "radical" approach. It only raises to a level of philosophic generality what, e.g., most psychoanalysts already do, when they suspend all "moral" judgments with a patient. That obviously does not produce an absolute indifference. In fact in many cases the patient only discovers what his "real" values are after the "moral" specters have been exorcised.

And similarly in the field of education. A. S. Neill explains in *Summerhill* that he makes every effort not to subject his children to "morality." What he means, of course, is not that he will abstain from "value judgments," but that he will not have recourse to "guilt," or "duty," or the like against them.

He tells the story of a boy who once attacked Neill's much-beloved grand piano with a hammer, and Neill takes the stand that it would have been unfair and ultimately harmful to raise a moral barricade before the child by telling him that this was "bad," and something that he "ought" not to do. That in effect would have identified the interests of the adult with an impersonal world-order. It would have allowed the adult to hide himself behind an implacable neutrality while pitting the boy against it. In Neill's estimation, precisely the reverse of the inherited view is true: "Morality" does not raise us above the jungle that is nature. On the contrary, there is more humanity in honestly setting desire against desire, and in making it an open struggle. Of course Neill stopped the boy, but he made it clear that he was simply rising to the defense of something that he cared for.

The same lines can be extended back to Nietzsche. He assaulted not only the pretensions of the specifically Christian ethic. To imagine that he meant to cauterize that single version of morality sets beyond his reach too much that may not be entitled to that safety. On the one hand, he wanted more than simply to substitute one morality for another, yet, on the other, he was obviously *not* an advocate of "all is the same," "there are no values." That attitude he ridiculed and scorned in countless passages. (Once he likened it to a sullen guest who attends a banquet and has not even the courtesy to bring a good appetite.) If the former interpretation is too narrow, then the latter is much too wide. Nietzsche's thinking on this point may be best represented by the claim that we just posed: he rejected not just the Christian, but all "morality." The weight and the authority of the specifically "moral" seemed to him unjustified, just as the base that we envision would not carry it. But its dismissal did not leave him with "Nihilism," or the inability to judge. More nearly the reverse: he thought that the mystic vapor of the "moral" had blinded and distracted us. It hid the genuine and living ground from which values grow, and we were, therefore, as individuals and as a culture at a costly disadvantage.

The same two main reorientations (i.e., [1] the genesis of values in the concrete, and [2] the identification of "morality" with the particular way of judging that has its center in "duty," "ought," and "guilt") also opens the discussion of utilitarianism from a different side. The kind of "objectivity" that we have claimed for value properties raises first a question about the reduction to one "measure," regardless of whether this be "pleasure" or "utility." The point that there are different and perhaps incommensurate pleasures has often been made. But that grants too much, and throws away the earlier and more telling question, how the singling out of "pleasure" can be justified? If art cannot be judged simply by the pleasure or the

satisfaction it yields, then why should this be good enough for actions, or for people? If an action has all the myriad properties that
we have discussed, then why would it be "rational" or "moral" to
make decisions on such limited and crude criteria?

But there is a deeper question which can now be pressed; it asks
whether utilitarianism was not sheltered by a misconception? As
long as one believed that some first principle was absolutely needed,
the first rule of utilitarianism may have looked more palatable than
most other candidates. But if values have their base in the concrete,
and do not require a deductive derivation, then the constraint
relaxes and one can open doors to several doubts. Is the idea that an
action is not right or moral unless it maximizes the benefits for *all*
mankind as innocuous and sensible as we habitually think? The tone
of the formula is so unpresuming that we perhaps no longer realize
what it means. Taken seriously, it involves my having to consider
all persons *equally*. In a given choice I have to weigh the effects of
my actions on the remotest stranger, with the same scale and
measure with which I weigh the consequences that they would have
on my own son, or my closest friend. If the *total* satisfaction to
mankind in the long run is the criterion then I must decide to do X,
if X gives slightly greater satisfaction (or whatever) to a stranger,
while Y would give a smaller quantity to someone whom I love.

It is not enough to say that this requirement is much too high,
that no one in practice could possibly live up to it, and that it
therefore inevitably makes hypocrisy the standard currency, or that
it renders the faculty for values impotent by engaging it with an un-
workable and useless "really should" which is so unattainable that
it produces only a Sunday morning melancholy, but leaves one's actual practical existence in darkness and without advice. It is not
just "too high." It is more seriously deficient. Ultimately one cannot stop short of the charge that it sanctifies with the halo of the
"moral" a leveling destructiveness. Love, affection, loyalty would
all find themselves in opposition and censured by this calculus.

One has to think concretely—I mean, close to life—to see why
this is so. I ask myself: should I continue to raise my two-year-old
son? He has the love of his mother, also material comfort, and his
life would still be like a sunny morning even with me gone. Set
against this the suffering of a single starving child. Is there any
question where I could make the greater difference? And even if it
were by other standards "wrong" to care so much more for two or
three human beings than for all the rest—could it be "moral" not to
discriminate at all, and to accord to every pain or pleasure the same
importance, regardless of who suffers it?

The utilitarian rule is at least not the easy, obvious axiom that can be laid down at the start. Of course, the severity of the requirements embedded in it do imply humane and charitable attitudes and actions. To prove that is child's play. The point is that the rule in fact entails immeasurably more—a self-effacement that reduces all of my relationships to a single plane. The meaningful question points therefore just the other way: this rule itself needs a justification far more than much of what it has often been used to justify. Regard, compassion, even love for others are easier to justify than the utilitarian rule.—But enough![4]

For a whole epoch of my life, between sixteen and twenty-four, I was sure that values were illusions. I had come to this conclusion much like most of us at some point do with religion. It seemed as natural as waking up when it grows light. I did not feel lost. The event was altogether not dramatic, more like a leaf turning to the sun. If there was an emotion, then only a sense of lightness, of a burden gone. I remember that those who still regarded themselves as accountable to values seemed to me then like grown men frightened of the dark. Not only that, of course; they also seemed bound by ropes that they could have unknotted. But for me there were "no limits." Actions moved like canoes in a river, judgments and values splashed against them as mere spray. "Everything was permitted."

For some years I really lived by this, but then I was changed by the thoughts that I have now put down. For a time the sheer reality of values, the comforting discovery that they did not require some transcendent realm, but had as plain and common an existence as buttons on a coat, seemed to settle things. The landscape of smooth snowdrifts was transformed, and the new, flamboyant, tropic world was no longer silent, but seemed to demand a quite specific attitude. It made an openness, a receptivity, a cautious gentleness the only natural and suitable response.

But then that too disappeared, and I began to realize that even the objectivity of values had no consequences for myself; that there were still no restraints and no arrows marking my direction, even if every possible assessment was firmly fixed in the very core of things. Everything still was possible. Even Camus's scornful distance, his lyrically pronounced determination *not* to make his peace with life, but to keep his eyes fixed on its disproportionality, and to revolt against it—even that was still an appropriate reaction. One that in fact was predicated precisely on the objectivity of values, though on an objectively existing clash, an objectively existing absence and deficiency. And if his stance was still consistent with the sheer fact of the actuality of values, and depended on the internal substance, on what specific value this or that thing had, then this was true as well for countless other ways to live.

The controversy over the subjectivity or objectivity of values thus became for me "academic" in this specific sense. The resulting greater firmity of guidance supposedly at stake—the reward that those who argue for the objectivity of values seek—is simply not received. It shifts elusively and is again on the far side of a gap when that battle has been won. The division between fact and value can perhaps be bridged, and values can perhaps be shown to be included in the realm of facts, but if so then there is still on *one* side the objectively existing value, and on the *other* my response to it. There is still the gap between the worth that something has and the action that I decide to take.

The whole trajectory of thoughts that we have so far traversed brings us, therefore, only to the start of a beginning. Up to this point we have only cleared the air of ghosts. No positive conclusion has yet emerged. The results of these preliminary probings are almost wholly negative: we know which questions are bones that have been chewed too long. Perhaps this understates it. Some are not merely theoretical exclusions. But the one that is to me the most decisive is also paradoxically almost invisible to many of my friends. A rather personal way of stating it would be to say that "there is no *should.*" I mean by this that there is no external sanction, that no court at all sits in judgment over our life. Everything we touch shines with a multiplicity of values, and everything we do moves in their flow. To breathe is an act of affirmation—but that is all. The qualities that our actions realize are the end. We do not place them one by one into a swaying scale, they are like pebbles over which a river flows.

I know that some will not perceive this as even an assertion, maybe because they lack the experience that it denies. Yet there are moments when it does seem, all the same, as if the large philosophical debates in ethics were finally a struggle over these alternatives. The more definable divisions—Are values objective or not? How absolute or relative should their existence be conceived? Can there be general rules?—these were of course the loudly stated conflicts. Still, it is possible that they were animated by the wish to exorcise this ghost. Those who argued outwardly against absoluteness and objectivity perhaps still inwardly protested that there was no court, that no one calls us to account. We can now see that none of this needs to be denied. Values may be objective, and of course there can be rules, and yet living may still be like a silent walk.

NOTES

1. Cf. William Frankena, *Ethics* (Englewood Cliffs, N.J.: Prentice-Hall, 1963), p. 81 and passim.
2. I owe this idea to Walter Kaufmann.
3. I have developed this view of human and civil rights more fully in a separate paper which I expect to publish soon.
4. Utilitarianism may be the important fork where the English-American and the continental philosophy of values (and not just they) separated, and went different ways: on the Continent, utilitarianism was dismissed, and the questions put to values, therefore, became radical. In England and America this did not happen; perhaps in part because utilitarianism seemed to provide a new and different base as soon as the religious legitimation had collapsed.

9

Bad Art

Quentin Bell

I

This may seem an eccentric and wrong-headed theme. Why, it may be asked, should we devote attention to that which, manifestly, does not deserve it? There are two answers to this question: one, which might lead me far astray from my main argument, is concerned with art history, for history so it seems to me, cannot afford to neglect any major historical phenomenon. The other answer, which in fact defines the purpose of this lecture, is that our perception of the goodness of good art is determined by some opposite quality with which we compare it. If this be accepted, the utility of such an enquiry will at once be apparent; it is always useful to take an object and look at it from a new point of view, to consider it, so to speak, backside on or upside down.

In order to avoid confusion it must at once be conceded that arguments concerning bad art are no more conclusive than arguments concerning good art. In the last analysis they must rest upon assertions that cannot be proved.[1] Nevertheless, I think that we can advance further upon common ground if we approach the matter from this direction than would be the case if we started by considering that which we admire. Lovers of art are likely to be fiercely divided when they discuss the work of their more distinguished contemporaries; but when it comes to the illustrations in a woman's magazine or the design on a box of chocolates they will be more or less unanimous. Unanimous judgements are not always reliable, but they do at least provide a point of departure.

I would like to begin by considering what happens when a pic-

This essay, a lecture delivered at Bretton Hall College of Higher Education, is reprinted by permission.

ture is copied. There are many kinds of copy; the copy which is better than the original, the copy that is worse, the copy that is different—but the kind of copy of which I would like to remind you is that which you may see if you go into any of the great Continental galleries where you will find a certain number of assiduous imitators who, with masterpieces before them, attempt to produce facsimiles. Some of these copyists are highly skilled, they match their tones with infinite care, they copy line for line even to the last *minutiae* of the brush. And yet, as they themselves would be the first to admit, some vital element of the original escapes them. No special knowledge is needed in order to distinguish between the masterpiece and the counterfeit, the second resembles the first only as a corpse resembles a living body.

Obviously the difference between the copy and the original must lie in the paint: a painting, whatever its content, is always a material thing, yet the difference, howsoever striking, is so minute that it may be hard to point to any one part of the picture that has not been perfectly reproduced. It is as though a glaze has been floated over the entire canvas, distorting and corrupting everything through the interposition of an alien personality. We can measure the extent of this drastic though impalpable metamorphosis by comparing a photograph with a copy such as I have described; the impersonal machine preserves far more of the original—even though it works through a different medium—than does the personal care of the imitator.

Now certain facts about bad art immediately become clear when we look at an example of this kind. There are certain qualities which the bad copyist can take from the good original without apparently making his own picture any better. The copy may be as carefully painted, as well composed, as faithful a mirror of the external world as that which it feigns and I think we may conclude from this that excellence in dexterity, verisimilitude and composition will not make a bad picture good. This, indeed, is sufficiently apparent from the original works of many lesser masters. None of the excellencies which we can enumerate will survive even the most careful transposition, although every quality that can be described in words may also be described by the copyist in paint. An essayist having in front of him a good coloured reproduction of a Rembrandt may write as complete an account of the picture as he could do in front of the original. But he will know very well that there is an immense—an indescribable, difference between the thing itself and the printed image.

If we want a word with which to describe this incommunicable element, then I think that the word must be "sentiment." Even here we must be careful; when, for instance, Van Gogh copied Gustave Doré's miserable engraving of a prison yard he undoubtedly attempted to conserve that vulgar artist's trite sentiment. And yet the sentiment is not the same. And it is here, I think, that we may come nearest to discovering the essential quality in bad art. The expression of sentiment as opposed to the pictorial narration of a given story is something which derives from a state of mind and just as, obviously, the same story illustrated by, say, Rembrandt and Rubens or even by artists who are comparatively close together, as for instance David and Prudhon, will undergo a profound metamorphosis as it passes into different hands, so a landscape by Constable or a still life by Cézanne is virtually uncopyable, except by mechanical means, because the sentient copyist must inevitably, and however much he attempts to subordinate himself to his original, retain sentiments of his own and these must inevitably affect his work.

So far I have probably commanded your assent rather than your attention. But the next stage of my argument is more questionable and less commonplace: I believe that the quality of badness in a work of art derives from an awareness of beauty, or rather, of that which society at large considers beautiful and which I will here call "social beauty." I must return and consider the implications of that word "beautiful," but first let me offer two examples which may help to clarify my meaning. The sentiment in a Van Gogh is in the highest degree personal, he is moved by a pure, irreflective and uncalculating desire to make pictorial statements, even today that which he says has a brutal and unexpected quality: in his own time his work was almost universally condemned for its ugliness and its ineptitude. Gustave Doré, on the other hand, refers continually to a whole common market of ideas, at no point are we disturbed by an original or a surprising sentiment. In fact his work was socially acceptable and was for many years widely and enthusiastically accepted, unlike Van Gogh he was considered "artistic."

Or again, take the work of almost any three-year-old child and compare it with the productions of an adolescent. The picture by the adolescent will almost certainly be more workmanlike, more intelligent, and, in certain respects, more profound than that of the child, but it will also have a quality of badness, of insincerity, which is completely absent from the first drawings that we make. The badness of the adolescent's drawing arises from what we call self-consciousness, but which is in fact consciousness of others, not necessarily an awareness of the teacher so much as an awareness of society, of all that society deems beautiful.

The situation of Gustave Doré or of the adolescent is that he is forced by his perception of social values to modify that frankly unconscious approach which belongs to those who are untroubled by social exigencies—the genius and the child. He is the victim of a dual standard of excellence which leads him, almost inevitably, to a compromise or to a capitulation which necessarily vitiates his sentiments.

Here I am led naturally back to the question of beauty. It is not necessary to define the term but merely to point to the existence—in certain historical conditions—of two standards of excellence. Return, once more, to the example of Van Gogh and Gustave Doré. In a sense it may be said that both artists sought beauty and that both achieved it, even though their aims seem to be diametrically opposed.

The beauty of Van Gogh is of a kind which, at first sight, seems to the general public to be the very negation of beauty, to be, in fact, pure, brutal, unmitigated ugliness. Only by degrees, as we learn to understand the meaning behind the violence of the artist's language, do we learn to accept it. When once it has been accepted we think, not, I hope, unreasonably, that it has become a permanent acquisition (but even in this we may be wrong).

The typical life history of every artistic movement of the past hundred years has consisted of a struggle against hostility and indifference, the good artist has fought against the popular conception of beauty, the bad artist has accepted it at once or after a brief struggle. There have been two measures of excellence and, as a necessary result, a struggle in which the artist must be continually driven to a compromise, to an insincere bargain which results in falsity of sentiment, in bad art. The typical aesthetic history of the child, that is to say, the suppression of pure irreflective emotion untroubled by any conscious pursuit of beauty and its replacement by an attitude of social deference allows us to suppose that, in modern society this conflict, and the almost inevitable victory of social taste, makes bad art a normal, if not a universal, phenomenon.

I think that we shall have come about as far as we can come towards an incontrovertible statement if we say that bad art arises from a failure of sentiment, that this is caused by some form of insincerity, and that this, in its turn, results from a form of social pressure in favour of that which society at large calls "beauty."

Consider now the obvious and overwhelming examples of the
last century: *The Monarch of the Glen, The Boyhood of Raleigh,* and
When did you last see your Father? Why is it that they are so ap-
pallingly bad? What was it that made Millais and Landseer and
Francis Yeams so deplorable? Why was it that two former artists,
both of whom showed enormous talent as young men, should have
become so dreadful in middle age? In each case the demands of
society were met, and met with enthusiasm. These artists had completely accepted the opinion of their age as to what constituted a
beautiful picture, and, having done so, addressed themselves to the
pursuit of the beautiful with horrifying success.

If we look further into the nineteenth century and consider that
work which, without being of the heroic stature of the Impressionists, is still valued for its charm—the dresses, the fashion
plates, and the cheap ornaments of the period—we find them far
preferable to the great historical machines of the Academies *precisely because they attempt far less.* We can perceive the same law in
operation even within the *oeuvre* of the most portentous masters. If
we compare the book illustrations or the rough sketches of a Millais,
a Poynter or a Leighton with their finished easel pictures, we shall
realise that they could only do their worst when they really exerted
themselves.

Take another example, this time from our own epoch. Go into a
big department store and look at the more expensive and highly
decorated objects, the garlanded lampshades and the moquette
television suites (trad. or contemp.), the apparatus of gracious living
and the reproductions of works by artists who paint a socially acceptable pastiche of the Impressionists. There, if you have a grain of
sensibility, your heart will sink. But it will rise again as you leave
this abominable abode of beauty and enter the hardware department. Here you may enjoy yourself for here there is no art. Take a
spade and admire its clean, athletic, trenchant appearance. It has
only one blemish—the manufacturer's label, for here there will be
some little pretence at ornament, some paltry shield or feeble scroll,
some artful distortion of the maker's name made in the cause of art.

Put the case in another way. *The Monarch of the Glen* is bad
because it is attempting to be so good; the conflict between social
and personal valuations is therefore exceptionally acute; the fashion
plate or the spade succeeds at its own level because the maker is
relatively unambitious and is therefore not compelled to seek beauty
with any large measure of enthusiasm. We may in fact postulate a

simple law of aesthetic gravity: the higher you fly the harder you fall.

II

If bad art results from an awareness of social demands, then we should expect to find that the incidence of bad art varies according to the social situation of the artist and in response to historical changes. I believe that a clear correspondence can be seen between historical developments and the growth or decline of bad art, and indubitably, bad art is a variable not a constant phenomenon.

At first sight, indeed, it appears that one of the advantages of discussing bad art lies in the abundance of material that lies ready to hand, and of course, it is true that we do not have to look far in order to find great quantities of miserable work produced in every part of the civilized world during the past hundred and fifty years. But, if we go back to the eighteenth and then to the seventeenth and sixteenth centuries, we shall, if we continue to apply the same standards, discover a substantial diminution of output, especially in architecture and the applied arts. In fact the abundant production of bad art which we now regard as a normal feature of European culture, hardly begins before the Renaissance. Implicitly we recognise this fact in our day to day judgements concerning art. If I were to say: there is some thirteenth-century glass in such and such a church, you would know without being told that it was good or very good. If I were to say that the glass was nineteenth century you would know that in all probability it was bad; it is only if I were to put the glass in some intermediate period between the fourteenth and the nineteenth centuries that you would require information concerning its aesthetic value.

In other words, there are long periods in which the statistical probability of a thing being good or bad is so great as to make further information superfluous. Moreover, I can make aesthetic judgements concerning whole cultures—Benin, Maya, Sassanian, twelfth century, T'ang, which are quite as reliable as the judgements that I might pass upon individuals such as Corot, Monet or Picasso.

Nor is this simply a matter of cultures and periods; in a stricter sense the social context of the artist determines his standards of achievement. While vast inequalities exist between one painter and another in a period such as the sixteenth century, only very slight differences will be found between masons, potters or cabinet makers of that epoch.

Here let me add a rider which in truth follows naturally from what I have already said. Social forces are nearly always inescapable. The whole method of art history is based on the assumption that one can usually date a work by its style. A nineteenth century copy of a sixteenth century painting will almost invariably be recognisable for what it is. One may see this principle of aesthetic determinism at work in historical reconstructions for stage or films where, despite the careful efforts of the designer to render a true image of the past, the present—the designer's present—constantly emerges. The date is "given away" by the fact that the artist cannot but want to make his work beautiful and that in so doing he must make concessions to the standards of his period. It is not until these standards have lost their validity that we perceive the shortcomings of the imitations. The case of art forgeries is particularly instructive here. The Van Meegeren Vermeers, forgeries of a most ingenious kind, did deceive a great number of the experts twenty or thirty years ago. Today we are amazed at their gullibility; this is not simply hindsight. The forger's deficiencies as an artist have become visible, as a patch on a piece of cloth becomes visible when it fades faster than the surrounding material. His style has begun to "date" and we see that, despite all his efforts to conjure himself into the seventeenth century, he remains always in the 1930s. Mr. Benedict Nicholson has even shown that his facial types are drawn from film stars of the period. Once again the artist is prevented from achieving his object by an inescapable deference to beauty.

Clearly, at this point, I am in some danger of contradicting myself. If the taste of any period is inescapable, then it is not only the bad artist who is affected by it. This is true enough and it is true that the work even of a nonconformist like Van Gogh dates in the sense that we can place it historically; but it dates far less than does a work by Gustave Doré. The emotional insincerity which makes Doré's work so deplorable arises from an enslavement to the standards of his age. Van Gogh was liberated from this because the intensity of his vision was such that he could rise above it. The twelfth century artist required no liberation because he could accept his age without inward questioning, for him there was no conflict, hence no insincerity.

Bad art, if this analysis be correct, arises from a rather sophisticated state of mind. In order to be insincere the artist must have some kind of choice and his choice must lie between two kinds of excellence, such as will occur only in certain conditions. We need not and should not imagine the bad artist deliberately setting out to please his public, we need not even think of him saying to himself: that looks attractive, that will please the critics. The damnable thing about bad art is that the insincerity that lies at its roots is not perceived by the artist himself.

It is not within my purpose, and perhaps it is beyond my capacity, to write a history of bad art. Today I will go no farther than to suggest that such a history would be confined to periods of high culture—I think we might discover examples of bad art in the later Egyptian and Chinese dynasties, the later Hellenic world, some forms of Islamic art and European art after Giotto. It follows or co-exists with very good art, and this for the simple reason that very good art creates a destructive admiration for beauty. A typical instance would, I think, be the Italianizing art of the Low Countries in the sixteenth century. If one were to take Messrs. Thieme-Becker's solid tomes and count the number of good artists who have flourished since the death of Michelangelo one would, I am afraid, be forced to the unwelcome conclusion that the great majority have been bad. This melancholy but most important fact about art is obscured by our tendency to forget those artists whose work no longer interests us.

In the case of the late nineteenth century, where we are interested only in a few rebellious figures who stood outside the main stream of contemporary work, we have today a completely distorted view. Look at the Encyclopaedia Britannica for 1912. A special section is devoted to recent developments in France. It was written by M. Leonce Bénédite, curator of the Luxembourg. He makes no mention of Seurat, Signac, Gauguin, Van Gogh, Vuillard, Berthe Morisot, or any of the Fauves, and for him the great French artists of the period after 1870 are Robert Fleury, Bastien Lepage, Meissonier, Rosa Bonheur, Gerome, Bouguereau, Fromentin, Bonvin, Cormon and Henner. The article on British painting is even more striking. You may perhaps have heard of Herkomer, Luke Fildes and Frank Dicksee but you will surely be surprised to learn that "in marine painting no one has appeared to rival Henry Moore, perhaps the greatest student of wave forms the world has ever seen," although apparently even he had a competitor in the late Edward Hayes. Pass from the vast catalogue of English and French nonentities to the equally numerous and even more undistinguished multitude of Belgian, Dutch, German, Swedish and Norwegian and

Russian painters and you will, I think, be appalled by the spectacle of misused paint and wasted effort. The French independents then appear in perspective, as a little candle in a vast and naughty world. They were bright indeed, but to most wanderers invisible. How could it be otherwise if we remember that the aim of painting is the production of beauty and that which these painters produced appeared ugly and inept.

This disquieting pattern of production and achievement is less obvious when we turn to more remote ages and certainly the nineteenth century is peculiar in having neglected nearly all its great painters and in having produced a school of art which finds no echo in the architecture and applied art of the epoch. Nevertheless something of the same inequality of performance and rarity of merit will be found in all the periods subsequent to the High Renaissance.

But the nineteenth century even now, when we are learning to consider it with more sympathy than was possible a generation ago, is still in a class of its own. I cannot account for this beyond saying that it seems to me clear that the reasons are to be found in the history of society itself; but I do want to point to the intensity of the nineteenth-century concern with beauty. No other age sought it with such assiduity, it clamoured for beauty as a child clamours for sweets; it produced beauty by the ton and by the square mile, it applied beauty with reckless profusion to every available surface in the form of frills and flounces, stucco and gutta percha mouldings, buttons, beading and Berlin wool, lincrusta, papier maché and Britannia metal, crockets, buttresses, cherubs, scroll work, arabesques and foliage. Look at any board school or bustle of eighty years ago and you will find more beauty than you know what to do with. It is true that the century produced some gaunt metallic structures which we can now admire, but from these, lovers of beauty—from Ruskin downwards—turned shudderingly away.

Here, perhaps, we may obtain a glimpse of the social mechanism that creates bad art. The mischievous sense of beauty arises from a corresponding perception of ugliness and a rejection of that ugliness. The art of the High Renaissance and, still more, that of the seventeenth-century academicians results from an aristocratic dislike of mean, base or villainous subjects, beauty here may almost be equated with "nobility." The idea was replaced by that which, first suggested by Diderot and then developed by Ruskin, asserts that beauty is indissolubly connected with morality. In both cases the critics were reacting against something that their society had made for itself—the vulgarities of plebeian life or the apparatus of industrialism—and they set against it an aesthetic ideal of a more tolerable kind. Thus we have a preoccupation with beauty which is eminently social in that it arises not from any delight in the visible world but from a species of social anxiety and social ostentation. I am not arguing that such motives are not productive of good art but that, while producing works of lasting value, they also engender much that is bad—the pretentious and histrionic confections of a Lebrun or a Van Loo, the sickly pomposities of Ary Scheffer or Joseph Albert Moore. These were an escape into social beauty and represented not personal feelings but polite evasions.

III

What about us? From what I have already said it will be clear that most of us like bad art and that we don't perceive that it is bad until our changing standards of social beauty have ceased to recommend it. This, obviously, makes assessment difficult and, when we try to use the principles that I have outlined, certain new elements in the social and aesthetic structure of twentieth-century society prevent us from applying them with certainty. It is easy enough to find an obvious and disastrous worship of beauty in the annual exhibitions at Burlington House, the pretentious banker's Georgian facades of our cities or in those emporia to which I have already alluded. But can we oppose to that an art which offends and shocks by its ugliness? Until recently we could do so, but now I am not so sure.

The art that we find in Bond Street, the art of the international dealers, the art that we find in our glossy magazines, the art that wins awards and prizes is *not* the art of the academician or of the salon painter. *That* art, indeed, seems almost to have sunk to the position of a naive and provincial survival from the past. For us the really agonising question is: are we uniquely blessed in having a truly enlightened public, a wealthy clientéle seeking a beauty which, for all its social acceptability, is truly personal; or shall we find that the international abstract school was but a school of social beauty, a more complete and drastic turning away from unpalatable realities than even the art of Frank Dicksee or Philip de Laszlo?

The completely abstract painting raises this question in an acute form, for the abstract painter—with perfect logic—has stripped art of all its irrelevancies—verisimilitude, ideology, content, everything save those essential qualities which make a painting valuable. Everything, in fact, save beauty.

If you have had the patience to follow my argument so far, you will perceive that this is the most dangerous situation in which any artist can find himself. It is here, in the total pursuit of beauty, that the aesthetic law of gravity exerts its maximum pull. Take a canvas and cover it with areas of colour, colour without figurative or symbolic intention, colour with no function save that of looking nice. On what principle will you add or subtract, erase or divide, on what principle save a principle of taste? There is no other check, no other discipline, no difficulty save that you have no difficulty. Everything in an abstract painting results from aesthetic decision which is inescapably social.

I think that much of the development of art during the past twenty years results from an awareness of the dangers of this situation. On the one hand we have had a rejection of decision, on the other a rejection of beauty, finally we have had a denial that the dilemma exists at all.

Let us begin first with this last symptom of aesthetic malaise. It is the least important; it consists on the one hand in a kind of playing at nonconformity, a pretence that abstract art is like Impressionism, the art of a persecuted minority. This, patently, is nonsense and is of interest only as a symptom. Secondly, there is a change of terminology—the word beauty has become taboo because of its alarming suggestions and the word art is tactfully changed to anti-art. These are circumlocutions which hide but do not resolve the dilemma.

Much more striking is the rejection of decision, an absurd, but in the circumstances understandable effort by the painter to avoid making any choice involving taste by refusing to make any choice at all, by allowing haphazard splashes, the imprints of a bicycle tyre, to take responsibility, by using the ready made object, the machine or the monkey, or by framing a piece of wallpaper and calling it a picture. Evasions of this kind, artful rejections of art, are also attempts to escape from beauty. The younger and more serious figurative painters—who are indeed something of a persecuted minority—face a less agonising decision. For them the image is at least a break, a distraction from the aesthetic demands; but here, too, I think that something of the same malaise has been felt. The work of Francis Bacon, of Bratby and of the young men who find their inspiration in "pop" art follows in a very long tradition of the picturesque which is in itself a form of escape from beauty, but in their wholehearted search for ugliness there is, I think, a more febrile attempt at liberation than we have seen before.

I wish that I could see a solution to the dilemma of the modern painter, but even if I could it would be of little service to him. It is not in theorising such as this but in the studio that solutions are found. All that I can do is to try to explain what it is that has made the art of previous ages bad and at the same time attempt to explain the danger in which, as I believe, we now stand. This, perhaps, is not entirely useless; to know what your problem is may be the first step to finding a solution to it, but the act of pointing it out is not one for which I can expect to be thanked.

NOTE

1. And also upon assertions to which we ourselves can no longer subscribe. Today, in 1982, I should no longer write, as I did in 1962, of the "sickly pomposities of . . . Joseph Albert Moore" (see p. 169).

10

On the Obsolescence
of the Concept of Honor

Peter Berger

Honor occupies about the same place in contemporary usage as
chastity. An individual asserting it hardly invites admiration, and
one who claims to have lost it is an object of amusement rather than
sympathy. Both concepts have an unambiguously outdated status
in the *Weltanschauung* of modernity. Especially intellectuals, by
definition in the vanguard of modernity, are about as likely to admit
to honor as to be found out as chaste. At best, honor and chastity
are seen as ideological leftovers in the consciousness of obsolete
classes, such as military officers or ethnic grandmothers.

The obsolescence of the concept of honor is revealed very sharply in the inability of most contemporaries to understand insult,
which in essense is an assault on honor. In this, at least in America,
there is a close parallel between modern consciousness and modern
law. Motives of honor have no standing in American law, and legal
codes that still admit them, as in some countries of southern
Europe, are perceived as archaic. In modern consciousness, as in
American law (shaped more than any other by that prime force of
modernization which is capitalism), insult in itself is not actionable,
is not recognized as a real injury. The insulted party must be able to
prove material damage. There are cases, indeed, where psychic harm
may be the basis for a legal claim, but that too is a far cry from a notion of offense against honor. The *Weltanschauung* of everyday life
closely conforms in this to the legal definitions of reality. If an individual is insulted and, as a result, is harmed in his career or his
capacity to earn an income, he may not only have recourse to the

This essay from the *Archives européennes de sociologie* 11 (1970):
339–47 is reprinted by permission.

courts but may count on the sympathy of his friends. His friends, and in some cases the courts, will come to his support if, say, the insult so unsettles him that he loses his self-esteem or has a nervous breakdown. If, however, neither kind of injury pertains, he will almost certainly be advised by lawyers and friends alike to just forget the whole thing. In other words, the *reality* of the offense will be denied. If the individual persists in maintaining it, he will be negatively categorized, most probably in psychiatric terms (as "neurotic," "overly sensitive," or the like), or if applicable in terms that refer to cultural lag (as "hopelessly European," perhaps, or as the victim of a "provincial mentality").

The contemporary denial of the reality of honor and of offenses against honor is so much part of a taken-for-granted world that a deliberate effort is required to even see it as a problem. The effort is worthwhile, for it can result in some, perhaps unexpected, new insights into the structure of modern consciousness.

The problem of the obsolescence of the concept of honor can be brought into better focus by comparing it with a most timely concept—that of dignity. Taken by itself, the demise of honor might be interpreted as part of a process of moral coarsening, of a lessening of respect for persons, even of dehumanization. Indeed, this is exactly how it looked to a conservative mind at the beginning of the modern era—for example, to the fifteenth-century French poet Eustache Deschamps: "Age of decline nigh to the end,/Time of horror which does all things falsely,/Lying age, full of pride and of envy,/*Time without honour and without true judgment.*"[1] Yet it seems quite clear in retrospect that this pessimistic estimate was, to say the least, very one-sided. The age that saw the decline of honor also saw the rise of new moralities and of a new humanism, and most specifically of a historically unprecedented concern for the dignity and the rights of the individual. The same modern men who fail to understand an issue of honor are immediately disposed to concede the demands for dignity and for equal rights by almost every new group that makes them—racial or religious minorities, exploited classes, the poor, the deviant, and so on. Nor would it be just to question the genuineness of this disposition. A little thought, then, should make clear that the problem is not clarified by ethical pessimism. It is necessary to ask more fundamentally: What is honor? What is dignity? What can be learned about modern consciousness by the obsolescence of the one and the unique sway of the other?

Honor is commonly understood as an aristocratic concept, or at least associated with a hierarchical order of society. It is certainly true that Western notions of honor have been strongly influenced by the medieval codes of chivalry and that these were rooted in the social structures of feudalism. It is also true that concepts of honor have survived into the modern era best in groups retaining a hierarchical view of society, such as the nobility, the military, and traditional professions like law and medicine. In such groups honor is a direct expression of status, a source of solidarity among social equals and a demarcation line against social inferiors. Honor, indeed, also dictates certain standards of behavior in dealing with inferiors, but the full code of honor only applies among those who share the same status in the hierarchy. In a hierarchically ordered society the etiquette of everyday life consists of ongoing transactions of honor, and different groups relate differently to this process according to the principle of "To each his due." It would be a mistake, however, to understand honor *only* in terms of hierarchy and its delineations. To take the most obvious example, the honor of women in many traditional societies, while usually differentiated along class lines, may pertain in principle to women of *all* classes.

J. K. Campbell, in his study of contemporary rural culture in Greece,[2] makes this very clear. While the obligations of honor (*timi*) differ as between different categories of individuals, notably between men and women, everyone within the community exists within the same all-embracing system of honor. Those who have high status in the community have particular obligations of honor, but even the lowly are differentiated in terms of honor and dishonor. Men should exhibit manliness and women shame, but the failure of either implies dishonor for the individual, the family and, in some cases, the entire community. For all, the qualities enjoined by honor provide the link, not only between self and community, but between self and the idealized norms of the community: "Honour considered as the possession by men and women of these qualities is the attempt to relate existence to certain archetypal patterns of behaviour."[3] Conversely, dishonor is a fall from grace in the most comprehensive sense—loss of face in the community, but also loss of self and separation from the basic norms that govern human life.

It is valid to view such a culture as essentially premodern, just as it is plausible to predict its disintegration under the impact of modernization. Historically, there are several stages in the latter process. The decline of medieval codes of honor did not lead directly to the contemporary situation in which honor is an all but meaningless concept. There took place first the *embourgeoisement* of honor, which has been defined by Norbert Elias as the process of "civilization," both a broadening and a mellowing process.[4] The contents had changed, but there was still a conception of honor in the age of the triumphant bourgeoisie. Yet it was with the rise of the bourgeoisie, particularly in the consciousness of its critical intellectuals, that not only the honor of the *ancien régime* and its hierarchical prototypes was debunked, but that an understanding of man and society emerged that would eventually liquidate *any* conception of honor.

Thus Cervantes' *Quixote* is the tragi-comedy of a particular obsolescence, that of the knight-errant in an age in which chivalry has become an empty rhetoric. The greatness of the *Quixote*, however, transcends this particular time-bound debunking job. It unmasks not only the "madness" of chivalry but, by extension, the folly of *any* identification of self with "archetypal patterns of behaviour." Put differently, Don Quixote's "enchanters" (whose task, paradoxically, is precisely what Max Weber had in mind as "*dis*enchantment") cannot be stopped so easily once they have started their terrible task. As Don Quixote tells Sancho in one of his innumerable homilies: "Is it possible that in the time you have been with me you have not yet found out that all the adventures of a knight-errant appear to be illusion, follies, and dreams, and turn out to be the reverse? Not because things are really so, but because in our midst there is a host of enchanters, forever changing, disguising and transforming our affairs as they please, according to whether they wish to favor or destroy us. So, what you call a barber's basin is to me Mambrino's helmet, and to another person it will appear to be something else."[5] These "enchanters," alas, have not stopped with chivalry. Every human adventure, in which the self and its actions have been identified and endowed with the honor of collective prototypes has, finally, been debunked as "illusion, follies, and dreams." Modern man is Don Quixote on his deathbed, denuded of the multicolored banners that previously enveloped the self and revealed to be *nothing but a man*: "I was mad, but I am now in my senses; I was once Don Quixote of La Mancha, but I am now, as I said before, Alonso Quixano the Good."[6] The same self, deprived or, if one prefers, freed from the mystifications of honor is hailed in Falstaff's "catechism": "Honour is a mere scutcheon."[7] It is modern consciousness that unmasks it as such, that "enchants" or "disenchants" it (depending on one's point of view) until it is shown as nothing but a painted artifact. Behind the "mere scutcheon" is the face of modern man—man bereft of the consolation of prototypes, *man alone*.

It is important to understand that it is precisely this solitary self that modern consciousness has perceived as the bearer of human dignity and of inalienable human rights. The modern discovery of dignity took place precisely amid the wreckage of debunked conceptions of honor. Now, it would be a mistake to ascribe to modern consciousness alone the discovery of a fundamental dignity underlying all possible social disguises. The same discovery can be found in the Hebrew Bible, as in the confrontation between Nathan and David ("Thou art the man"); in Sophocles, in the confrontation between Antigone and Creon; and, in a different form, in Mencius' parable of a criminal stopping a child from falling into a well. The understanding that there is a humanity behind or beneath the roles and the norms imposed by society, and that this humanity has profound dignity, is not a modern prerogative. What is peculiarly modern is the manner in which the reality of this intrinsic humanity is related to the realities of society.

Dignity, as against honor, always relates to the intrinsic humanity divested of all socially imposed roles or norms. It pertains to the self as such, to the individual regardless of his position in society. This becomes very clear in the classic formulations of human rights, from the Preamble to the Declaration of Independence to the Universal Declaration of Human Rights of the United Nations. These rights always pertain to the individual "irrespective of race, color or creed"—or, indeed, of sex, age, physical condition or any conceivable social status. There is an implicit sociology and an implicit anthropology here. The implicit sociology views all biological and historical differentiations among men as either downright unreal or essentially irrelevant. The implicit anthropology locates the real self over and beyond all these differentiations.

It should now be possible to see these two concepts somewhat more clearly. Both honor and dignity are concepts that bridge self and society. While either pertains to the individual in a very intimate way, it is in relations with others that both honor and dignity are attained, exchanged, preserved or threatened. Both require a deliberate effort of the will for their maintenance—one must *strive* for them, often against the malevolent opposition of others—thus honor and dignity become goals of moral enterprise. Their loss, always a possibility, has far-reaching consequences for the self. Finally, both honor and dignity have an infectious quality that extends beyond the moral person of the individual possessing them.

The infection involves his body ("a dignified gait"), his material ambience (from clothing to the furnishings of his house) and other individuals closely associated with him ("He brought honor on his whole family"). What, then, is the difference between these two concepts of the social self? Or, substituting a more current term to avoid the metaphysical associations of "self," how do these two conceptions of identity differ?

The concept of honor implies that identity is essentially, or at least importantly, linked to institutional roles. The modern concept of dignity, by contrast, implies that identity is essentially independent of institutional roles. To return to Falstaff's image, in a world of honor the individual *is* the social symbols emblazoned on his escutcheon. The true self of the knight is revealed as he rides out to do battle in the full regalia of his role; by comparison, the naked man in bed with a woman represents a lesser reality of the self. In a world of dignity, in the modern sense, the social symbolism governing the interaction of men is a disguise. The escutcheons *hide* the true self. It is precisely the naked man, and even more specifically the naked man expressing his sexuality, who represents himself more truthfully. Consequently, the understanding of self-discovery and self-mystification is reversed as between these two worlds. In a world of honor, the individual discovers his true identity in his roles, and to turn away from the roles is to turn away from himself—in "false consciousness," one is tempted to add. In a world of dignity, the individual can only discover his true identity by emancipating himself from his socially imposed roles—the latter are only masks, entangling him in illusion, "alienation" and "bad faith." It follows that the two worlds have a different relation to history. It is through the performance of institutional roles that the individual participates in history, not only the history of the particular institution but that of his society as a whole. It is precisely for this reason that modern consciousness, in its conception of the self, tends toward a curious ahistoricity. In a world of honor, identity is firmly linked to the past through the reiterated performance of prototypical acts. In a world of dignity, history is the succession of mystifications from which the individual must free himself to attain "authenticity."

It is important not to lose sight here of continuities in the constitution of man—of "anthropological constants," if one prefers. Modern man is not a total innovation or a mutation of the species. Thus he shares with any version of archaic man known to us both his intrinsic sociality and the reciprocal process with society through which his various identities are formed, maintained and changed. All the same, within the parameters set by his fundamental constitution, man has considerable leeway in constructing, dismantling and reassembling the worlds in which he lives. Inasmuch as identity is always part of a comprehensive world, and a humanly *constructed* world at that, there are far-reaching differences in the ways in which identity is conceived and, consequently, experienced. Definitions of identity vary with overall definitions of reality. Each such definition, however, has reality-generating power: Men not only define themselves, but they actualize these definitions in real experience—*they live them.*

No monocausal theory is likely to do justice to the transformation that has taken place. Very probably most of the factors commonly cited have in fact played a part in the process—technology and industrialization, bureaucracy, urbanization and population growth, the vast increase in communication between every conceivable human group, social mobility, the pluralization of social worlds and the profound metamorphosis in the social contexts in which children are reared. Be this as it may, the resultant situation has been aptly characterized by Arnold Gehlen with the terms "de-institutionalization" and "subjectivization." The former term refers to a global weakening in the holding power of institutions over the individual. The institutional fabric, whose basic function has always been to provide meaning and stability for the individual, has become incohesive, fragmented and thus progressively deprived of plausibility. The institutions then confront the individual as fluid and unreliable, in the extreme case as unreal. Inevitably, the individual is thrown back upon himself, on his own subjectivity, from which he must dredge up the meaning and the stability that he requires to exist. Precisely because of man's intrinsic sociality, this is a very unsatisfactory condition. Stable identities (and this also means identities that will be subjectively plausible) can only emerge in reciprocity with stable social contexts (and this means contexts that are structured by stable institutions). Therefore, there is a deep uncertainty about contemporary identity. Put differently, there is a built-in identity crisis in the contemporary situation.

It is in this connection that one begins to understand the implicit sociology and the implicit anthropology mentioned above. Both are rooted in actual experience of the modern world. The literary, philosophical and even social-scientific formulations are ex post facto attempts to come to terms with this experience. Gehlen has shown this convincingly for the rise of the modern novel as the literary form most fully reflecting the new subjectivism. But the conceptualizations of man and society of, for instance, Marxism and existentialism are equally rooted in this experience. So is the perspective of modern social science, especially of sociology. Marx's "alienation" and "false consciousness," Heidegger's "authenticity" and Sartre's "bad faith," and such current sociological notions as David Reisman's "other-direction" or Erving Goffman's "impression management" could only arise and claim credibility in a situation in which the identity-defining power of institutions has been greatly weakened.

The obsolescence of the concept of honor may now be seen in a much more comprehensive perspective. The social location of honor lies in a world of relatively intact, stable institutions, a world in which individuals can with subjective certainty attach their identities to the institutional roles that society assigns to them. The disintegration of this world as a result of the forces of modernity has not only made honor an increasingly meaningless notion, but has served as the occasion for a redefinition of identity and its intrinsic dignity apart from and often *against* the institutional roles through which the individual expresses himself in society. The reciprocity between individual and society, between subjective identity and objective identification through roles, now comes to be experienced as a sort of struggle. Institutions cease to be the "home" of the self; instead they become oppressive realities that distort and estrange the self. Roles no longer actualize the self, but serve as a "veil of *maya*" hiding the self not only from others but from the individual's own consciousness. Only in the interstitial areas left vacant, as it were, by the institutions (such as the so-called private sphere of social life) can the individual hope to discover or define himself. Identity ceases to be an objectively and subjectively given fact, and instead becomes the goal of an often devious and difficult quest. Modern man, almost inevitably it seems, is ever in search of himself. If this is understood, it will also be clear why both the sense of "alienation" and the concomitant identity crisis are most vehement among the young today. Indeed, "youth" itself, which is a matter of social definition rather than biological fact, will be seen as an interstitial area vacated or "left over" by the large institutional structures of modern society. For this reason it is, simultaneously, the locale of the most acute experiences of self-estrangement and of the most intensive quest for reliable identities.

A lot will depend, naturally, on one's basic assumptions about man whether one will bemoan or welcome these transformations.

What to one will appear as a profound loss will be seen by another as the prelude to liberation. Among intellectuals today, of course, it is the latter viewpoint that prevails and that forms the implicit anthropological foundation for the generally "left" mood of the time. The threat of chaos, both social and psychic, which ever lurks behind the disintegration of institutions, will then be seen as a necessary stage that must precede the great "leap into freedom" that is to come. It is also possible, in a conservative perspective, to view the same process as precisely the root pathology of the modern era, as a disastrous loss of the very structures that enable men to be free and to be themselves. Such pessimism is expressed forcefully, if somewhat petulantly, in Gehlen's latest book, a conservative manifesto in which modernity appears as an all-engulfing pestilence.[8]

We would contend here that both perspectives—the liberation myth of the "left" and the nostalgia of the "right" for an intact world—fail to do justice to the anthropological and indeed the ethical dimensions of the problem. It seems clear to us that the unrestrained enthusiasm for total liberation of the self from the "repression" of institutions fails to take account of certain fundamental requirements of man, notably those of order—that institutional order of society without which both collectivities and individuals must descend into dehumanizing chaos. In other words, the demise of honor has been a very costly price to pay for whatever liberations modern man may have achieved. On the other hand, the unqualified denunciation of the contemporary constellation of institutions and identities fails to perceive the vast moral achievements made possible by just this constellation—the discovery of the autonomous individual, with a dignity deriving from his very being, over and above all and any social identifications. Anyone denouncing the modern world tout court should pause and question whether he wishes to include in that denunciation the specifically modern discoveries of human dignity and human rights. The conviction that even the weakest members of society have an inherent right to protection and dignity; the proscription of slavery in all its forms, of racial and ethnic oppression; the staggering discovery of the dignity and rights of the child; the new sensitivity to cruelty, from the abhorrence of torture to the codification of the crime of genocide—a sensitivity that has become politically significant in the outrage against the cruelties of the war in Vietnam; the new recognition of individual responsibility for all actions, even those assigned to the individual with specific institutional roles, a recognition that attained the force of law at

Nuremberg—all these, and others, are moral achievements that would be unthinkable without the peculiar constellations of the modern world. To reject them is unthinkable ethically. By the same token, it is not possible to simply trace them to a false anthropology.

The task before us, rather, is to understand the empirical processes that have made modern man lose sight of honor at the expense of dignity—and then to think through both the anthropological and the ethical implications of this. Obviously these remarks can do no more than point up some dimensions of the problem. It may be allowed, though, to speculate that a rediscovery of honor in the future development of modern society is both empirically plausible and morally desirable. Needless to say, this will hardly take the form of a regressive restoration of traditional codes. But the contemporary mood of anti-institutionalism is unlikely to last, as Anton Zijderveld implies.[9] Man's fundamental constitution is such that, just about inevitably, he will once more construct institutions to provide an ordered reality for himself. A return to institutions will ipso facto be a return to honor. It will then be possible again for individuals to identify themselves with the escutcheons of their institutional roles, experienced now not as self-estranging tyrannies but as freely chosen vehicles of self-realization. The ethical question, of course, is what these institutions will be like. Specifically, the ethical test of any future institutions, and of the codes of honor they will entail, will be whether they succeed in embodying and in stabilizing the discoveries of human dignity that are the principal achievements of modern man.

NOTES

1. Cited in J. Huizinga, *The Waning of the Middle Ages* (New York: Doubleday-Anchor, 1954), p. 33 [my italics].
2. J. K. Campbell, *Honour, Family and Patronage* (Oxford, 1964).
3. Ibid., pp. 271 sq.
4. Norbert Elias, *Der Prozess der Zivilisation* (Bern: Francke, 1969).
5. Cervantes, *Don Quixote,* trans. Walter Starkie (New York: New American Library, 1964), I:25, p. 243.
6. Ibid., II:74.
7. W. Shakespeare, *Henry IV,* Part I, V:I.
8. Arnold Gehlen, *Moral and Hypermoral* (Frankfurt: Athenäum, 1969).
9. Anton Zijderveld, *Abstract Society* (New York: Doubleday, 1970).

11

Biblical Revelation and Medical Decisions

Richard J. Mouw

"Fear God, and keep His commandments; for this is the whole duty of man." The writer of Ecclesiastes thus summarizes a significant perspective on the nature of the good life. At the heart of this perspective is the conviction that there is a God who has offered directives to human beings, which they must acknowledge as they shape the patterns of their lives. As many Christians view things, this posture of obedience to a God who reveals his will is foundational to an adequate understanding of morality. For those who assume such a posture, it is unthinkable that we could reflect at any length on a moral issue without asking, "What does the Lord require of us?"

If divine commands have a crucial bearing on "the whole duty of man," then they must surely be taken into account when we seek to do our duty in the area of medical decision making. On such a view, Christian medical ethics cannot be pursued without careful reflection upon divine commandments as they bear on the medical dimensions of human life.

To view medical ethics in this light is to adopt a perspective whose plausibility—or even intelligibility—is not immediately obvious to all contemporary ethicists. As Peter Geach has observed: "In modern ethical treatises we find hardly any mention of God; and the idea that if there really is a God, his commandments might be morally relevant is wont to be dismissed by a short and simple argument" (Geach 1969, p. 117). Indeed, the assumption that divine commands are morally irrelevant even operates among contemporary Christian writers of ethical treatises.

My concern here is not so much to defend obedience to divine

This essay from *Journal of Medicine and Philosophy* 4, no. 4 (1979): 367–82 is reprinted by permission.

commands against either impious or pious critics as it is to explain one way in which divine commandments might be viewed as morally relevant and as important for shaping attitudes in the area of medical decision making. Indeed, while I will address some of my initial comments to the topic of divine commands, I am actually concerned to elucidate a somewhat broader perspective, namely, the pattern of submitting to divine revelation as it is mediated by the Bible. Divine commands, strictly speaking, constitute only part of what is involved in Biblical revelation; but I will begin by focusing on divine commandments.

My concern here is to explain a certain kind of *sola scriptura* emphasis as it applies to medical problems. This emphasis, which was a prominent feature of the Protestant Reformation and is still dear to the hearts of many conservative Protestants, differs—at least in tone and procedure—from other ways of understanding obedience to the revealed will of God. For example, some Christians understand "natural law" in such a manner that when someone makes moral decisions with reference to natural law that person is obeying divine commands. Others hold that submission to the *magisterium* of a specific ecclesiastical body counts as obedience to divine directives. Others hold that individual Christians, even those who are not members of ecclesiastical hierarchies, can receive specific and extrabiblical commands from God, such as "Quit smoking!" or "Get out of New Haven!" Still others hold that the will of God can be discerned by examining our natural inclinations or by heeding the dictates of conscience.

None of these is, strictly speaking, incompatible with a *sola scriptura* emphasis. One could hold, for example, that the Bible itself commands us to conform to natural law, or to submit to the church's teachings, or to consult our conscience. Or one could simply view these alternative sources as necessary supplements to biblical revelation. The view which I will be attempting to elucidate is not intended as a denial of the legitimacy of appeals to these other sources. Rather, I am assuming a perspective from which the Bible is viewed as a clarifier of these other modes; the Bible is viewed here as an authoritative source against which deliverances from these other sources must be tested.

OBEYING DIVINE COMMANDS

Before proceeding to discuss questions of medical decision making, some clarifications are in order concerning the relevance of divine commands to moral reasoning.

Christian ethicists of the past have often assumed that the Bible offers a plurality of divine commands which have continuing relevance for the moral life. That assumption seems to have been under attack in recent years by Christian ethicists who contend that there is only one divine commandment which is morally relevant, namely, the command to love God and neighbor. This seems to be Joseph Fletcher's contention when he describes himself as "rejecting all 'revealed' norms but the one command—to love God in the neighbor" (1966, p. 26).

The issue at stake here is important for a field like medical ethics. If the command to love is the only biblical command which has normative relevance for medical decision making, then much of the substance of Christian medical ethics can be established without reference to the Scriptures. But if the Bible offers other commands and considerations which bear on medical decision making, then the task will be one of finding correlations between biblical revelation and medical issues at many different points.

It is important to note, however, that when Fletcher explains the grounds for his mono-imperativism, his arguments are not so much directed against the moral relevance of other divine commands as they are against their alleged "absoluteness." To hold, however, that there is a plurality of divine commands which are morally relevant and binding is not to commit oneself to the view that each of these commands is indefeasible. It may well be that there is only one indefeasible command, the so-called "law of love"—such that in any situation in which the course of action prescribed by the law of love is one's duty, it is one's actual duty, and that only the law of love has this property. But this does not rule out the possibility—and, based on the view being assumed here, the likelihood—that there are other divine commandments which prescribe courses of action which are one's prima facie duties to perform in those situations in which the commands in question are morally relevant.

We must also insist that not all commandments which are found in the Bible are to be obeyed by contemporary Christians. For example, God commanded Abram to leave Ur of the Chaldees, and he commanded Jonah to preach in Nineveh; it would be silly to suppose that it is part of every Christian's duty to obey these commandments.

Furthermore, it would be wrong to attempt to ascertain what God commands in the Bible simply by looking at sentences which are in the imperative mood. The Bible is much more than a compendium of commandments. It contains history, prayers, sagas, songs, parables, letters, complaints, pleadings, visions, and so on. The moral relevance of the divine commandments found in the Scriptures can only be understood by viewing them in their interrelatedness with these other types of biblical writing. Divine commands, as recorded in the Bible, must be contextually understood. The history, songs, predictions, and so on of the Bible serve to sketch out the character of the biblical God; from the diversity of materials we learn what kind of God he is, what his creating and redeeming purposes are, what sorts of persons and actions he approves of, and so on. Divine commands must be evaluated and interpreted in this larger context.

But it is also the case that we will miss some of the commands which are to be "found" in the Bible if we attend only to sentences which are grammatically imperative. For example, nowhere in the New Testament is there a literal command to the followers of Jesus to stop discriminating against Samaritans. But the New Testament record has Jesus telling stories and engaging in activities which make it very clear that he is directing his followers to change their attitudes toward the Samaritans. Thus, it is accurate to say that Jesus "commanded" his disciples to love the Samaritans, even though the words (or their Greek or Aramaic equivalents) "Stop discriminating against Samaritans" never appear in the Bible.

When the writer of Ecclesiastes, then, insists that our whole duty consists in obeying God's "commandments," we must not understand him to be instructing us to attend only to divine utterances which have a specific grammatical form. He is telling us, rather, that we must conform to what God requires of us, to what he instructs us to do—whether the instruction is transmitted through parables, accounts of divine dealings with nations and individuals, or sentences which somebody commands.

Something must also be said about the relationship between obedience to divine commands and the question of moral justification. It is not within the scope of this discussion to give anything like a fully adequate account of this relationship. Instead, I will sketch out one possible way of viewing the situation.

Let us say that a person has a *direct* moral justification for a given course of action if that person directly ascertains that the course of action in question, in the light of all relevant and available factual information, satisfies what he takes to be the correct fundamental moral criteria or criterion. Furthermore, let us understand normative theories such as utilitarianism, deontology, and virtue ethics as providing different understandings of what constitutes the correct fundamental moral criterion or criteria. (This account of direct moral justification is intended as a formal one. Nothing is implied about the truth of those beliefs which are supported by direct moral justifications. A person, then, may have a direct moral justification for a course of action without being justified in pursuing that course of action.)

Thus, in one version of utilitarianism, a person who is wondering whether to keep a specific promise will ask whether the keeping of that promise will bring about a situation in which there is a greater excess of good over bad consequences than the situation which would result if the promise is not kept. Or a deontologist would ask whether, say, telling Peter that I will give him twenty-five dollars on Wednesday conforms to a rule of practice whose obligatoriness is rationally defensible (or intuitively obvious), and whether in conforming to that rule I would not be violating another rule whose obligatoriness is weightier in that situation.

When a person has gone through the proper moral operations regarding a course of action, with direct reference to fundamental moral criteria, we can say that a person has a direct moral justification for what he decides. But there are situations in which persons do not have direct moral justifications—where, for example, sufficient factual information is unavailable, or where there is no time to calculate consequences or to engage in appropriate rational reflection. Nonetheless, in such situations there may be other grounds for making justified moral judgments.

Let us say that a person has an indirect moral justification for a course of action under conditions of this sort: The course of action possesses some property distinct from the property of being supportable by fundamental moral criteria, and the person reasonably believes that the possession of this property by a course of action makes it either logically certain or inductively probable that the action has the property of satisfying the correct moral criteria.

Perhaps an analogy will be helpful. Suppose that my car engine's being fixed consists in certain adjustments having been made to the engine. But suppose I do not possess the skills to ascertain whether those adjustments have been made. But if I believe that when my mechanic, Mary, says that the engine is fixed then it is in all likelihood fixed—so that Mary's saying that it is fixed makes it highly probable that it is fixed—then knowing that Mary says so constitutes an indirect justification for the claim that it is fixed. Mary herself, in this case, has a direct justification for that claim.

The following might be a situation in which I have an indirect moral justification for some course of action: I am a utilitarian and have not calculated the consequences of some act, but I know that Jane Fonda, whom I believe to be a skilled utilitarian calculator, wants me to perform that act. Or I am a deontologist and have not engaged in the proper reflection regarding some course of action, but I know that Ralph Nader, whose intuitive powers I greatly respect, generally reacts with favor when that course of action is recommended in similar circumstances. In these cases, knowing that Jane Fonda or Ralph Nader approves of a given course of action would count as an indirect justification for my approving of that course of action.

It is important to distinguish between two questions which relate to moral decision making: What makes an action right, and how do I decide that an action is right? We can decide, of course, that an action is right by directly investigating whether it possesses what we take to be the proper right-making characteristics. But often the two questions receive very different answers. Very often people decide what to do by listening to moral authorities or by looking at moral examples. This is sometimes a dangerous basis for decision making. But not always. Sometimes, as I am suggesting, the appeal to an authority or an example can constitute an indirect justification for a specific decision. In both car repair and morality, appeals to authority or example must take into account the credentials of the person to whom reference is made.

What I mean to be arguing here is that the Christian does not have to insist that God's commanding something is what makes it morally right. It is not necessary to argue that knowing that God has commanded something constitutes a direct moral justification for that course of action; one could believe that God himself, in commanding a course of action, does so on the basis of ascertaining that that course of action satisfies certain moral criteria (which are distinct from his having commanded it). For example, God's commanding marital fidelity may not necessarily be what makes marital fidelity morally right. Indeed, in the terms which I am outlining here, the Christian believer could remain open to a number of different theoretical accounts of what constitutes a direct moral justification for a course of action. God himself might be a utilitarian, or a deontologist, or a virtue ethicist. Of course, it could be the case that God's commanding something is the correct fundamental moral criterion. But, in the view which I am suggesting, the Christian need only hold that God's commanding something is either a direct or an indirect moral justification for that course of action.

Ordinary Christian piety often leads believers to say things of this sort: "I don't know why God wants me to do that, but I am confident that he knows best." What I am suggesting here is that what goes into God's "knowing best" is subject to theoretical—even metaethical—speculation; and we do not have to answer that question in order to accept God's commands as reliable moral guidelines.

There are some who will object to this way of viewing the moral life, not so much because of any logical weakness that they perceive in it, but because of its "feel" or tone. For example, it might be thought that this perspective lacks plausibility because it is much too "heteronomous," or even "military," in its emphasis on the moral agent as a commandee, submitting to the authority of a moral commander.

Some Christian apologists seem inclined to meet this challenge head-on, claiming that if the posture of obedience to divine commands is indeed a heteronomous one, then heteronomy deserves a better reputation than it is often granted. This seems to be the thrust of Peter Geach's comments on this subject: "I shall be told by [some] philosophers that since I am saying . . . [that] it is insane to set about defying an Almighty God, my attitude is plain power-worship. So it is: but it is the worship of the Supreme Power, and as such is wholly different from, and does not carry with it, a cringing attitude towards earthly powers. An earthly potentate does not compete with God, even unsuccessfully: he may threaten all manner of afflictions, but only from God's hands can any affliction actually come upon us" (1969, p. 127). This is a very Hobbesian account of the relationship between God and his human creatures; we submit to God's will out of fear of his power—the appeal is not so much to a sense of the moral fittingness of that submission as it is to a prudential awareness of what is in our self-interest.

But the defense need not move along these lines. Rather, we can insist that, viewed from "inside" the Christian life, it seems quite inappropriate to describe a Christian's relationship to God as one where a human being receives commands from an "external other," although it is not difficult to see how things can be viewed in that light from other points of view (e.g., existentialism and Marxism).

In both the Old and New Testaments, there is a sense of clear movement toward an "inner-directedness" in moral decision making. The Law at Sinai may have been "handed down" from heaven on tables of stone; but it was not long before those who had received that law were talking about a word of guidance that was to be "written on the heart"—a sense of inner-directedness which culminates in the New Testament concerning the indwelling of the Holy Spirit (or receiving "the mind of Christ"). From within such a perspective, it may be difficult to identify one's posture as that of submitting to commands which are simply "handed down from above."

Similarly, a heteronomous account of Christian morality does not capture the intimacy of the relationship between commander and commandee as it is described in the Bible. The God who commands is one who has taken the human condition upon himself, who has been tempted in all of the ways in which his human creatures are tempted. The believer in turn receives his law as a gift, becoming the temple of his Spirit. The intimacy here is not, of course, one of metaphysical merger; it is an interpersonal intimacy, a unity of purpose within the context of covenant. This intimacy is such that the term "heteronomy" will seem, to those who experience it, much too formal and lifeless to account for the facts of the case.

MEDICAL PERSPECTIVES IN THE BIBLE

How do we move from the Bible to contemporary medical decision making? How do we apply divine commandments, which were addressed to people whose cultural situations are far removed from our own, to medical questions as they arise today?

It will certainly not do to take each medically oriented divine command in the Bible and apply it directly to contemporary situations. For one thing, not all biblical directives regarding medical matters have direct application to contemporary situations. Leviticus 13 prescribes that any man who has itchy spots on the skin under his beard should present himself to the priest for examination; there follows a series of directions concerning the examination and quarantine of such persons. The elaborate steps described here are obviously developed because of a fear of various contagious diseases, grouped together under the term "leprosy." The stipulated methods and underlying concerns are clearly linked to a certain stage of disease identification and are spelled out in terms of social roles which are quite foreign to our present situation. (This is, e.g., one of the few instances in which the cultic priest is called upon to serve as both medical examiner and quarantine officer.) It would be ludicrous to view this passage as important to contemporary Christian views of skin care.

Indeed, the divine commands in the Bible which are most directly relevant to contemporary medical decision making may be commands which are not, in their biblical context, explicitly "medical" in nature. In dealing with such contemporary issues as abortion, or national health plans, or the question of a patient's consent in various situations, the most morally relevant biblical considerations may have to do with the command to love one's neighbor, or to show mercy to the oppressed, or to seek justice.

The Bible, in the view being represented here, is both a record of God's past revelation and a vehicle for his present revelation. But in some cases it takes considerable work to decide exactly what God is saying today by way of his deliverances to an ancient people. We discover what he is saying to twentieth-century Christians by attending to the record of his dealings with Semitic nomads and Palestinian fishermen, but not without considerable interpretive work.

Those who want to explore the relevance of the biblical message to contemporary medical decision making must begin by attempting to understand the Bible on its own terms. This involves at least two tasks: first, we must engage in the piecemeal descriptive task of understanding various elements of the biblical record; then, we must organize the results of that descriptive study theologically.

Let us briefly examine some elements of the first task. We have already insisted on the importance of understanding the divine commands found in the Bible in relation to their larger biblical context. This involves attempts to establish what exactly was meant by biblical directives for the people to whom they were originally addressed. The task of achieving a properly contextualized understanding of divine commands within their biblical setting must necessarily draw upon a full range of disciplines and subdisciplines which bear upon "biblical studies." With reference to medical (and I use this term in a broad sense to cover, e.g., hygienic, preventative, and curative activities) issues, this means that the Bible must be studied with the purpose of grasping the milieu within which divine commands were originally viewed as normative for medical concerns.

The descriptive task of giving an account of intrabiblical medical perspectives is an extensive one. It includes linguistic and conceptual studies focusing on biblical language regarding disease, health, bodily functions, medicinal practices, and the like. It must also involve developing something like a "historical medical sociology" of biblical cultures, which would provide accounts of the actual medical institutions, functions, and practices of, say, Israel and her neighbors.

Perspectives on the changing conceptions and practices regarding medical matters within the history covered by biblical literature are also important here. Israel experienced several major geographical and cultural shifts in her mode of social, political, and economic interaction: from slavery to nomadic life, to "landed" theocracy, to exile and diaspora, to life in Palestine under an occupying force. The New Testament also has writings which are descriptive of, and addressed to, a variety of cultural situations, with the transition from Jewish to Gentile Christianity being a dominant factor.

It should be noted that in our attempts to understand the cultural context of the biblical writings it is not always easy to distinguish or separate medical factors from other dimensions of the culture in question. This is due, in good part, to a lack of cultural differentiation in the biblical literature. The medical dimensions of life are intimately intertwined with cultic, culinary, sexual, and economic matters. What may strike us at first glance as a "medical" matter may be closely related to a cultic concern: for example, hygienic instructions may be intimately aligned to a desire for "ritual purity."

The importance of these descriptive concerns can be seen in relation to Saint Paul's reference to homosexuality in Romans 1:26-27. The apostle there describes homosexual acts as being "against nature"; and since these acts are viewed by him as being committed out of a spirit of willful rebellion against God, many Christians have understood him to be taking an unambiguous stand on the question of whether homosexuality is "sin" or "disease" or a morally neutral matter of personal preference. Some commentators have suggested, however, that what Paul is condemning here is homosexual activity as it occurred in certain specific pagan temple rituals. Others have argued that he is referring only to homosexual acts committed by persons who are "naturally" heterosexual. If either of these accounts is correct (which I personally doubt), then it would have the effect of limiting the relevance of this passage to only one subset of acts of genital contact between homosexual persons. Thus, the question of the range of acts to which Paul is referring is crucial to an understanding of the scope of his moral condemnation.

The second task which we have noted is that of organizing the results of this descriptive study theologically. This task includes elements of both "biblical theology" and "systematic theology." It might be helpful to think here in terms of a biblical-systematic theology of medicine. Such an enterprise would be rooted in a descriptive account of the variety of medical references in the Scriptures, and it would attempt to discern the overall patterns of biblical medical thought. The goal here would be that of attaining as clear an account as possible of the various nuances, and perhaps even tensions or conflicts, which emerge in considering the variety of biblical medical data.

From a conservative theological perspective, this activity would be characterized by a desire to find some coherent way of understanding the diversity of biblical data. As James Gustafson has noted, Karl Barth attempted to develop a Christian ethical perspective based on obedience to divine commands, but he did so with the insistence that those commands be viewed as fitting into the overall patterns of biblical theology. Barth recognized, as Gustafson puts it, that "while God gives specific commands on each occasion, he is not capricious; thus his commands are likely to be consistent with the Decalogue and the Sermon on the Mount" (Gustafson 1975, p. 84). The same desire for coherence should characterize (but, of course, not distort) the attempt to interpret the variety of biblical medical data.

An analogy can be drawn here to the attempt to construct a biblical understanding of poverty (see de Santa Ana 1979). Some biblical references to poverty—most notably those in the Wisdom literature of the Old Testament—view economic deprivation as brought about by laziness. Proverbs 6:10–11 provides a good example of this theme: "A little sleep, a little slumber, a little folding of the hands to rest, and poverty will come upon you like a vagabond, and want like an armed man." There are many other passages, however, in which the poor are viewed as victims of injustice, as kept in bondage to poverty by the greed and hardheartedness of the rich and powerful.

A proper theological understanding of biblical references to poverty must take these differing nuances into account. One possibility, of course, is to insist that the Bible offers conflicting accounts of the causes of poverty. Or one could look (as seems quite proper) for some way of fitting these nuances into a coherent overview of poverty. One plausible way of doing so is to understand the Bible as calling human beings to engage in serious labor in order to attain their livelihood: If some refuse to do so out of sloth, they are condemned; if others are prohibited from doing so by greed of the rich and powerful, they are to be considered victims of injustice.

Similarly, a biblical theology of medicine must attempt to account for various nuances in the biblical references to disease and physical health. There is much to be explored here, since attitudes toward the role of disease in human life are closely linked to the major biblical themes of creation, sin, and redemption.

The Bible views the beginnings of creation in terms of a garden paradise in which God looked at all of the things which he had created and pronounced them to be "good." The rebellion of the first human pair against the will of the Creator shattered the original harmony of Eden. The divine curse which they brought upon themselves by their disobedience introduced experiences of physical discomfiture which they had hitherto not known: the woman would experience great pain in childbearing, while the man would eat bread "in the sweat of your face" (Gen. 3:16, 19).

Disease and serious injury are obviously viewed as incompatible with God's original creating purposes. And the hope for redemption which emerges in the life of Israel includes the expectation that human beings will be delivered from physical disease: "Bless the Lord, O my soul, and forget not all his benefits, who forgives all your iniquity, who heals all your diseases" (Ps. 103:2-3).

The New Testament consistently views Jesus as a healer. Indeed, this healing mission is viewed as one dimension of a larger confrontation with the effects of sin on human life. In the Gospel of Mark, for example, Jesus' successful efforts at healing diseases seem to be portrayed as one aspect of a ministry which has a cosmic scope: Jesus not only heals physical ailments, but he casts out demons, tames the angry sea, combats hunger and economic injustice, and even raises the dead. The elimination of disease as an element of a cosmic redemption is an important element in the eschatalogical expectation of a new age, in which God "will wipe every tear from their eyes, and death shall be no more, neither shall there be mourning nor crying nor pain any more, for the former things have passed away" (Rev. 21:4).

This sketchy account of the place of disease in the Bible's view of God's creating and redeeming activity points to matters which almost everyone would agree are present in the biblical perspective: intense physical suffering was not a part of the original creation; disease enters into human affairs as a result of sin and rebellion; the work of divine redemption aims at the elimination of disease from the creation.

The nuances in the biblical picture of the place of disease in human life arise primarily with regard to the significance of suffering for "this present age," that is, for the period which is no longer the original fallen creation, but not yet the new age in which disease will be eliminated. How do we account for a specific physical affliction which enters into the life of a particular individual? How ought the contemporary Christian to deal with disease in his or her own life? The New Testament church clearly expected that Christians would be miraculously cured of physical ailments: "Is any among you sick? Let him call for the elders of the church, and let them pray over him, anointing him with oil in the name of the Lord; and the prayer of faith will save the sick man, and the Lord will raise him up" (James 5:14-15).

But even within the New Testament this encouragement to expect miraculous healing is countered by the suggestion that God sometimes desires that Christians endure physical suffering. Thus, Paul reports that he received a "thorn in the flesh," for whose removal he prayed three times, only to be convinced that God did not want to remove it, so that divine power would be manifested in Paul's weakness (2 Cor. 12:7-9).

The formulation of a clear and coherent theological account of biblical perspectives on this issue, and a variety of other topics, is necessary to provide some of the essential data for yet another task, that of wrestling with contemporary medical issues in the light of biblical teaching.

THE LIMITATIONS OF "ETHICS"

It is not uncommon for writers of books and articles on medical ethics to give the impression that the right sort of medical decisions will be made if only we ensure that medical professional or technical expertise is wedded to an awareness of moral values. If this is to be considered an adequate portrayal of the way things ought to be, then the term "moral values" will have to carry considerable freight—which, of course, it often does—and will be a misleading label for designating that body of considerations which must supplement technical skill.

The Christian who wants to understand the full human significance of medicine will have to look to more than ethics, even to the theological and philosophical disciplines of ethics, for aid. For one thing, medical issues must be viewed from the perspectives of political, legal, and economic thought; for this reason, we can be grateful for the increased attention being given recently to "medical rights" and "the politics of health care."

But the contributions of several other philosophical and theological disciplines and subdisciplines are also important. Here is only a small sampling of issues with regard to which medicine intersects with various areas of theological and philosophical inquiry: metaphysical, epistemological, and anthropological questions concerning the genesis and cessation of human life; dualistic and monistic accounts of human composition, as they touch on basic issues concerning the significance of medical treatments in the careers of human persons; questions about the role of science in human society; issues having to do with the nature, merits, and demerits of human "technique"; analyses of the function of medical institutions in human cultural formation; theological and aesthetic criteria for deciding what counts as "deformity" and "normalcy."

We have already insisted that God's moral commands must be understood in their larger biblical context. A parallel point here is this: Christian philosophical and theological medical ethics must be understood in the context of the broader reaches of the philosophy and theology of medicine.

The upshot of all this seems to be that Christian medical decision making must take place in a context characterized by comprehensive concerns and a rather broad interdisciplinary dialogue. It will not do simply to apply biblical proof-texts to contemporary issues. Nor is "doing ethics" adequate. Admittedly, the appropriate alternative is difficult to state in terms of a precise methodology. A number of catchphrases seem, to me at least, to point in the right methodological direction: Tillich's notion of "correlating" the biblical message with contemporary problems; the call to engage in "dialogue before the Word"; the emphasis on seeking to have our contemporary struggles "disciplined" by our submission to biblical authority.

Of course, the Bible itself points in these directions. Christians are called to participate in the life of a community, in whose midst

196	Richard J. Mouw

they are to "prove what is the will of God, and what is good and acceptable and perfect" (Rom. 12:2). This community is given a mandate to exercise the "gifts of the spirit," such as—to use the list of 1 Corinthians 12—"the utterance of wisdom," "the utterance of knowledge," "faith," "healing," "the working of miracles," "prophecy," "the ability to distinguish between spirits," "tongues," and the "interpretation of tongues." Perhaps it is no accident that the gift of healing is linked here to the gifts of prophecy and discernment—to say nothing of the gifts of wisdom and knowledge.

BASIC ASSUMPTIONS IN MEDICINE

The Bible is a book about God and about his relationship to the creation in general and to human creatures in particular. To accept the biblical message is to grasp hold of facts—"extraordinary" facts, perhaps, but accounts nonetheless of what is the case—which, because of our sinfulness and finitude, we would not otherwise take hold of.

To believe what the Bible says about God and creation and human persons is to be thrust into a network of relationships and obligations of which we would not otherwise be aware. For example, the biblical writers describe God as a shepherd, a father (and on some occasions, a mother), a king. As James Gustafson notes, these "analogies to social roles imply certain relations, which, in turn, are sources for delineating certain moral purposes or duties" (Gustafson 1975, p. 17). The duties and purposes generated by these relationships bear on medical matters in a variety of ways.

Much attention has been given by Christian medical ethicists to questions of how biblical purposes and duties bear on medical matters as they occur within the present patterns of medical care. How is the surgeon to show agape to the patient? How can the clergyperson better coordinate his or her efforts with those of medical specialists? What does service to one's neighbor mean for the Christian social worker? How can we achieve more just and righteous patterns of health-care delivery?

My own impression is that a good many of such discussions have a rather "priestly" tone to them. They assume, for the most part at least, the legitimacy of current standards and norms for medical practice, asking how we can be more loving or just within those patterns. The "prophetic" task of offering a critique of the fundamental patterns themselves has been left to groups who are beyond the pale of Christian medical ethics "orthodoxy." Three such prophetic groups come to mind: (a) various Marxist- and anarchist-oriented writers; (2) those who have been diagnosing the alleged "iatrogenic diseases" of Western societies; and (3) medical "fundamentalists," such as the Jehovah's Witnesses, Christian Scientists, Seventh Day Adventists, the Amish, and the "Old Reformed" Dutch Calvinists, each of whom rejects some significant item of contemporary medical orthodoxy.

If we were to take the basic concerns of these prophetic groups seriously, a result would be the development of a full-scale critique of the patterns of contemporary medicine from a point of view characterized by political, cultural, spiritual, and theological sensitivities. Attention here would be given to some of the fundamental "givens" of contemporary medical thought and practice.

This is not to say that Christian medical ethicists (or, more generally, theorists) should merely mimic the criticisms of any or all of the three groups mentioned above. In a broad-ranging dialogue on these issues, Christian thinkers will undoubtedly disagree among themselves on the merits of this or that prophetic pronouncement. The goal here is to expose contemporary medical patterns to a critical scrutiny which is disciplined by submission to biblical authority.

Take, for example, Ivan Illich's recent critique of "the medicalization of life." Illich insists that the development of medical bureaucracies leads to (among other things) conditions of this sort; "disabling dependence" on medical experts, the lowering of "levels of tolerance for discomfort or pain," the abolition of "the right to self-care," the "hospitalization" of suffering, and the labeling of "suffering, mourning, and healing outside the patient role" as "a form of deviance" (Illich 1977, p. 33).

Illich may be misperceiving or distorting the empirical situations, as Thomas Szasz may also be doing when he insists that "medicine now functions as a state religion" (Szasz 1977, p. 146). But even if these writers are locating possible tendencies rather than actual states of affairs, the factors they point to are worthy of criticial reflection.

Similarly, there is something to be said for the instincts, if not the hermeneutics, of the medical fundamentalists. For example, the Old Reformed refuse polio immunization, and other preventative measures, by appealing to Jesus' claim that "those who are well have no need of a physician, but those who are sick" (Matt. 9:12). Their error here is not that they think that claims made by Jesus have relevance for contemporary medical decision making, but that they misconstrue his actual intention in making this particular observation. Nonetheless, there is a kind of integrity in their insistence upon exposing medical "technique" to theological and spiritual scrutiny.

On the most favorable reading of the claims of the medical fundamentalists, what is being resisted is the absorption of the individual's struggle with suffering into the context of the patient-role. Unfortunately, many of the most vocal secular critics of the same pattern of absorption view the proper alternative in terms of the "autonomy" of the individual. Thus, the fundamental conflict is often viewed as one between medicalization and the right to self-care.

Christians (at least some Christians) will want to join the fundamentalists in viewing the basic situation in different terms. The Christian is a creature of God, "belonging" to him by virtue of God's creating and redeeming activity. All other relationships and duties and roles must be assessed in the light of this primary relationship with its attendant duties. If medical "intervention" by experts poses a threat, then, it is not to one's autonomy but rather to one's fidelity to the primary convenantal relationship with God. The danger is not so much a loss of freedom as it is a temptation to place idolatrous trust in medical technology.

Take the standard textbook case of the woman who has terminal cancer, but whose doctors think it not in her best interest to know the facts about her condition. If the patient is a Christian, then certain factors have to be taken into account in deciding what is in her best interest. For one thing, it is in the Christian's interest to be allowed to struggle with the spiritual significance of a specific affliction. Like Paul in his struggles with his "thorn in the flesh," the Christian must ask, "Why has God allowed this to happen to me, and what constitutes a faithful response to this development?" In this case, the woman must be allowed to assess the role which this experience of disease plays in her overall career as a human being. And because of what she believes by virtue of her acceptance of a Christian view of things, she will understand her own "career" as extending into the age of the Resurrection. She must go through the struggle of evaluating her own suffering and impending death in the light of the apostle's declaration: "I consider that the sufferings of this present time are not worth comparing with the glory that is to be revealed to us" (Rom. 8:18).

It is obvious simply from reading the Bible that there is an important emphasis placed there on the merits of a fully informed struggle, in the presence of God, with the issues of personal suffering and the questions of life and death. It is an important part of the Christian experience to bargain, like King Hezekiah, for an extension of life, or to plead in agony, like Jesus himself, "Let this cup pass from me." The spiritual significance of suffering corresponds, for the Christian, to a right to know the facts about one's physical condition.

Of course, not all medical experts or ethicists will consider this view of suffering to be legitimate or plausible. But the question here is not one of asking everyone to agree with the Christian; it is a question of finding a just pattern of distributing medical information, a pattern which is built on an awareness of the existing plurality of perspectives on the issues of life and death, health and suffering.

The recent establishment of hospices and "holistic medicine clinics" may well be a positive sign in the direction of new forms of medical organization which can serve as practical alternatives for Christians who want to view health care from a self-consciously Christian perspective. These practical experiments in medical alternatives should perhaps also be viewed as a challenge and stimulus for new directions in Christian medical theorizing.

If some Christians are going to insist that their right to approach suffering in a Christian manner be respected, this has implications for broader issues having to do with medical justice. If, as the Heidelberg Catechism puts it, "I, with body and soul, both in life and death, am not my own, but belong unto my faithful Savior Jesus Christ," then questions about what other persons do to my own body will have theological—even "ideological"—significance for me. And if I claim medical rights as over against those who have differing views concerning the meaning and nature of my suffering, justice would seem to require that I be willing to generalize from my own case.

Thus, it would seem quite plausible to suggest that Christians who sense some conflict between their own medical perspectives and those of a "medicalized" society should be willing to formulate policies which grant rights to those who have even different ideologies than their own. Norman Cantor's excellent discussion (1973) of a patient's right to decline lifesaving medical treatment seems to me to be an excellent starting point for a discussion that should be extended into a number of other areas which relate to issues of medical pluralism.

MEDICAL POLITICS

My main concern in this discussion has been to show some of the ways in which medical questions might be approached by Christians who hold a "high" view of biblical inspiration and authority. My comments have been primarily programmatic in nature; consequently, I have skimmed over some important topics and left others untouched.

It is perhaps significant that this discussion has drifted in the direction of the sociopolitical dimensions of medical questions. The fact is that Protestant Christians who claim allegiance to a conservative or "traditional" theological perspective have not, in this century at least, demonstrated many clear sensitivities to the political dimensions of the biblical message, to say nothing of the application of that political message to medical questions.

But in very recent years many theologians—Roman Catholic, Eastern Orthodox, and Protestant (including some conservative Protestants)—have contributed to a renewed interest in the biblical address to political matters. From this ecumenical theological exploration, at least three important emphases have emerged, and each seems to have important implications for medical issues, although the connections have as yet been largely ignored.

First, and perhaps most important, has been the emphasis on the biblical call to identify with the concerns of the "poor and oppressed." Biblical passages dealing with this theme often single out specific types of persons as special objects of God's compassion and redemptive concern: the widow, the orphan, the prisoner, the sojourner, the hungry beggar (see, e.g., Ps. 146). What these types seem to have in common is that they are without rights or legal "standing" before the political, economic, and cultural structures of society.

The second emphasis is on the phenomenon of "contextualization"—a prominent notion in recent discussions carried on by Third World Christians. What is at stake here is the contention that the Christian Gospel is inevitably received in a context characterized by, among other things, the political, economic, and "class" orientation of the hearer. This emphasis has been accompanied by the insistence that Western (or "North Atlantic") Christians examine the biases which have influenced, and even distorted, their theological reflections.

A third emphasis has grown out of the work of the post-World War II "biblical theology" movement. Here there is a growing number of studies of the New Testament, especially Pauline, references to "principalities and powers," which are understood to be "invisible authorities" who influence the "minds" and structures of a society and who, as "the rulers of darkness," tempt human beings into patterns of corporate idolatry (racism, sexism, consumerism, militarism). This emphasis has led some commentators to stress the need for a discernment of the spirits as they show their influence in the systemic patterns of human interaction.

Each of these emphases—much too briefly described here—embodies a concern which deserves a special place on the agenda of contemporary Christian medical thought. No moral perspective which takes divine commands seriously can ignore the overwhelming number of occasions on which God has commanded his people to defend the cause of those who are helpless before the structures of society. Some crucial questions for medical ethics are: Who are the helpless ones in the area of medical care? Whose cries for medical attention are currently going unheeded? How best can the physically oppressed be liberated within a framework of justice?

The emphasis on contextualization indicates the need for Christian thinkers to be conscious of their own class and cultural biases in discussing medical questions—and perhaps to search for the kinds of pluralistic structures appropriate to the fact of medical contextualization. And all of this must be done out of a desire to be spiritually discerning, even if that requires us to question the basic "minds" which are often at work in medical discussions.

REFERENCES

Cantor, Norman L. "A Patient's Decision to Decline Lifesaving Medical Treatment: Bodily Integrity versus the Preservation of Life." *Rutgers Law Reveiw* 26 (1973): 228–64. Reprinted in Stanley Joel Reiser, Arthur J. Dyck, and William J. Curran, eds. *Ethics in Medicine: Historical Perspectives and Contemporary Concerns.* Cambridge, Mass.: M.I.T. Press, 1977.

de Santa Ana, Julio. *Good News to the Poor: The Challenge of the Poor in the History of the Church.* Maryknoll, N.Y.: Orbis Books, 1979.

Fletcher, Joseph. *Situation Ethics: The New Morality.* Philadelphia: Westminster Press, 1966.

Geach, Peter. *God and the Soul.* New York: Schocken Books, 1969.

Gustafson, James M. *The Contributions of Theology to Medical Ethics.* 1975 Père Marquette Theology Lecture, Marquette University, Theology Department, 1975.

Illich, Ivan. *Medical Nemesis: The Expropriation of Health.* New York: Bantam Books, 1977.

Szasz, Thomas. *The Theology of Medicine: The Political-Philosophical Foundations of Medical Ethics.* New York: Harper & Row, 1977.

12

Secular Faith

Annette Baier

1. THE CHALLENGE

Both in ethics and in epistemology one source of scepticism in its contemporary version is the realization, often belated, of the full consequences of atheism. Modern non-moral philosophy looks back to Descartes as its father figure, but disowns the *Third Meditation.* But if God does not underwrite one's cognitive powers, what does? The largely unknown evolution of them, which is just a version of Descartes's unreliable demon? "Let us . . . grant that all that is here said of God is a fable, nevertheless in whatever way they suppose that I have arrived at the state of being that I have reached, whether they attribute it to fate or to accident, or make out that it is by a continual succession of antecedents, or by some other method—since to err and deceive oneself is a defect, it is clear that the greater will be the probability of my being so imperfect as to deceive myself ever, as is the Author to whom they assign my being the less powerful" (Meditation I, Haldane and Ross, tr.). Atheism undermines a solitary thinker's single-handed cognitive ambitions, as it can undermine his expectation that unilateral virtue will bring happiness. The phenomenon of atheism in unacknowledged debt to theism can be seen both in ethical theory and in epistemology, and the threat of scepticism arises in a parallel manner.

In a provocative article, David Gauthier[1] has supported the charge made two decades ago by Anscombe,[2] that modern secular moral philosophers retain in their theories concepts which require a theological underpinning. "The taking away of God . . . in thought dissolves all," said Locke, and Gauthier agrees that it dissolves all those duties or obligations whose full justification depends upon a

This essay from *The Canadian Journal of Philosophy* 10, no. 1 (March 1980): 131–48 is reprinted by permission.

general performance of which one has no assurance. He quotes
Hobbes: "He that would be modeste and tractable and perform all
he promises in such time and place where no man els should do so,
should but make himself the prey to others, and procure his own
ruin, contrary to all Lawes of Nature, which tend to Nature's preservation" (*Leviathan*, chap. 15). The problem arises not merely when
"no man els" does his[3] duty, but when a significant number do not,
so that the rest, even a majority, make themselves prey to the immoral ones, and procure their own exploitation, if not their own ruin.
The theist can believe, in his cool hour, that unilateral, or minority,
or exploited majority morality will not procure his ultimate ruin,
that all things work together for good, but what consolation can a
secular philosopher offer for the cool thoughtful hour, in the absence
of God? If Gauthier is right, either false or insufficient consolation.
He says that in those modern theories which preserve some vestige
of a duty to do what others are not known to be doing, or known to
be failing to do, "God is lurking unwanted, even unconceived, but
not unneeded."[4]

I shall suggest that the secular equivalent of faith in God, which
we need in morality as well as in science or knowledge acquisition, is
faith in the human community and its evolving procedures—in the
prospects for many-handed cognitive ambitions and moral hopes.
Descartes had deliberately shut himself away from other thinkers,
distrusting the influence of his teachers and the tradition in which
he had been trained. All alone, he found he could take no step
beyond a sterile self certainty. Some other mind must come to his
aid before he could advance. Descartes sought an absolute
assurance to replace the human reassurance he distrusted, and I
suggest that we can reverse the procedure. If we distrust the
theist's absolute assurance we can return to what Descartes spurned,
the support of human tradition, of a cross-generational community.
This allows us to avoid the narrow and self-destructive self-seeking
which is the moral equivalent of solipsism. But Gauthier's challenge
is precisely to the reasonableness of community-supportive action
when we have no guarantee of reciprocal public-spirited or commun-
ally-minded action from others. Not only may we have no such
guarantee, we may have evidence which strongly *dis*confirms the
hypothesis that others are doing their part. We may have neither
knowledge nor inductively well based belief that others are doing
their part. Faith and hope I take to involve acceptance of belief on
grounds other than deductive or inductive evidence of its truth.
Faith is the evidence of things unseen. It will be faith, not

knowledge, which will replace religious faith. I shall try to make clear exactly what that faith is faith in, and what it would be for it to be (a) ill-founded or unreasonable, (b) reasonable, but in vain. I shall be defending the thesis that the just must live by faith, faith in a community of just persons.

2. FAITH: THE SUBSTANCE OF THINGS HOPED FOR

Faith, not knowledge, was and is needed to support those "plain duties" whose unilateral observation sometimes appears to procure the dutiful person's ruin. But faith, for rational persons, must appear reasonable before it can be attained. If it is to be reasonable, it must not fly in the face of inductive evidence, but it may go beyond it, when there are good reasons of another sort to do so. We may have such good reasons to hope for an empirically very unlikely but not impossible eventuality. Reasonableness is relative to the alternative beliefs or policies one might adopt, or be left with, if one rejected the candidate for the status of reasonable belief. One of the chief arguments for the moral faith I shall present is the great unreasonableness of any alternative to it. The *via negativa* which leads to secular faith has been clearly indicated in Hobbes' description of the state of nature, the state of persons without the constraint of justice. Hobbes' modern commentators, including Gauthier, have underlined the futility of the alternatives to morality. Yet if everyone insisted on knowing in advance that any sacrifice of independent advantage which they personally make, in joining or supporting a moral order, will be made up for by the returns they will get from membership in that moral order, that order could never be created nor, if miraculously brought about, sustained. Only by conquest could a Hobbesian *Leviathan* ever be created, if the rational man must have secure knowledge that others are doing likewise before he voluntarily renounces his right to pursue independent advantage. How, except by total conquest, could one ever know for sure that other would-be war makers will lay down their arms when one does so?

In fact Hobbes' first Law of Nature requires every man to endeavor peace, not when he has certainty of attaining it, but "as fare as he has *hope* of attaining it" (*Leviathan*, chap. 14, emphasis added). Hope had been previously defined as "appetite with opinion of attaining" (op.cit., chap. 6) and opinion is contrasted with science (op.cit., chap. 7), which alone is the outcome of correct reckoning or calculation. It is then, for Hobbes, a Law of Nature, or a counsel of rational prudence, to act on hope when what is at stake is escape from the Hobbesian state of nature.

Faith, Hobbes tells us "is in the man, Beleefe both of the man and of the truth of what he says" (ibid.). It is faith in its Hobbesian sense, in men, not merely belief in the truth of what they say which I shall argue is the only 'substance' of the hoped-for cooperation which avoids the futility and self-destructiveness of its alternatives. Faith, in a non-Hobbesian sense, that is a belief which runs beyond the inductive evidence for it, when it is faith in the possibility of a just cooperative scheme being actualized, is the same as that hope whose support is trust "in the man."

Trust in people, and distrust, tends to be self-fulfilling. Faith or lack of faith in any enterprise, but especially one requiring trust in fellow-workers, can also be self-fulfilling. Confidence can produce its own justification, as William James[5] persuasively argued. The question whether to support a moral practice without guarantee of full reciprocity is, in James' terminology, live, momentous, and forced, and the choice made can be self-verifying whichever way we choose. Every new conversion to moral scepticism strengthens the reason for such scepticism, since, if acted on, it weakens the support of moral practices and so diminishes their returns to the morally faithful. Similarly, every person who continues to observe those practices provides some reason for belief that they are supported, and so strengthens the foundation for his own belief that their support is sufficient, and provides some justification for his own dependence on that support. *Some* justification, but not enough, surely, to be decisive, since he is unlikely to be the critical straw to save or break the camel's back. The case for the self-confirmation of moral faith is less clear than for the self-confirmation, the band wagon effect, of moral scepticism. Immorality breeds immorality, but need moral action, especially if *unilateral*, breed more of the same? The sense in which the exemplary unilateral act *does* provide its own support, even if the example it gives is not followed by one's contemporaries, will be explored later. For the moment the best one can say for the reasonableness of willing to believe in the value of (possibly) unilateral moral action is that the alternative, giving up on that crucial part of the moral enterprise which secures cooperation, must lead eventually to an outcome disastrous to all, although those with a taste for gun-running may make a good profit before doomsday dawns. There are different styles of shoring fragments against one's ruin, and some choose to exploit the presumed failure of morality, while others or even the same ones, retreat into a narrow circle where virtues can still be cultivated. But when, even granted the badness of its alternatives, would it be unreasonable to keep faith in the moral enterprise, in particular in the attempt to achieve a fair scheme of human cooperation? I turn next to consider the coherence of the ideal of justice.

3. MORE OR LESS JUST SOCIETIES

When would an actual cooperative scheme between persons be a just one, one which gave its participants the *best reasons* to support it? When the goods, for each, gained by cooperation outweigh the individual advantage any sacrificed, and where all partakers in the benefits make their fair contribution, pay their dues, observe the rules which ensure production and fair distribution of benefits. Even in a society where this was true, there would still be a place for a descendant of Hobbes' *Leviathan*, to enforce rules, since there may still be persons who act irrationally, and who have a perverse taste for bucking the system, whatever the system. A stable, efficient, equitable[6] and democratic scheme of cooperation would give its conforming members security, delectation, non-exploitation and freedom, but some may still try to get a free ride, or to break the rules out of what Hobbes called "the stubborness of their passions." His fifth Law of Nature commands "compleasance," that every man strive to accommodate himself to the rest, and unilateral breach of this rule is contrary to Hobbesian reason whose dictates include the laws of nature, since it calculates that the individual can count on preserving himself only if steps are taken to ensure the conservation of men in multitudes, and so to ensure peace. "He that having sufficient security, that others observe the same laws towards him, observes them not himself, seeketh not peace, but war; and consequently the destruction of his own nature by violence" (*Leviathan*, chap. 15, immediately following the passage quoted by Gauthier, which points out the folly of unilateral conformity to the laws of nature).

Both unilateral conformity and unilateral non-conformity are, according to Hobbes, contrary to reason, but man's natural intractability inclines him to the latter. In any state of affairs short of perfect and perfectly secure justice such intractability provides a healthy challenge to an imperfect *status quo*, but if a satisfactory form of cooperation were attained such a character trait would serve no useful function. And even if Hobbes is wrong in claiming that one who refuses to do his part thereby irrationally seeks his own violent destruction, his claim that only a fool believes he can profit by breaking the rules his fellows keep is plausible to this extent, that if those rules were just in a stronger sense than any Hobbes can provide, then however attractive the promised gains of a free ride, or of exploiting others, only a fool would believe that he has more to gain by risking the enmity of his fellows by such a policy than by cultivating a taste for the pleasures of cooperation and regulated fair competition. It may not be positively irrational to break the fifth Law of Nature, especially in a would-be totalitarian Leviathan state, but it would be against reason to think one would do better by breaking the rules of a decent just scheme of cooperation. There is no reason *not* to be sociable in a decent society, and nothing to be gained there by non-irrational unsociability, by going it alone, by entering into a state of war with one's fellows. But some will act contrary to reason, "by asperity of Nature," and be "Stubborn, Insociable, Forward, Intractable." Such stubborness is perversity, not superior rationality, when the rules are just. We could define a perfectly just society as one where it takes such intractability to motivate disobedience.

How do we measure how close an actual society is to the adequately just society? Unless we can do this it would seem impossible ever to judge a society so unjust that its institutions merit disrespect, or to have confidence that any change made in existing institutions is a change for the better. Yet there are grave problems in establishing any coherent measure of comparative justice. These problems arise because of the tension between two ways in which an existing state of things may approximate the just society. In one sense an institution is just to the extent that it *resembles* one we expect to be part of the adequately just society. In another sense an institution is better to the extent that it is instrumental in moving the society closer in time to that adequacy. But the institutions a society needs, to change itself, may be quite other than those it needs, once improvement is no longer needed. Yet if we opt for this dynamic measure of relative justice, and say that institutions are good to the extent that they facilitate movement towards adequate justice, we run up against the possibility, explored by Hegel and developed by Marx, that historical movement towards a social idea may be dialectical, that the institutions which best facilitate movement towards an ideal may be ones which least embody that ideal.

The ideal of *justice*, however, is one which cannot generate a sense of 'more just than' in which intolerable exploitation is counted more just than a lesser degree of exploitation, merely because it is more likely to precipitate rebellion and change. Those who advocate making things worse in order that they may get better, cannot claim that what their strategies increase is justice. Is justice then an ideal which is committed to a perhaps groundless liberal faith in progress, faith in its own gradual attainment by moves, each of which represents *both* an increase in qualitative approximation to the ideal, and *also* a step closer, historically and causally, to its attainment? If these two measures of approximation are both proper, yet can come apart, can come into irresolvable conflict with one another, then the ideal of justice may be confused and incoherent,[7] may rest on a faith which is false. I think there is a genuine issue here, but it is not one which I shall discuss further. Social science, not philosophy, would shore up the liberal's faith, or show it to be false. If it is false, if there is no coherent measure of relative justice, then the modern moral philosophy Gauthier criticises is in even worse straits than he claims. But I shall proceed within the limits of the comforting liberal faith which I take Gauthier to share, faith that some institutions can be judged less just than others, and that improving them can count as progress towards a just society. It is worth pointing out that this is part of the *faith* the just live by, but it is not that part of it which is controversial to Gauthier and those he criticises, none of whom embrace the radical moral scepticism to which the Marxist argument leads, nor the new non-moral revolutionary faith which can fill the vacuum it creates.

Where else does faith enter into the motivation to act, in a less than fully just society, for the sake of justice, to conform to more or less just institutions which not all conform to, or to act, possibly unilaterally to reform salvageable institutions, and to protest corrupt ones? What must the just person believe, which must turn out to be true if his action is not to be pointless or futile? Before we can discuss the question of whether and when personal advantage is pointlessly sacrificed, we must first discuss the nature and varieties of advantage and personal good. I shall in this discussion adopt a hedonist terminology, to stay as close as possible to the Hobbesian point of departure.

4. GOODS: SECURE AND INSECURE

Hobbes speaks not of advantage but of *power,* namely "present means to obtain some future apparent good." Advantage strictly is advantage over, or against, others, and Hobbes' emphasis on man's "diffidence" or need to assure himself that there is "no other power great enough to endanger him" (op.cit., chap. 13) turns power-seeking into the attempt to attain advantage, competitive edge, a position superior to one's fellows, since even in civil society he believes that men "can relish nothing but what is eminent" (op.cit., chap. 17). I shall keep the term 'advantage' for this competitive good, superiority over others, and use Hobbes' word 'power' for the more generic concept of possession of present means to obtain some future, apparent, possibly noncompetitive, good. (I think that when Gauthier speaks of 'advantage' he is using it in a looser way, more equivalent simply to 'good', that is to a combination of possession of present good and power or present means to attain a future good, whether or not these goods are scarce and competed for.)

Hobbes says that prudence, the concern for power rather than for immediate good, is concern for the future, which is "but a fiction of the mind" (op.cit., chap. 3), and moreover is based on an uncertain presumption that we can learn, from the past, what to expect in the future. "And though it be called Prudence, when the Event answereth our Expectation; yet in its own nature is but Presumption" (ibid.). Hobbes is surely correct in pointing out the risks inherent in prudence. One may invest in a form of power which turns out to be a passing not a lasting one. Hobbes (op.cit., chap. 10) catalogs the many forms power takes, and it is fairly obvious that accidents of chance and history may add to, and subtract from, this list, as well as determine the relative importance of different items on it. Even if one's choice of a form of power to obtain is a lucky one, one may not live into that future where the power could be spent in delectation, or even in misery-avoidance. At some point, in any case, the restless pursuit of power after power must end in death, so *some* future good for which the prudent person saved is bound, if he remains prudent to the end, not to be enjoyed by him. In theory one might, when imminent death is anticipated, make a timely conversion to imprudence, cash one's power in for delectation and die gratified and powerless, but persons with Hobbesian, or with our actual, psychology are not likely to be capable of such a feat. One may have advantage, and have power, which is no good to one, or no longer any good to one, if to be good it must be cashed in delectation.

How are we to judge what is and what is not good to a person? Must good, to be such, be converted, eventually, from apparent good into real indubitable good, and from future into present good?

These are hard questions, and it would take a full theory of the good of a person, the place in it of pleasure, interest, power, advantage, to answer them. I have no such theory,[8] and will offer only a few remarks about the complexity of all goods other than present simple pleasures. In all human motivation, other than the gratification of current appetite, there is a potential multi-tier structure. In the case of action designed to make possible the gratification of future desires, that is in prudent action, the good for the sake of which one acts is the expected future gratification, but usually also, derivatively, the present satisfaction of feeling secure, of believing that one has taken thought for the future, secured its needs. So even if the prudent investor does not live into that future for which he provided, he may still enjoy a sense of security while he lives. Prudence, like virtue, may be, and sometimes has to be, its own reward. It is possible, but unlikely, that prudent persons take no present satisfaction in their prudent action, that they develop no taste for a sense of security. The normal accompaniment of prudence is the pleasure of a sense of security. I shall call such pleasures, which make reference to other, possibly non-present pleasures, 'higher' pleasures (Hobbes' "pleasures of the mind"). By calling these pleasures 'higher' I do not mean to imply that they should necessarily be preferred to lower ones. The special class of them which makes reference to future pleasures are power-derivative higher pleasures (Hobbes' "glory"). Such pleasures can coexist with regret that the cost of prudence was renunciation of a present available lower pleasure, and even with doubt whether such costs were unavoidable, and whether one will live to enjoy the future for which one has saved. It would be incorrect to say that the prudent person trades in present lower pleasure for higher pleasure—the higher pleasure is merely a bonus which can come with the power for which the lower pleasure was traded. But hedonic bonuses count for *something*, when the rationality of the action is to be judged.

When one acts for the sake of some good for others, be that good pleasure or power, present or future, there is a similar immediate bonus or "glory" possible, the pleasure of believing that someone else's present or future is improved by one's action. Persons who perform such altruistic acts usually do develop a taste for altruism, a fellow-feeling whereby they share in the good they do others. Just as the sense of personal security usually pleases the prudent person, the awareness of others' pleasure and the sense of their security usually pleases the altruist. It may be possible to do good to others because the moral law is thought to require it, without thereby getting any satisfaction for oneself, but such bonus-refusing psychology seems neither likely nor desirable. It is best if virtue is at least *part* of its own reward, and a waste if it is not.

5. ARTIFICES TO SECURE THE INSECURE

To be a normal human person is to be capable of higher pleasures, both self-derived and other-derived, to be able to make the remote in time and the remote from oneself close enough in thought and concern not merely to affect present action but to give present pleasure. Hume explored the mechanisms whereby concern for the remote, both from the present, and from oneself and one's family, can be strengthened by its coincidence with concern for the contiguous, so that the "violent propension to prefer the contiguous to the remote," (*Treatise*, p. 537) may be combatted, its unfortunate and sometimes violent effects avoided. These mechanisms include not merely psychological ones, imagination and sympathy, which turn the useful into the also agreeable, and the agreeable for others into the agreeable for oneself also, but also social practices of training and education, and social artifices. Such artifices—promise, property, allegiance—turn the useful for people in general into what is useful for oneself, and this requires both convention, or agreement between people as to *what* the artifice is, and general conformity to its constitutive rules. Convention requires both communication and coordination. Hume believed, perhaps wrongly, that all of justice was in this sense artificial and that only with respect to the artificial virtues did a person risk being "the cully of his integrity" (*Treatise*, p. 535) if he acted unilaterally, without assurance that others were similarly virtuous. Since the actions of a kind or a generous person do the good they do, to individual others, case by case, whereas just or honest actions *need* do no good to any specified individual, and do what good they do, for people in general, for the public interest, only when they are supported by other just acts, it is an easy but false move from this valid contrast between the ways the natural and the artificial virtues do good, to a contrast at the level of motivation for the agent, and to the claim that an individual always has good reason to display a natural virtue whether or not others do, while one has no reason to display an artificial virtue, unless others are displaying the same version of it. Non-violence, or gentleness, is a natural virtue, but non-violence toward the violent can be as self-destructive as unilateral promise keeping. Moreover, the higher pleasure of knowing that one's attacker has not suffered at one's hands is not merely insufficient to outweigh the loss of life or limb, it will also be lessened by the awareness that, when violence is the rule, the good to the violent man done by one's own non-violence is shortlived and insignificant, unless it inspires others to non-violence.

The natural virtues can, in individual cases, lose most of their point if the degree of non-virtuousness of others is great enough. They still contrast with the artificial virtues, however, in that their good-promoting power will vary from case to case, given the same degree of general conformity. When there is general conformity to non-violence, one may still have reason not to trust individual persons, if there is reason to believe that those ones reciprocate non-violence with violence. When there is general violence, one may still have reason to expect a non-violent response to non-violence in selected cases, so that isolated pockets of gentleness and mutual trust can grow up within a climate of general violence. The same is true, up to a point, of the artificial virtues, in that respect for property rules, or promise keeping, or allegiance, may be dependable within a restricted circle—say among members of the mafia—although they do not observe rules outside that group. The artificial virtues differ from the natural ones, however, in that there is never excuse for *selective non-observance,* within a generally conforming circle, as there can be reason for selective non-observance of non-violence, generosity, helpfulness. A debt owed to a vicious man, a miser, a profligate debauchee, or a dishonest man, is still owed. "Justice, in her decisions never regards the fitness or unfitness of objects to particular persons, but conducts herself by more extensive views. Whether a man be generous, or a miser, he is equally well receiv'd by her, and obtains with the same facility a decision in his favor, even for what is entirely useless to him" (Hume, *Treatise,* p. 502). To grant that the conformity of others does affect the value of the natural as well as the artificial virtues is not to deny Hume's point here, that selective non-observance, based on "fitness or unfitness of objects to particular persons," is reasonable with natural but not with artificial virtues. "Taking any single act, my justice may be pernicious in every respect; and 'tis only on the supposition, that others are to imitate my example, that I can be persuaded to embrace that virtue; since nothing but this combination can render justice advantageous or afford me any motives to conform myself to its rules" (op.cit., p. 498).

6. THE PLEASURES OF CONFORMITY

One must suppose, then, that enough others will imitate one's just action if a just act is to be "advantageous," is to advance any interest, or give anyone, however altruistic or public-spirited, rational motive to perform it. When that supposition or faith is reasonable, then there will be a new higher pleasure obtainable by virtuous persons: the satisfaction of knowing that they have contributed to the preservation of the condition of general conformity needed for justice to deliver its utility. This higher pleasure of conformity will be obtainable not only from acts conforming to established more or less just artifices, but also from acts displaying those natural virtues whose full point requires the reasonable expectation that others will not return vice for virtue. The higher pleasure of conformity can, in those latter cases, be added to those of altruism and prudence, and it exceeds them in 'height.' As prudence and altruism facilitate delectation, so conformity facilitates prudence and altruism, as well as extending their range through artifices.

There are, then, a series of hedonic bonus pleasures which we can enjoy, if we cultivate our spiritual palates and develop a relish for them, as Locke puts it (*Essay*, Bk. II, 21, 69). They can accompany the non-hedonic goods which are powers, the non-self directed goods, and conformity to those artifices which create public "powers" to increase the powers and pleasures of individuals. Such present occurrent pleasures, once obtained, cannot be taken away from the prudent man, the altruist, or the conformist, even if the non-present or other-dependent good *in* which the pleasure is taken does not eventuate. Bonus pleasures are non-negligible contributors to the goodness of a life. As pains are indicators of other ills, these pleasures are indicators, not guarantees, of other presumed goods, and they add to them as well as indicate them. But the indication may be false, the glory may be vainglory. Only insofar as one can reasonably hope for the success of one's prudent policy, altruistic project, or for the successful achievement of *general* conformity to an institution, can one derive a higher pleasure from prudent, altruistic or conforming action. Should the hopes on which they were, reasonably, based become later known to be false, the already obtained bonus pleasures may be devalued. They cannot be cancelled, but they may count for less, perhaps count negatively, in the person's proper assessment of the goodness of the life. If hopes turn out to have been what Hobbes calls vain "presumptions," the pleasures dependent on them may come to have been vainglory. If, on one's deathbed, one were persuaded that the person whose apparent love and devotion had given one much pleasure had really been uncaring, perhaps even had despised one, it would not, I think, be reasonable to react with the thought "thank God I didn't know till now." False pleasures, pleasures based on what comes to be seen as a lie, can, if the lie is serious and has reverberating implications for many of one's concerns, be worse than the absence of pleasure. Better no glory than vainglory.

Would the prudent man's bonus pleasure of feeling secure come to have been, like the friend's trusting pleasure, fool's gold, if he comes to realize that he will not live into the future for which he saved? If the bonus pleasure had been pleasure in the anticipated spendings of his savings, it would certainly be degraded by realization that he will not spend it, but to the extent that his bonus pleasure in his sense of security was in that which freed him from anxiety about his future, that bonus pleasure is not devalued by any knowledge he may acquire about his imminent early death. The power he had was a good, even if not exercised, because its absence would have been an ever present felt evil. One might say, of the trusting friend, that his trust that his love was reciprocated was a good similar to the prudent man's security, in that its absence would have been an evil for him. But could the evil of suspicion or distrust, or of the absence of affection, be as great as the evil the friend suffers if he bases his life on a false trust? The difference, I think, lies in the fact the unnecessarily prudent man is not *betrayed* by events, as the friend is by the false friend. The prudent man saves, because of the *possibility* that he may live long, but the friend loved in the confidence that love was returned. Prudence is, and knows itself to be, a reaction to risk and uncertainty, so its goods are not devalued if the possibility the prudent man provided for does not come about. But friendship does not, typically, see itself as content with the mere *possibility* of returned trust and love.

Can the man who acts for the sake of justice, when he knows or suspects that others are not conforming, get any bonus pleasures which are not fool's gold? We need to distinguish the cases where most but not all others are conforming from the cases where the conformists are in a minority, and, within the latter class, between the few who are trying to *inaugurate* a needed practice, and the few who are clinging to a once accepted but now imperilled institution. The last case, of fidelity to a once supported practice, faces less severe problems than those of the moral innovator, who must both get agreement on what should be conformed to, and also try to get sufficient conformity to it to secure the rewards of conformity. At least the moral conservative, the would-be supporter of a once established practice, does not face what have been called[9] the isolation and coordination problems, he faces only the problem of assurance of compliance. I shall not discuss the problems, faced by Hobbesian natural men, of simultaneously achieving communication, agreeing on what institutions are desirable (what coordination scheme to adopt) and also getting assured compliance to them. Let us, optimistically, assume that we have got, by the fact of past established conventions, their later reform, and their agreed need for specific further reforms, a solution to the isolation and coordination problems, that is, we have agreement on how we *should* all be acting. The compliance problem then arises—namely whether to act as we all should if we all are to get the best state of things for us, when there is no assurance that the rest of us are going to comply. If I comply and the rest of you don't, then the main good, for the sake of which that cooperative scheme was seen to be acceptable, will not be fully obtained, by any of us. To the extent it is partially attained it will be attained by noncompliers as well as compliers. I will have been the cully of my integrity. So, it seems, the pleasure of conformity is fool's gold unless others do in fact conform in sufficient numbers.

One thing which might save those pleasures from becoming false is the psychological taste of the individual for conformity. Not everyone can enjoy gun-running. Just as the prudent man who doesn't live to enjoy his savings may nevertheless have been saved by his prudence from unpleasant anxiety, so conformity to the old ways may soothe the timid who would be alarmed, not gratified, by the immortalists' life style.

But suppose I *could* develop a relish for gun-running, would it be irrational for me to decide to stick by, not to abandon, the threatened moral practices? Can unilateral, (or minority-wide) conformity to just, or potentially just, institutions have any genuine lure for me?

7. THE HIGHER PLEASURE OF QUALIFYING FOR MEMBERSHIP IN THE KINGDOM OF ENDS

Hume's point, a valid one, is that only a fool supports widely unsupported institutions whose only good depends on their getting wide support. But support from whom? My contemporaries and only them? It is fairly evident, I think, that the support of the majority of his contemporaries is not *sufficient* to guard the conformist from being taken in by fool's gold, especially when the institution is one which *conserves* goods for future generations. Whole generations can be retroactively made into cullies of their joint integrity by later generations' waste and destruction. What I want to stress is that conformity by the majority of one's contemporaries is not *necessary* to save the moral man from having been a fool.

Here, at last, I turn to the obvious source of a reply to Gauthier: Kant. He spelled out more clearly than any other modern philosopher the wholly secular basis for a strong set of plain duties. It is wholly secular, and it is also faith-requiring.

Kant says that although a rational being, when he acts on the maxim he can will as a universal law, "cannot for that reason expect every other rational being to be true to it; nor can he expect the realm of nature and its orderly design to harmonize with him as a fitting member of a realm of ends which is possible through himself. That is, he cannot count on its favoring his expectation of happiness. Still the law: Act according to the maxims of a universally legislative member of a merely potential realm of ends, remains in full force, because it commands categorically. And just in this lies the paradox, that merely the dignity of humanity as rational nature without any end or advantage to be gained by it, and thus respect for a mere idea, should serve as the inflexible precept of the will. There is the further paradox that the sublimity and worthiness of every rational subject to be a legislative member in the realm of ends consists precisely in independence of maxims from all such incentives" (Kant, *Foundation of the Metaphysics of Morals*, trans. Lewis White Beck). In this remarkable passage Kant appears to be claiming that the willingness to act as *if* one were a member of an actual kingdom of ends, when one knows that one is in fact a member of a society which falls short of this ideal, alone makes one worthy to be a legislating member of an actual kingdom of ends, or just society. But unless there can be such sublime and worthy persons, no just society is possible. The kingdom of ends is "possible through oneself." The existence of persons with the ability to act from respect for that "mere idea," is, then, the condition of the idea's actualization. Apparently just institutions would not guarantee a just society, if those persons living under them fail Kant's motivational test. A just society must be comprised of just men whose lives are ordered by just institutions.

On this account, apparently futile unilateral and possibly self-sacrificing action is neither futile nor unilateral. Not futile, because it keeps alive the assurance of the possibility of qualified members for a just society. Not unilateral, because the one just man has a 'cloud of witnesses,' all those others whose similar acts in other times kept alive the same hope. The actions of individuals who, unsupported by their contemporaries, act for the sake of justice do not necessarily hasten the coming of a just society, but they do rule out one ground on which it might be feared impossible. In this very modest way the just man's actions confirm his faith, demonstrate that *one* condition of the existence of a just society can be met, that human psychology can be a psychology of sovereigns. And the one just man is not alone, his isolation problem is solved if he recalls that enough others have already acted as he is acting. Thus every action in conformity to a just but threatened institution, or in protest against an unjust but supported one, furthers the cause, keeps the faith. The highest pleasure or 'relish' of all is that of qualifying for membership in the kingdom of ends.[10] It is not just a priggish pleasure if the demonstration that there are and can be qualified members has the role which Kant as I interpret him claimed for it. (The blood of the martyrs is the seed of the church.)

8. THE FAITH THE JUST LIVE BY

The secular faith which the just live by is, then, a faith in the possibility of a society for membership in which their just action theoretically qualifies them. They believe, in part, because of the previous demonstration that there can be such qualified members, so they join a movement already started. Each new member gives other potential members new assurance that the faith is not in vain, and it also confirms the faith of that new member himself, in that, after his act, the club of which he is an 'honorary' member is the larger by one, and its point depends on the size and persistence of its membership.

The qualified, so honorary, member of the kingdom of ends, usually hopes that some actual society, perhaps long after his death, will embody the kingdom of ends on earth, that the possible will become actual. Such a society would, in general intention, honor all those who acted for the sake of justice, who qualified for membership but did not survive to be members. They would be participants in the secular variant of the communion of the saints. This higher pleasure is a variant of that pleasure of imagination, delight in the prospect of posthumous recognition, which even Hobbes allows as a real pleasure. "Though after death there be no sense of the praise given us on earth, as being joys that are either swallowed up in the unspeakable joys of heaven or extinguished in the extreme torments of hell, yet is not such fame vain; because men have a present delight therein from the foresight of it and of the benefit that may redound thereby to their prosperity, which, though they see not, yet they imagine; and anything that is pleasure to the sense, the same is also pleasure in the imagination" (*Leviathan*, chap. 11). Hobbes would not be content with anonymous recognition—presumably only the foresight that one's name will live on, preserved on some honor roll, could give Hobbesian man this pleasure of imagination. Fame is one thing, membership in the faceless communion of the saints quite another for one who values nothing but what is eminent. Still, the qualification for praise and recognition by a posterity to whom benefits redound is at least part of what the Hobbesian can glory in, and for a Kantian it suffices for glory.

Does this pleasure of imagination require expectation that posterity *will* benefit? Does the faith the just live by include confidence that some society on earth will some day actually be just? As already acknowledged, the ideal of justice includes a demand, which may be Utopian, that its historical approximation coincide with its qualitative approximation. In addition to this demand, which the just person must, for the moment at least, merely *hope* can be met, there is another more serious difficulty in the idea of an actual just society which would meet the Kantian requirements. This is that, to the extent that there *is* conformity among one's contemporaries to apparently just practices, to precisely that extent none of the conformers can be assured that they, each of them, qualify for membership in the kingdom of ends. If they are acting, not for a mere idea, but in support of an actual practice, they cannot be sure they meet Kant's paradoxical test for qualification for membership in a just society, that is they cannot be sure how they *would* act if there were not general conformity. But the apparently just conforming society will not be just, in Kant's sense, if its sovereign-subjects are not qualified to be members. Kant's paradox is real, and so, once again, the ideal of a just society threatens to become incoherent. The threat, this time, is not one which can be allayed by sociological and historical findings, but is more fundamental—a *necessary* conflict between the criteria for qualification as the just society comprised of qualified members, and the criteria for its actualization.

Must the just man then conclude 'credo quia absurdum est?' He might—as he might develop a relish for acting for necessarily lost causes—but he can keep his faith from being the absurd hope for the impossible, by acceptance of the fact that one can live without certainty. As the just man *now*, in an unjust world, has no certainty, only faith and hope, that there really can and will be a just society of the living, so, in any apparently attained just society, that is in one with just institutions, its members will rely on the faith and hope that they could if necessary act for a mere idea, and so that they really qualify for membership. A new variant of Hobbesian faith in man will be needed. Both in the absence and in the presence of an actual just society, then, the just will live by faith.[11]

NOTES

1. "Why Ought One Obey God, Reflections on Hobbes and Locke," *Canadian Journal of Philosophy* 7 (1977): 425–46.

2. G. E. M. Anscombe, in "Modern Moral Philosophy" (*Philosophy*, 1958, pp. 1–18, reprinted in *The Definition of Morality*, ed. Wallace and Walker, London, 1970) claimed that all deontological moral concepts are empty words unless there is a divine lawgiver and duty-determiner. Gauthier's thesis concerns not *all* moral laws and duties, but only those involving "moral convention," where mutual benefits depend upon general observance. I accept this assumption that all moral duties require some rational basis, that we do not simply intuit moral absolutes.

3. Throughout this paper I use 'his' to mean 'his or her' and sometimes use 'man' to mean 'person'. This is especially regrettable in a paper about justice, but needed allusions to the words of Hobbes and other sexists dictated my usage. I am not, it seems, willing to make the sacrifices in communication needed to help gain as n..ch currency for 'the one just woman' as already gained for the one just man.

4. Gauthier, op. cit., p. 428.

5. William James, "The Will to Believe," in *The Will to Believe and Other Essays in Popular Philosophy* (New York and London, 1897). In this paper I am really saying no more than James said about moral faith. I suppose the justification for saying it again, and adapting it to a Hobbesian context, is the perennial character of the issue. I have benefited from discussion with Richard Gale on James' position, and from his comments on an earlier version of this paper.

6. It is not an easy matter to formulate an acceptable criterion of the equitable, but I have assumed that we can get a stronger test for justice than that provided by Hobbes—"What all men have accepted, no man can call unjust." If we cannot, then maybe only the fool says in his heart that there is more to justice than fidelity to possibly forced agreement. If the

ideal of the equitable or fair is empty or incoherent, then the more inclusive ideal of justice in a strong sense, which I am invoking, will also be empty or incoherent.

7. As has been pointed out by a reader for this journal, coherence could be preserved by letting one test apply on some occasions, the other on others, whenever the two tests would give conflicting decisions if both were applied. This would preserve only a weak formal coherence, unless some clear principle could be formulated which selects which test is applicable, and unless this principle itself expressed some component element in our hazy intuitive idea of justice.

8. Although in what follows I try to depart as little as possible from the hedonism of Hobbes and Locke (not because I agree with it, but because of the context of the present discussion), I do however depart very significantly from Hobbes in accepting, as rational motivation, not only self preservation of the natural man, or "nature's preservation" but also preservation, not of Leviathan, but of a moral community, and of the very idea of such a community. A special 'pleasure of the mind' would have to be added to Hobbes' list to accommodate such Kantian motivation.

9. Kurt Baier, "Rationality and Morality," *Erkenntnis* 11 (1977): 197, where the 'isolation', 'coordination', and 'assurance' problems are distinguished.

10. I have not discussed the question, raised by Gauthier's example of unilateral abstention from preemptive nuclear strike, of what should be done when the decision taken may commit others besides the decision-maker to the higher pleasures of martyrdom for a good cause. This is the *really* difficult question.

11. I have tried, throughout this paper, to evoke some Biblical echoes, to show how the secular faith I describe parallels its theological forerunners. The effort to speak both the language of Hobbes and that of the King James Bible has resulted in a style which some readers have found obscure. This I regret, but I do want to keep, for those in a position to recognize them, allusions to, e.g., St. Paul's Epistle to the Hebrews chaps. 10 and 11.

13

The Iliad or The Poem of Force

Simone Weil

The true hero, the true subject, the center of the *Iliad* is force. Force employed by man, force that enslaves man, force before which man's flesh shrinks away. In this work, at all times, the human spirit is shown as modified by its relations with force, as swept away, blinded, by the very force it imagined it could handle, as deformed by the weight of the force it submits to. For those dreamers who considered that force, thanks to progress, would soon be a thing of the past, the *Iliad* could appear as an historical document; for others, whose powers of recognition are more acute and who perceive force, today as yesterday, at the very center of human history, the *Iliad* is the purest and the loveliest of mirrors.

To define force—it is that x that turns anybody who is subjected to it into a *thing*. Exercised to the limit, it turns man into a thing in the most literal sense: it makes a corpse out of him. Somebody was here, and the next minute there is nobody here at all; this is a spectacle the *Iliad* never wearies of showing us:

> . . . the horses
> Rattled the empty chariots through the files of battle,
> Longing for their noble drivers. But they on the ground
> Lay, dearer to the vultures than to their wives.

The hero becomes a *thing* dragged behind a chariot in the dust:

> All around, his black hair
> Was spread; in the dust his whole head lay,
> That once-charming head; now Zeus had let his enemies
> Defile it on his native soil.

The bitterness of such a spectacle is offered us absolutely undiluted. No comforting fiction intervenes; no consoling prospect of immor-

This essay translated by Mary McCarthy in *Politics*, November 1945, pp. 3–37 is reprinted by permission.

tality; and on the hero's head no washed-out halo of patriotism
descends.

> His soul, fleeing his limbs, passed to Hades,
> Mourning its fate, forsaking its youth and its vigor.

Still more poignant—so painful is the contrast—is the sudden
evocation, as quickly rubbed out, of another world: the faraway,
precarious, touching world of peace, of the family, the world in
which each man counts more than anything else to those about him.

> She ordered her bright-haired maids in the palace
> To place on the fire a large tripod, preparing
> A hot bath for Hector, returning from battle.
> Foolish woman! Already he lay, far from hot baths,
> Slain by grey-eyed Athena, who guided Achilles' arm.

Far from hot baths he was indeed, poor man. And not he alone.
Nearly all the *Iliad* takes place far from hot baths. Nearly all of
human life, then and now, takes place far from hot baths.

Here we see force in its grossest and most summary form—the
force that kills. How much more varied in its processes, how much
more surprising in its effects is the other force, the force that does
not kill, i.e., that does not kill just yet. It will surely kill, it will
possibly kill, or perhaps it merely hangs, poised and ready, over the
head of the creature it *can* kill, at any moment, which is to say at
every moment. In whatever aspect, its effect is the same: it turns a
man into a stone. From its first property (the ability to turn a
human being into a thing by the simple method of killing him) flows
another, quite prodigious too in its own way, the ability to turn a
human being into a thing while he is still alive. He is alive; he has a
soul; and yet—he is a thing. An extraordinary entity this—a thing
that has a soul. And as for the soul, what an extraordinary house it
finds itself in! Who can say what it costs it, moment by moment, to
accommodate itself to this residence, how much writhing and bend-
ing, folding and pleating are required of it? It was not made to live
inside a thing; if it does so, under pressure of necessity, there is not
a single element of its nature to which violence is not done.

A man stands disarmed and naked with a weapon pointing at
him; this person becomes a corpse before anybody or anything
touches him. Just a minute ago, he was thinking, acting, hoping:

> Motionless, he pondered. And the other drew near,
> Terrified, anxious to touch his knees, hoping in his heart
> To escape evil death and black destiny . . .

> With one hand he clasped, suppliant, his knees,
> While the other clung to the sharp spear, not letting
> go . . .

Soon, however, he grasps the fact that the weapon which is pointing at him will not be diverted; and now, still breathing, he is simply matter; still thinking, he can think no longer:

> Thus spoke the brilliant son of Priam
> In begging words. But he heard a harsh reply:
> He spoke. And the other's knees and heart failed him.
> Dropping his spear, he knelt down, holding out his arms.
> Achilles, drawing his sharp sword, struck
> Through the neck and breastbone. The two-edged sword
> Sunk home its full length. The other, face down,
> Lay still, and the black blood ran out, wetting the ground.

If a stranger, completely disabled, disarmed, strengthless, throws himself on the mercy of a warrior, he is not, by this very act, condemned to death; but a moment of impatience on the warrior's part will suffice to relieve him of his life. In any case, his flesh has lost that very important property which in the laboratory distinguishes living flesh from dead—the galvanic response. If you give a frog's leg an electric shock, it twitches. If you confront a human being with the touch or sight of something horrible or terrifying, this bundle of muscles, nerves, and flesh likewise twitches. Alone of all living things, the suppliant we have just described neither quivers nor trembles. He has lost the right to do so. As his lips advance to touch the object that is for him of all things most charged with horror, they do not draw back on his teeth—they cannot:

> No one saw great Priam enter. He stopped,
> Clasped the knees of Achilles, kissed his hands,
> Those terrible man-killing hands that had slaughtered so
> many of his sons.

The sight of a human being pushed to such an extreme of suffering chills us like the sight of a dead body:

> As when harsh misfortune strikes a man if in his own
> country
> He has killed a man, and arrives at last at someone else's
> door,

> The door of a rich man; a shudder seizes those who see
>   him.
> So Achilles shuddered to see divine Priam;
> The others shuddered too, looking one at the other.

But this feeling lasts only a moment. Soon the very presence of the
suffering creature is forgotten:

> He spoke. The other, remembering his own father, longed
>   to weep;
> Taking the old man's arm, he pushed him away.
> Both were remembering. Thinking of Hector, killer of
>   men,
> Priam wept, abased at the feet of Achilles.
> But Achilles wept, now for his father,
> Now for Patroclus. And their sobs resounded through the
>   house.

It was not insensibility that made Achilles with a single movement
of his hand push away the old man who had been clinging to his
knees; Priam's words, recalling his own old father, had moved him
to tears. It was merely a question of his being as free in his attitudes
and movements as if, clasping his knees, there were not a suppliant
but an inert object. Anybody who is in our vicinity exercises a certain power over us by his very presence, and a power that belongs to
him alone, that is, the power of halting, repressing, modifying each
movement that our body sketches out. If we step aside for a passer-
by on the road, it is not the same thing as stepping aside to avoid a
billboard; alone in our rooms, we get up, walk about, sit down again
quite differently from the way we do when we have a visitor. But
this indefinable influence that the presence of another human being
has on us is not exercised by men whom a moment of impatience can
deprive of life, who can die before even thought has a chance to pass
sentence on them. In their presence, people move about as if they
were not there; they, on their side, running the risk of being reduced
to nothing in a single instant, imitate nothingness in their own persons. Pushed, they fall. Fallen, they lie where they are, unless
chance gives somebody the idea of raising them up again. But supposing that at long last they have been picked up, honored with cor-
dial remarks, they still do not venture to take this resurrection
seriously; they dare not express a wish lest an irritated voice return
them forever to silence:

> He spoke; the old man trembled and obeyed.

At least a suppliant, once his prayer is answered, becomes a human being again, like everybody else. But there are other, more unfortunate creatures who have become things for the rest of their lives. Their days hold no pastimes, no free spaces, no room in them for any impulse of their own. It is not that their life is harder than other men's nor that they occupy a lower place in the social hierarchy; no, they are another human species, a compromise between a man and a corpse. The idea of a person's being a thing is a logical contradiction. Yet what is impossible in logic becomes true in life, and the contradiction lodged within the soul tears it to shreds. This thing is constantly aspiring to be a man or a woman, and never achieving it—here, surely, is death but death strung out over a whole lifetime; here, surely is life, but life that death congeals before abolishing.

This strange fate awaits the virgin, the priest's daughter:

> I will not give her up. Sooner shall old age come upon her
> In our house in Argos, far from her native land,
> Tending the loom and sharing my bed.

It awaits the young wife, the young mother, the prince's bride:

> And perhaps one day, in Argos, you will weave cloth for
>   another,
> And the Messeian or Hyperian water you will fetch,
> Much against your will, yielding to a harsh necessity.

It awaits the baby, heir to the royal scepter:

> Soon they will be carried off in the hollow ships,
> I with them. And you, my child, will either go with me,
> To a land where you will work at wretched tasks,
> Laboring for a pitiless master. . . .

In the mother's eyes, such a fate is, for her child, as terrible as death; the husband would rather die than see his wife reduced to it; all the plagues of heaven are invoked by the father against the army that subjects his daughter to it. Yet the victims themselves are beyond all this. Curses, feelings of rebellion, comparisons, reflections on the future and the past, are obliterated from the mind of the captive; and memory itself barely lingers on. Fidelity to his city and his dead is not the slave's privilege.

And what does it take to make the slave weep? The misfortune of his master, his oppressor, despoiler, pillager, of the man who laid waste his town and killed his dear ones under his very eyes. This man suffers and dies; *then* the slave's tears come. And really why not? This is for him the only occasion on which tears are permitted, are, indeed, required. A slave will always cry whenever he can do so with impunity—his situation keeps tears on tap for him.

> She spoke, weeping, and the women groaned,
> Using the pretext of Patroclus to bewail their own torments.

Since the slave has no license to express anything except what is pleasing to his master, it follows that the only emotion that can touch or enliven him a little, that can reach him in the desolation of his life, is the emotion of love for his master. There is no place else to send the gift of love; all other outlets are barred, just as, with the horse in harness, bit, shafts, reins bar every way but one. And if, by some miracle, in the slave's breast a hope is born, the hope of becoming, some day, through somebody's influence, *someone* once again, how far won't these captives go to show love and thankfulness, even though these emotions are addressed to the very men who should, considering the very recent past, still reek with horror for them:

> My husband, to whom my father and respected mother gave me,
> I saw before the city transfixed by the sharp bronze.
> My three brothers, children, with me, of a single mother,
> So dear to me! They all met their fatal day.
> But you did not allow me to weep, when swift Achilles
> Slaughtered my husband and laid waste the city of Mynes.
> You promised me that I would be taken by divine Achilles,
> For his legitimate wife, that he would carry me away in his ships,
> To Pythia, where our marriage would be celebrated among the Myrmidons,
> So without respite I mourn for you, you who have always been gentle.

To lose more than the slave does is impossible, for he loses his whole inner life. A fragment of it he may get back if he sees the possibility of changing his fate, but this is his only hope. Such is the empire of force, as extensive as the empire of nature. Nature, too, when vital needs are at stake, can erase the whole inner life, even the grief of a mother:

But the thought of eating came to her, when she was tired
of tears.

Force, in the hands of another, exercises over the soul the same
tyranny that extreme hunger does; for it possesses, and *in perpetuo,*
the power of life and death. Its rule, moreover, is as cold and hard as
the rule of inert matter. The man who knows himself weaker than
another is more alone in the heart of a city than a man lost in the
desert.

Two casks are placed before Zeus's doorsill,
Containing the gifts he gives, the bad in one, the good in
     the other . . .
The man to whom he gives baneful gifts, he exposes to
     outrage;
A frightful need drives across the divine earth;
He is a wanderer, and gets no respect from gods or men.

Force is as pitiless to the man who possesses it, or thinks he
does, as it is to its victims; the second it crushes, the first it intox-
icates. The truth is, nobody really possesses it. The human race is
not divided up, in the *Iliad*, into conquered persons, slaves, sup-
pliants, on the one hand, and conquerors and chiefs on the other. In
this poem there is not a single man who does not at one time or
another have to bow his neck to force. The common soldier in the *Iliad* is free and has the right to bear arms; nevertheless he is subject
to the indignity of orders and abuse:

But whenever he came upon a commoner shouting out,
He struck him with his scepter and spoke sharply:
"Good for nothing! Be still and listen to your betters,
You are weak and cowardly and unwarlike,
You count for nothing, neither in battle nor in council."

Thersites pays dear for the perfectly reasonable comments he
makes, comments not at all different, moreover, from those made by
Achilles:

He hit him with his scepter on back and shoulders,
So that he doubled over, and a great tear welled up,
And a bloody welt appeared on his back
Under the golden scepter. Frightened, he sat down,
Wiping away his tears, bewildered and in pain.
Troubled though they were, the others laughed long at
     him.

Achilles himself, that proud hero, the undefeated, is shown us at the outset of the poem, weeping with humiliation and helpless grief—the woman he wanted for his bride has been taken from under his nose, and he has not dared to oppose it:

> ... But Achilles
> Weeping, sat apart from his companions,
> By the white-capped waves, staring over the boundless ocean.

What has happened is that Agamemnon has deliberately humiliated Achilles, to show that he himself is the master:

> ... So you will learn
> That I am greater than you, and anyone else will hesitate
> To treat me as an equal and set himself against me.

But a few days pass and now the supreme commander is weeping in his turn. He must humble himself, he must plead, and have, moreover, the added misery of doing it all in vain.

In the same way, there is not a single one of the combatants who is spared the shameful experience of fear. The heroes quake like everybody else. It only needs a challenge from Hector to throw the whole Greek force into consternation—except for Achilles and his men, and they did not happen to be present:

> He spoke and all grew still and held their peace,
> Ashamed to refuse, afraid to accept.

But once Ajax comes forward and offers himself, fear quickly changes sides:

> A shudder of terror ran through the Trojans, making their limbs weak;
> And Hector himself felt his heart leap in his breast.
> But he no longer had the right to tremble, or to run away. . . .

Two days later, it is Ajax's turn to be terrified:

> Zeus the father on high, makes fear rise in Ajax.
> He stops, overcome, puts behind him his buckler made of seven hides,
> Trembles, looks at the crowd around, like a wild beast. . . .

Even to Achilles the moment comes; he too must shake and stammer with fear, though it is a river that has this effect on him, not a man. But, with the exception of Achilles, every man in the *Iliad* tastes a moment of defeat in battle. Victory is less a matter of valor than of blind destiny, which is symbolized in the poem by Zeus's golden scales:

> Then Zeus the father took his golden scales,
> In them he put the two fates of death that cuts down all
>   men,
> One for the Trojans, tamers of horses, one for the bronze-
>   sheathed Greeks.
> He seized the scales by the middle; it was the fatal day of
>   Greece that sank.

By its very blindness, destiny establishes a kind of justice. Blind also is she who decrees to warriors punishment in kind. He that takes the sword, will perish by the sword. The *Iliad* formulated the principle long before the Gospels did, and in almost the same terms:

> Ares is just, and kills those who kill.

Perhaps all men, by the very act of being born, are destined to suffer violence; yet this is a truth to which circumstance shuts men's eyes. The strong are, as a matter of fact, never absolutely strong, nor are the weak absolutely weak, but neither is aware of this. They have in common a refusal to believe that they both belong to the same species: the weak see no relation between themselves and the strong, and vice versa. The man who is the possessor of force seems to walk through a non-resistant element; in the human substance that surrounds him nothing has the power to interpose, between the impulse and the act, the tiny interval that is reflection. Where there is no room for reflection, there is none either for justice or prudence. Hence we see men in arms behaving harshly and madly. We see their sword bury itself in the breast of a disarmed enemy who is in the very act of pleading at their knees. We see them triumph over a dying man by describing to him the outrages his corpse will endure. We see Achilles cut the throats of twelve Trojan boys on the funeral pyre of Patroclus as naturally as we cut flowers for a grave. These men, wielding power, have no suspicion of the fact that the consequences of their deeds will at length come home to them—they too will bow the neck in their turn. If you can make an old man fall silent, tremble, obey, with a single word of your own, why should it occur to you that the curses of this old man, who is after all a priest, will have their own importance in the gods' eyes? Why should you refrain from taking Achilles' girl away from him if you know that neither he nor she can do anything but obey you? Achilles rejoices over the sight of the Greeks fleeing in misery and confusion. What could possibly suggest to him that this rout, which will last exactly as long as he wants it to and end when his mood indicates it, that this very rout will be the cause of his friend's death, and, for that matter, of his own? Thus it happens that those who have force on loan from fate count on it too much and are destroyed. But at the time their own destruction seems impossible to them. For they do not see that the force in their possession is only a limited quantity; nor do they see their relations with other human beings as a kind of balance between unequal amounts of force. Since other people do not impose on their movements that halt, that interval of hesitation, wherein lies all our consideration for our brothers in humanity, they conclude that destiny has given complete license to them, and none at all to their inferiors. And at this point they exceed the measure of the force that is actually at their disposal. Inevitably they exceed it, since they are not aware that it is limited. And now we see them committed irretrievably to chance; suddenly things cease to obey them. Sometimes chance is kind to them, sometimes cruel. But in any case there they are, exposed, open to misfortune; gone is the armor of power that formerly protected their naked souls; nothing, no shield, stands between them and tears.

This retribution, which has a geometrical rigor, which operates automatically to penalize the abuse of force, was the main subject of Greek thought. It is the soul of the epic. Under the name of Nemesis, it functions as the mainspring of Aeschylus's tragedies. To the Pythagoreans, to Socrates and Plato, it was the jumping-off point of speculation upon the nature of man and the universe. Wherever Hellenism has penetrated, we find the idea of it familiar. In Oriental countries which are steeped in Buddhism, it is perhaps this Greek idea that has lived on under the name of Kharma. The Occident, however, has lost it, and no longer even has a word to express it in any of its languages: conceptions of limit, measure, equilibrium, which ought to determine the conduct of life are, in the West, restricted to a servile function in the vocabulary of technics. We are only geometricians of matter; the Greeks were, first of all, geometricians in their apprenticeship to virtue.

The progress of the war in the *Iliad* is simply a continual game of seesaw. The victor of the moment feels himself invincible, even though, only a few hours before, he may have experienced defeat; he forgets to treat victory as a transitory thing. At the end of the first

day of combat described in the *Iliad*, the victorious Greeks were in a
position to obtain the object of all their efforts, i.e., Helen and her
riches—assuming of course as Homer did, that the Greeks had
reason to believe that Helen was in Troy. Actually, the Egyptian
priests, who ought to have known, affirmed later on to Herodotus
that she was in Egypt. In any case, that evening the Greeks are no
longer interested in her or her possessions:

> "For the present, let us not accept the riches of Paris;
> Nor Helen; everybody sees, even the most ignorant,
> That Troy stands on the verge of ruin."
> He spoke, and all the Achaeans acclaimed him.

What they want is, in fact, everything. For booty, all the riches of
Troy; for their bonfires, all the palaces, temples, houses; for slaves,
all the women and children; for corpses, all the men. They forget one
detail, that *everything* is not within their power, for they are not in
Troy. Perhaps they will be there tomorrow; perhaps not. Hector, the
same day, makes the same mistake:

> For I know well in my entrails and in my hearts,
> A day will come when Holy Troy will perish
> And Priam, and the nation of Priam of the good lance.
> But I think less of the grief that is in store for the Trojans,
> And of Hecuba herself, and of Priam the king,
> And of my brothers, so numerous and so brave,
> Who will fall in the dust under the blows of the enemy,
> Than of you that day when a Greek in his bronze breast-
>   plate
> Will drag you away weeping and deprive you of your
>   liberty.
>
> But as for me, may I be dead, and may the earth have
>   covered me
> Before I hear you cry out or see you dragged away!

At this moment what would he not give to turn aside those hor-
rors which he believes to be inevitable? But at this moment nothing
he *could* give would be of any use. The next day but one, however,
the Greeks have run away miserably, and Agamemnon himself is in
favor of putting to the sea again. And now Hector, by making a very
few concessions, could readily secure the enemy's departure; yet
now he is even unwilling to let them go empty-handed:

Set fires everywhere and let the brightness mount the
  skies
Lest in the night the long-haired Greeks,
Escaping, sail over the broad back of ocean . . .
Let each of them take home a wound to heal
. . . thus others will fear
To bring dolorous war to the Trojans, tamers of horses.

His wish is granted; the Greeks stay; and the next day they reduce
Hector and his men to a pitiable condition:

As for them—they fled across the plain like cattle
Whom a lion hunts before him in the dark midnight . . .
Thus the mighty Agamemnon, son of Atreus, pursued
  them,
Steadily killing the hindmost; and still they fled.

In the course of the afternoon, Hector regains the ascendancy,
withdraws again, then puts the Greeks to flight, then is repulsed by
Patroclus, who has come in with his fresh troops. Patroclus, pressing his advantage, ends by finding himself exposed, wounded and
without armor, to the sword of Hector. And finally that evening the
victorious Hector hears the prudent counsel of Polydamas and
repudiates it sharply:

Now that wily Kronos's son has given me
Glory at the ships; now that I have driven the Greeks to
  the sea,
Do not offer, fool, such counsels to the people.
No Trojan will listen to you; nor would I permit it . . .
So Hector spoke, and the Trojans acclaimed him. . . .

The next day Hector is lost. Achilles has harried him across the field
and is about to kill him. He has always been the stronger of the two
in combat; how much the more so now, after several weeks of rest,
ardent for vengeance and victory, against an exhausted enemy?
And Hector stands alone, before the walls of Troy, absolutely alone,
alone to wait for death and to steady his soul to face it:

Alas, were I to slip through the gate, behind the rampart,
Polydamas at once would heap dishonor on me . . .
And now that through my recklessness I have destroyed
  my people,

> I fear the Trojans and the long-robed Trojan women,
> I fear to hear from some one far less brave than I:
> "Hector, trusting his own strength too far, has ruined his
>   people." . . .
> Suppose I were to down my bossed shield,
> My massive helmet, and, leaning my spear against the
>   wall,
> Should go to meet renowned Achilles? . . .
> But why spin out these fancies? Why such dreams?
> I would not reach him, nor would he pity me,
> Or respect me. He would kill me like a woman
> If I came naked thus . . .

Not a jot of the grief and ignominy that fall to the unfortunate is Hector spared. Alone, stripped of the prestige of force, he discovers that the courage that kept him from taking to the shelter of the walls is not enough to save him from flight:

> Seeing him, Hector began to tremble. He had not the heart
> To stay . . .
> . . . It is not for a ewe nor the skin of an ox,
> That they are striving, not these ordinary rewards of the
>   race;
> It is for a life that they run, the life of Hector, tamer of
>   horses.

Wounded to death, he enhances his conqueror's triumph by vain supplications:

> I implore you, by your soul, by your knees,
>   by your parents. . . .

But the auditors of the *Iliad* knew that the death of Hector would be but a brief joy to Achilles, and the death of Achilles but a brief joy to the Trojans, and the destruction of Troy but a brief joy to the Achaeans.

Thus violence obliterates anybody who feels its touch. It comes to seem just as external to its employer as to its victim. And from this springs the idea of a destiny before which executioner and victim stand equally innocent, before which conquered and conqueror are brothers in the same distress. The conquered brings misfortune to the conqueror, and vice versa:

> A single son, short-lived, was born to him.
> Neglected by me, he grows old—for far from home
> I camp before Troy, injuring you and your sons.

A moderate use of force, which alone would enable man to escape being enmeshed in its machinery, would require superhuman virtue, which is as rare as dignity in weakness. Moreover, moderation itself is not without its perils, since prestige, from which force derives at least three quarters of its strength, rests principally upon that marvelous indifference that the strong feel toward the weak, an indifference so contagious that it infects the very people who are the objects of it. Yet ordinarily excess is not arrived at through prudence or politic considerations. On the contrary, man dashes to it as to an irresistible temptation. The voice of reason is occasionally heard in the mouths of the characters in the *Iliad.* Thersites' speeches are reasonable to the highest degree; so are the speeches of the angry Achilles:

> Nothing is worth my life, not all the goods
> They say the well-built city of Ilium contains. . . .
> A man can capture steers and fatted sheep
> But, once gone, the soul cannot be captured back.

But words of reason drop into the void. If they come from an inferior, he is punished and shuts up; if from a chief, his actions betray them. And failing everything else, there is always a god handy to advise him to be unreasonable. In the end, the very idea of wanting to escape the role fate has allotted one—the business of killing and dying—disappears from the mind:

> We to whom Zeus
> Has assigned suffering, from youth to old age,
> Suffering in grievous wars, till we perish to the last man.

Already these warriors, like Craonne's so much later, felt themselves to be "condemned men."

It was the simplest trap that pitched them into this situation. At the outset, at the embarkation, their hearts are light, as hearts always are if you have a large force on your side and nothing but space to oppose you. Their weapons are in their hands; the enemy is absent. Unless your spirit has been conquered in advance by the reputation of the enemy, you always feel yourself to be much stronger than anybody who is not there. An absent man does not impose the yoke of necessity. To the spirits of those embarking no necessity yet presents itself; consequently they go off as though to a game, as though on holiday from the confinement of daily life.

Where have they gone, those braggadocio boasts
We proudly flung upon the air at Lemnos,
Stuffing ourselves with flesh of horned steers,
Drinking from cups brimming over with wine?
As for Trojans—a hundred or two each man of us
Could handle in battle. And now one is too much for us.

But the first contact of war does not immediately destroy the illusion that war is a game. War's necessity is terrible, altogether different in kind from the necessity of peace. So terrible is it that the human spirit will not submit to it so long as it can possibly escape; and whenever it can escape it takes refuge in long days empty of necessity, days of play, of revery, days arbitrary and unreal. Danger then becomes an abstraction; the lives you destroy are like toys broken by a child, and quite as incapable of feeling; heroism is but a theatrical gesture and smirched with boastfulness. This becomes doubly true if a momentary access of vitality comes to reinforce the divine hand that wards off defeat and death. Then war is easy and basely, coarsely loved.

But with the majority of the combatants this state of mind does not persist. Soon there comes a day when fear, or defeat, or the death of beloved comrades touches the warrior's spirit, and it crumbles in the hand of necessity. At that moment war is no more a game or a dream; now at last the warrior cannot doubt the reality of its existence. And this reality, which he perceives, is hard, much too hard to be borne, for it enfolds death. Once you acknowledge death to be a practical possibility, the thought of it becomes unendurable, except in flashes. True enough, all men are fated to die; true enough also, a soldier may grow old in battles; yet for those whose spirits have bent under the yoke of war, the relation between death and the future is different than for other men. For other men death appears as a limit set in advance on the future; for the soldier death *is* the future, the future his profession assigns him. Yet the idea of man's having death for a future is abhorrent to nature. Once the experience of war makes visible the possibility of death that lies locked up in each moment, our thoughts cannot travel from one day to the next without meeting death's face. The mind is then strung up to a pitch it can stand for only a short time; but each new dawn reintroduces the same necessity; and days piled on days make years. On each one of these days the soul suffers violence. Regularly, every morning, the soul castrates itself of aspiration, for thought cannot journey through time without meeting death on the way. Thus war effaces all conceptions of purpose or goal, including even its own "war aims." It effaces the very notion of war's being brought to an end. To be outside a situation so violent as this is to find it inconceivable; to be inside it is to be unable to conceive its end. Consequently, nobody does anything to bring this end about. In the presence of an armed enemy, what hand can relinquish its weapon? The mind ought to find a way out, but the mind has lost all capacity to so much as look outward. The mind is completely absorbed in doing itself violence. Always in human life, whether war or slavery is in question, intolerable sufferings continue, as it were, by the force of their own specific gravity, and so look to the outsider as though they were easy to bear; actually, they continue because they have deprived the sufferer of the resources which might serve to extricate him.

Nevertheless, the soul that is enslaved to war cries out for deliverance, but deliverance itself appears to it in an extreme and tragic aspect, the aspect of destruction. Any other solution, more moderate, more reasonable in character, would expose the mind to suffering so naked, so violent that it could not be borne, even as memory. Terror, grief, exhaustion, slaughter, the annihilation of comrades—is it credible that these things should not continually tear at the soul, if the intoxication of force had not intervened to drown them? The idea that an unlimited effort should bring in only a limited profit or no profit at all is terribly painful.

What? Will we let Priam and the Trojans boast
Of Argive Helen, she for whom so many Greeks
Died before Troy, far from their native land?
What? Do you want us to leave the city, wide-streeted
    Troy,
Standing, when we have suffered so much for it?

But actually what is Helen to Ulysses? What indeed is Troy, full of riches that will not compensate him for Ithaca's ruin? For the Greeks, Troy and Helen are in reality mere sources of blood and tears; to master them is to master frightful memories. If the existence of an enemy has made a soul destroy in itself the thing nature

put there, then the only remedy the soul can imagine is the destruction of the enemy. At the same time the death of dearly loved comrades arouses a spirit of somber emulation, a rivalry in death:

> May I die, then, at once! Since fate has not let me
> Protect my dead friend, who far from home
> Perished, longing for me to defend him from death.
> So now I go to seek the murderer of my friend,
> Hector. And death shall I find at the moment
> Zeus wills it—Zeus and the other immortal.

It is the same despair that drives him on toward death, on the one
hand, and slaughter on the other:

> I know it well, my fate is to perish here,
> Far from father and dearly beloved mother;
>   but meanwhile
> I shall not stop till the Trojans have had their fill of war.

The man possessed by this twofold need for death belongs, so long
as he has not become something still different, to a different race
from the race of the living.

What echo can the timid hopes of life strike in such a heart?
How can it hear the defeated begging for another sight of the light
of day? The threatened life has already been relieved of nearly all its
consequence by a single, simple distinction: it is now unarmed; its
adversary possesses a weapon. Furthermore, how can a man who
has rooted out of himself the notion that the light of day is sweet to
the eyes respect such a notion when it makes its appearance in some
futile and humble lament?

> I clasp tight your knees, Achilles. Have a thought, have
>   pity for me.
> I stand here, O son of Zeus, a suppliant, to be respected.
> In your house it was I first tasted Demeter's bread,
> That day in my well-pruned vineyard you caught me
> And sold me, sending me far from father and friends,
> To holy Lemnos; a hundred oxen was my price.
> And now I will pay you three hundred for ransom.
> This dawn is for me my twelfth day in Troy,
> After so many sorrows. See me here, in your hands,
> Through some evil fate. Zeus surely must hate me
> Who again puts me into your hands. Alas, my poor
>   mother, Laothoe,

Daughter of the old man, Altes—a short-lived son you
have borne.

What a reception this feeble hope gets!

Come, friend, you too must die. Why make a fuss about it?
Patroclus, he too has died—a far better man than you are.
Don't you see how handsome I am, how mighty?
A noble father begat me, and I have a goddess for mother.
Yet even I, like you, must some day encounter my fate,
Whether the hour strikes at noon, or evening, or sunrise,
The hour that comes when some arms-bearing warrior
will kill me.

To respect life in somebody else when you have had to castrate
yourself of all yearning for it demands a truly heartbreaking exertion of the powers of generosity. It is impossible to imagine any of
Homer's warriors being capable of such an exertion, unless it is that
warrior who dwells, in a peculiar way, at the very center of the
poem—I mean Patroclus, who "knew how to be sweet to everybody,"
and who throughout the *Iliad* commits no cruel or brutal act. But
then how many men do we know, in several thousand years of
human history, who would have displayed such god-like generosity?
Two or three?—even this is doubtful. Lacking this generosity, the
conquering soldier is like a scourge of nature. Possessed by war, he,
like the slave, becomes a thing, though his manner of doing so is different—over him too, words are as powerless as over matter itself.
And both, at the touch of force, experience its inevitable effects:
they become deaf and dumb.

Such is the nature of force. Its power of converting a man into a
thing is a double one, and in its application double-edged. To the
same degree, though in different fashions, those who use it and
those who endure it are turned to stone. This property of force
achieves its maximum effectiveness during the clash of arms, in battle, when the tide of the day has turned, and everything is rushing
toward a decision. It is not the planning man, the man of strategy,
the man acting on the resolution taken, who wins or loses a battle;
battles are fought and decided by men deprived of these faculties,
men who have undergone a transformation, who have dropped
either to the level of inert matter, which is pure passivity, or to the
level of blind force, which is pure momentum. Herein lies the last
secret of war, a secret revealed by the *Iliad* in its similes, which liken

the warriors either to fire, flood, wind, wild beasts, or God knows
what blind cause of disaster, or else to frightened animals, trees,
water, sand, to anything in nature that is set into motion by the
violence of external forces. Greeks and Trojans, from one day to the
next, sometimes even from one hour to the next, experience, turn
and turn about, one or the other of these transmutations:

> As when a lion, murderous, springs among the cattle
> Which by thousands are grazing over some vast marshy
>   field. . . .
> And their flanks heave with terror; even so the Achaians
> Scattered in panic before Hector and Zeus, the great
>   father.

> As when a ravening fire breaks out deep in a bushy wood
> And the wheeling wind scatters sparks far and wide,
> And trees, root and branch, topple over in flames;
> So Atreus' son, Agamemnon, roared through the ranks
> Of the Trojans in flight. . . .

The art of war is simply the art of producing such transformations,
and its equipment, its processes, even the casualties it inflicts on
the enemy, are only means directed toward this end—its true object
is the warrior's soul. Yet these transformations are always a
mystery; the gods are their authors, the gods who kindle men's imagination. But however caused, this petrifactive quality of force,
two-fold always, is essential to its nature; and a soul which has
entered the province of force will not escape this except by a
miracle. Such miracles are rare and of brief duration.

The wantonness of the conqueror that knows no respect for any
creature or thing that is at its mercy or is imagined to be so, the
despair of the soldier that drives him on to destruction, the oblitera-
tion of the slave or the conquered man, the wholesale slaughter—all
these elements combine in the *Iliad* to make a picture of uniform
horror, of which force is the sole hero. A monotonous desolation
would result were it not for those few luminous moments, scattered
here and there throughout the poem, those brief, celestial moments
in which man possesses his soul. The soul that awakes then, to live
for an instant only and be lost almost at once in force's vast
kingdom, awakes pure and whole; it contains no ambiguities,
nothing complicated or turbid; it has no room for anything but
courage and love. Sometimes it is in the course of inner delibera-

tions that a man finds his soul: he meets it, like Hector before Troy, as he tries to face destiny on his own terms, without the help of gods or men. At other times, it is in a moment of love that men discover their souls—and there is hardly any form of pure love known to humanity of which the *Iliad* does not treat. The tradition of hospitality persists, even through several generations, to dispel the blindness of combat.

> Thus I am for you a beloved guest in the breast of Argos. . .
> let us turn our lances away from each other, even in
>   battle.

The love of the son for the parents, of father for son, of mother for son, is continually described, in a manner as touching as it is curt:

> Thetis answered, shedding tears,
> "You were born to me for a short life, my child, as you
>   say . . ."

Even brotherly love:

> My three brothers whom the same mother bore for me,
> So dear. . . .

Conjugal love, condemned to sorrow, is of an astonishing purity. Imaging the humiliations of slavery which await a beloved wife, the husband passes over the one indignity which even in anticipation would stain their tenderness. What could be simpler than the words spoken by his wife to the man about to die?

> . . . Better for me
> Losing you, to go under the earth. No other comfort
> Will remain, when you have encountered your death-
>   heavy fate,
> Only grief, only sorrow. . . .

Not less touching are the words expressed to a dead husband:

> Dear husband, you died young, and left me your widow
> Alone in the palace. Our child is still tiny,
> The child you and I, crossed by fate, had together.
> I think he will never grow up . . .
> For not in your bed did you die, holding my hand
> And speaking to me prudent words which forever
> Night and day, as I weep, might live in my memory.

The most beautiful friendship of all, the friendship between comrades-at-arms, is the final theme of The Epic:

> ... But Achilles
> Wept, dreaming of the beloved comrade; sleep, all-
>   prevailing,
> Would not take him; he turned over again and again.

But the purest triumph of love, the crowning grace of war, is the friendship that floods the hearts of mortal enemies. Before it a murdered son or a murdered friend no longer cries out for vengeance. Before it—even more miraculous—the distance between benefactor and suppliant, between victor and vanquished, shrinks to nothing:

> But when thirst and hunger had been appeased,
> Then Dardanian Priam fell to admiring Achilles.
> How tall he was, and handsome; he had the face of a god;
> And in his turn Dardanian Priam was admired by Achilles,
> Who watched his handsome face and listened to his words.
> And when they were satisfied with contemplation of each
>   other ...

These moments of grace are rare in the *Iliad*, but they are enough to make us feel with sharp regret what it is that violence has killed and will kill again.

However, such a heaping-up of violent deeds would have a frigid effect, were it not for the note of incurable bitterness that continually makes itself heard, though often only a single word marks its presence, often a mere stroke of the verse, or a run-on line. It is in this that the *Iliad* is absolutely unique, in this bitterness that proceeds from tenderness and that spreads over the whole human race, impartial as sunlight. Never does the tone lose its coloring of bitterness; yet never does the bitterness drop into lamentation. Justice and love, which have hardly any place in this study of extremes and of unjust acts of violence, nevertheless bathe the work in their light without ever becoming noticeable themselves, except as a kind of accent. Nothing precious is scorned, whether or not death is its destiny; everyone's unhappiness is laid bare without dissimulation or disdain; no man is set above or below the condition common to all men; whatever is destroyed is regretted. Victors and vanquished are brought equally near us; under the same head, both are seen as counterparts of the poet, and the listener as well. If there is any difference, it is that the enemy's misfortunes are possibly more sharply felt.

> So he fell there, put to sleep in the sleep of bronze,
> Unhappy man, far from his wife, defending his own
>   people. . . .

And what accents echo the fate of the lad Achilles sold at
Lemnos!

> Eleven days he rejoiced his heart among those he
>   loved,
> Returning from Lemnos; the twelfth day, once more,
> God delivered him into the hands of Achilles,
> To him who had to send him, unwilling, to Hades.

And the fate of Euphorbus, who saw only a single day of war.

> Blood soaked his hair, the hair like to the Graces' . . .

When Hector is lamented:

> . . . guardian of chaste wives and little children. . . .

In these few words, chastity appears, dirtied by force, and child-
hood, delivered to the sword. The fountain at the gates of Troy
becomes an object of poignant nostalgia when Hector runs by, seeking to elude his doom:

> Close by there stood the great stone tanks,
> Handsomely built, where silk-gleaming garments
> Were washed clean by Troy's lovely daughters and
>   housewives
> In the old days of peace, long ago, when the Greeks
>   had not come.
> Past these did they run their race, pursued and pursuer.

The whole of the *Iliad* lies under the shadow of the greatest calamity
the human race can experience—the destruction of a city. This
calamity could not tear more at the heart had the poet been born in
Troy. But the tone is not different when the Achaeans are dying, far
from home.

   Insofar as this other life, the life of the living, seems calm and
full, the chief evocations of the world of peace are felt as pain:

> With the break of dawn and the rising of the day,
> On both sides arrows flew, men fell.
> But at the very hour that the woodcutter goes home to
>   fix his meal

> In the mountain valleys when his arms have had enough
> Of hacking great trees, and disgust rises in his heart,
> And the desire for sweet food seizes his entrails,
> At that hour, by their valor, the Danaans broke the front.

Whatever is not war, whatever war destroys or threatens, the *Iliad* wraps in poetry; the realities of war, never. No reticence veils the step from life to death:

> Then his teeth flew out; from two sides,
> Blood came to his eyes; the blood that from lips and
>   nostrils
> He was spilling, open-mouthed; death enveloped him in
>   its black cloud.

The cold brutality of the deeds of war is left undisguised; neither victors nor vanquished are admired, scorned, or hated. Almost always, fate and the gods decide the changing lot of battle. Within the limits fixed by fate, the gods determine with sovereign authority victory and defeat. It is always they who provoke those fits of madness, those treacheries, which are forever blocking peace; war is their true business; their only motives, caprice and malice. As for the warriors, victors or vanquished, those comparisons which liken them to beasts or things can inspire neither admiration nor contempt, but only regret that men are capable of being so transformed.

There may be, unknown to us, other expressions of the extraordinary sense of equity which breathes through the *Iliad;* certainly it has not been imitated. One is barely aware that the poet is a Greek and not a Trojan. The tone of the poem furnishes a direct clue to the origin of its oldest portions; history perhaps will never be able to tell us more. If one believes with Thucydides that eighty years after the fall of Troy, the Achaeans in their turn were conquered, one may ask whether these songs, with their rare references to iron, are not the songs of a conquered people, of whom a few went into exile. Obliged to live and die, "very far from the homeland," like the Greeks who fell before Troy, having lost their cities like the Trojans, they saw their own image both in the conquerors, who had been their fathers, and in the conquered, whose misery was like their own. They could still see the Trojan war over that brief span of years in its true light, unglossed by pride or shame. They could look at it as conquered and as conquerors simultaneously, and so perceive what neither conqueror nor conquered ever saw, for both were blinded. Of course, this is mere fancy; one can see such distant times only in fancy's light.

In any case, this poem is a miracle. Its bitterness is the only justifiable bitterness, for it springs from the subjections of the human spirit to force, that is, in the last analysis, to matter. This subjection is the common lot, although each spirit will bear it differently, in proportion to its own virtue. No one in the *Iliad* is spared by it, as no one on earth is. No one who succumbs to it is by virtue of this fact regarded with contempt. Whoever, within his own soul and in human relations, escapes the dominion of force is loved but loved sorrowfully because of the threat of destruction that constantly hangs over him.

Such is the spirit of the only true epic the Occident possesses. The *Odyssey* seems merely a good imitation, now of the *Iliad,* now of Oriental poems; the *Aeneid* is an imitation which, however brilliant, is disfigured by frigidity, bombast, and bad taste. The *chansons de geste,* lacking the sense of equity, could not attain greatness: in the *Chanson de Roland,* the death of an enemy does not come home to either author or reader in the same way as does the death of Roland.

Attic tragedy, or at any rate the tragedy of Aeschylus and Sophocles, is the true continuation of the epic. The conception of justice enlightens it, without ever directly intervening in it; here force appears in its coldness and hardness, always attended by effects from whose fatality neither those who use it nor those who suffer it can escape; here the shame of the coerced spirit is neither disguised, nor enveloped in facile pity, nor held up to scorn; here more than one spirit bruised and degraded by misfortune is offered for our admiration. The Gospels are the last marvelous expression of the Greek genius, as the *Iliad* is the first: here the Greek spirit reveals itself not only in the injunction given mankind to seek above all other goods, "the kingdom and justice of our Heavenly Father," but also in the fact that human suffering is laid bare, and we see it in a being who is at once divine and human. The accounts of the Passion show that a divine spirit, incarnate, is changed by misfortune, trembles before suffering and death, feels itself, in the depths of its agony, to be cut off from man and God. The sense of human misery gives the Gospels that accent of simplicity that is the mark of the Greek genius, and that endows Greek tragedy and the *Iliad* with all their value. Certain phrases have a ring strangely reminiscent of the epic, and it is the Trojan lad dispatched to Hades, though he does not wish to go, who comes to mind when Christ says to Peter: "Another shall gird thee and carry thee whither thou wouldst not." This accent cannot be separated from the idea that inspired the Gospels, for the sense of human misery is a pre-condition of justice and love. He who does not realize to what extent shifting fortune and necessity hold in subjection every human spirit, cannot regard as fellow-creatures nor love as he loves himself those whom chance separated from him by an abyss. The variety of constraints pressing upon man give rise to the illusion of several distinct species that cannot communicate. Only he who has measured the dominion of force, and knows how not to respect it, is capable of love and justice.

The relations between destiny and the human soul, the extent to which each soul creates its own destiny, the question of what elements in the soul are transformed by merciless necessity as it tailors the soul to fit the requirements of shifting fate, and of what elements can on the other hand be preserved, through the exercise of virtue and through grace—this whole question is fraught with temptations to falsehood, temptations that are positively enhanced by pride, by shame, by hatred, contempt, indifference, by the will to oblivion or to ignorance. Moreover, nothing is so rare as to see misfortune fairly portrayed; the tendency is either to treat the unfortunate person as though catastrophe were his natural vocation, or to ignore the effects of misfortune on the soul, to assume, that is, that the soul can suffer and remain unmarked by it, can fail, in fact, to be recast in misfortune's image. The Greeks, generally speaking, were endowed with spiritual force that allowed them to avoid self-deception. The rewards of this were great; they discovered how to achieve in all their acts the greatest lucidity, purity, and simplicity. But the spirit that was transmitted from the *Iliad* to the Gospels by way of the tragic poets never jumped the borders of Greek civilization; once Greece was destroyed, nothing remained of this spirit but pale reflections.

Both the Romans and the Hebrews believed themselves to be exempt from the misery that is the common human lot. The Romans saw their country as the nation chosen by destiny to be mistress of the world; with the Hebrews, it was their God who exalted them and they retained their superior position just as long as they obeyed Him. Strangers, enemies, conquered peoples, subjects, slaves, were objects of contempt to the Romans; and the Romans had no epics, no tragedies. In Rome gladiatorial fights took the place of tragedy.

With the Hebrews, misfortune was a sure indication of sin and hence a legitimate object of contempt; to them a vanquished enemy was abhorrent to God himself and condemned to expiate all sorts of crimes—this is a view that makes cruelty permissible and indeed indispensable. And no text of the Old Testament strikes a note comparable to the note heard in the Greek epic, unless it be certain parts of the book of Job. Throughout twenty centuries of Christianity, the Romans and the Hebrews have been admired, read, imitated, both in deed and word; their masterpieces have yielded an appropriate quotation every time anybody had a crime he wanted to justify.

Furthermore, the spirit of the Gospels was not handed down in a pure state from one Christian generation to the next. To undergo suffering and death joyfully was from the very beginning considered a sign of grace in the Christian martyrs—as though grace could do more for a human being than it could for Christ. Those who believe that God himself, once he became man, could not face the harshness of destiny without a long tremor of anguish, should have understood that the only people who can give the impression of having risen to a higher plane, who seem superior to ordinary human misery, are the people who resort to the aids of illusion, exaltation, fanaticism, to conceal the harshness of destiny from their own eyes. The man who does not wear the armor of the lie cannot experience force without being touched by it to the very soul. Grace can prevent this touch from corrupting him, but it cannot spare him the wound. Having forgotten it too well, Christian tradition can only rarely recover that simplicity that renders so poignant every sentence in the story of the Passion. On the other hand, the practice of forcible proselytization threw a veil over the effects of force on the souls of those who used it.

In spite of the brief intoxication induced at the time of the Renaissance by the discovery of Greek literature, there has been, during the course of twenty centuries, no revival of the Greek genius. Something of it was seen in Villon, in Shakespeare, Cervantes, Moliere, and—just once—in Racine. The bones of human suffering are exposed in *L'Ecole des Femmes* and in *Phèdre,* love being the context—a strange century indeed, which took the opposite view from that of the epic period, and would only acknowledge human suffering in the context of love, while it insisted on swathing with glory the effects of force in war and in politics. To the list of writers given above, a few other names might be added. But nothing the peoples of Europe have produced is worth the first known poem that appeared among them. Perhaps they will yet rediscover the epic genius, when they learn that there is no refuge from fate, learn not to admire force, not to hate the enemy, nor to scorn the unfortunate. How soon this will happen is another question.

14

The Meaning of Law
in the Book of Job

Herbert Fingarette

The law, its themes, concepts, images, and language, permeates
the Book of Job.[1] Moreover, the Book of Job is unique among the
Hebrew-Christian canonical texts in the manner of its concern with
law. Other canonical texts are dogmatic: they promulgate substantive law, God's particular laws or commands; or they make eloquent
but relatively brief and cryptic assertions as to the nature of God's
law for us.[2] Job, however, is analytical, philosophical. Even in so
legalistic a culture as that of ancient Israel, Job is the only
canonical work devoted to an extended, radically critical exploration of such fundamental concepts as law, justice, and retribution in
relation to the human context, the divine context, and the way in
which these two contexts interpenetrate one another. What is surprising is that in the commentaries of Job we find very little
systematic analysis directed to the conception of law as central to
the argument of the book.[3]

Yet, provocatively, although the Book of Job is explicitly cast
in the concepts, language, and imagery of the law, it is presented in
the mode of a dramatic poem rather than in the mode of
philosophical argument or in the form of a legal brief. The poetic
dramatic mode is no mere façade; this work is widely acknowledged
as surpassingly great in the history of literature. The Book of Job
towers among the great sacred texts.[4] It is intense, it is grand, it is
ruthless in its scorn for falsehood and sham. The medium of the
message is itself part of the message: the Book of Job is antilegalist.
The poem teaches, instead, a passionate personal integrity as the
ground essential to achieving an ultimate wisdom and salvation
that reveal law as an essentially human, not divine, enterprise.

This essay from *Hastings Law Journal* 29 (July 1978): 1581–1617 is
reprinted by permission.

As a corollary, the book teaches candid awe and humility before the inexhaustible mysteries, marvels, and terrors revealed when, on occasion, the tempests of our mortal crisis rip the veil from before our soul and reality thunders forth and shakes us. Then, as in terrible flashes of lightning, we see with the eye of our own illuminated consciousness; then we divine existence, even though we do not understand it. In this book, God speaks to us through suffering, through dreams and visions and songs in the night. Revelation, not litigation, is the way to reconciliation with the ultimate reality of our world. But this idea we see only after having pressed to the limit, along with Job, that familiar, even orthodox vision of existence as ultimately lawlike, of God as ultimate lawgiver.

Old Testament religion is one of the great sources of the idea that a primary mode, perhaps *the* primary mode, of our relation to God is that of responsibility to His law. According to this view, God's Will is our Law;[5] the authority even of human law lies in its claim to express, or at least to implement, God's Will. The idea of the pious man who suffers is found in Babylonian[6] and other Near Eastern[7] religions, and in this regard the story of Job—without the theme of law—was of a familiar pattern far beyond Israelite culture. But the life and culture of the Israelites became increasingly permeated by priestly legalism.[8] From the Genesis story of the very first human beings, which centers on disobedience to God's Will and the punishment that results, to the Commandments and many auxiliary laws and regulations elaborated upon by the Lord in the course of Old Testament history, there is a widening, deepening, and intensifying consciousness of the human relation to God as one that is defined and embodied in His Will as our law. Israel itself is bound by a covenant:[9] Yahweh set out His laws for Israel, and Israel undertakes to live "righteously," that is, to live according to God's Law. Keeping the covenant assures God's blessings, whereas failing to do so assures His retribution. This orthodoxy, though at first defined with reference to the nation, later comes to be interpreted as referring to the individual as well.[10]

The idea of existence as framed by God's Law also emerges in the doctrines of great Christian thinkers, both Catholic and Protestant.[11] It still permeates Jewish and Christian folk attitudes today.

A perennially troublesome issue for this view has arisen specifically in connection with the concept of retribution, the concept that we are to be punished for unlawful ways and rewarded for uprightness. To many people the doctrine of retribution has seemed a self-evident corollary of the belief in God the Lawgiver, just as it has seemed a corollary of human law.[12] But even before Job, true believers had raised the piercing query: why, then, do the wicked seem to prosper? And why do the righteous seem to suffer?[13]

Unbelievers may be inclined to stand aside, bemused by what seems to them a specious and unnecessary dilemma in the first place, because God Almighty, the Lawgiver, is to them either an unnecessary or positively misguided assumption. But it turns out that things, even so, are not that simple. Job has things to say to the unbeliever, too.

Certainly Job's three "comforters" insist that our life here on earth is ruled by God's law and His justice and that as a consequence He makes the righteous to prosper and the unrighteous to perish.[14] Job, too, has always believed this, and indeed this belief is what eventually motivates his challenges to God in the course of the dialogues.[15] The centrality throughout the debate of this belief in inevitable reward or retributive punishment may weaken the philosophical persuasiveness of it for readers in so irreligious, or at least so unorthodox, an age as ours. I believe we need to learn to appreciate the intellectual power of the friends' and Job's view; we need to see that it has an aspect of profound and necessary truth. I aim to show in this article that the doctrine of retribution is not an archaic naivete or a magical view of existence.[16]

On the other hand, we also need to learn to appreciate the inadequacy of this orthodoxy as an ultimate perspective on law, or on the divine. We need to understand the thundering challenge with which, in the end, the Lord addresses Job: "Who is this that darkeneth counsel by words without knowledge?"[17]

But here I have been talking of final things, and it is the voyage that gives sense and significance to the end. We must go back to the beginning, because the Book of Job is fraught with paradox. The logic of the entire affair is easily obscured. The very text itself is "probably more corrupt than that of any other biblical book."[18] So let us return to the beginning and pursue the case from the first moment when "the satan," the prosecutor,[19] accuses Job before Yahweh's court.

The book begins by setting the ultimate issue for us. That issue must remain unknown to Job and his friends if the prosecutor is to develop the evidence. Therefore the ultimate issue is defined in secret; that is, it is defined in a context that is sharply separated from the context of Job's ordeal. The book begins with a prologue.

The prologue,[20] based on folk legend, swiftly explains, in a selfconsciously folk-tale style, that once upon a time there was a great

and prosperous and pious man of Uz, named Job, who was mentioned as a very model by the Lord Yahweh himself, to his assembled
court in heaven. Yahweh callenges the satan, His prosecutor, and
asks him, "Have you considered my servant Job? You will find no
one like him on earth, a man of blameless and upright life, who fears
God and sets his face against wrongdoing." The satan takes up the
challenge, puts a new twist on the facts, and accuses: "Has not Job
good reason to be God-fearing?" He then points out how God has
protected Job from all dangers, piled up his possessions, and
showered him with honor, good fortune, and great family.[21] It is no
more than rational self-interest to follow God's law under the circumstances. The evidence that this behavior is motivated by self-
interest and not genuine piety is easily obtainable, says the satan:
"Only take away all these good things from Job, and I'll stand
pledge if Job doesn't end up cursing you, my Lord."[22] "Make him
ache and suffer in his very bones and flesh and skin! You'll see, I
swear!"[23]

The issue, in short, is this: true perfection before God, blameless
following of His law, should be selfless. It should be done simply out
of commitment in good faith to the Lord:

> What then O Israel, does the Lord your God ask of you?—Only
> to fear the Lord your God, to conform to all his ways, to love
> him and to serve him with all your heart and soul. This you will
> do by keeping the commandments of the Lord and his
> statutes . . . which I give you this day for your good.[24]

Thus said the Lord; but the satan has now presented a radical
challenge to the entire enterprise. It is one thing to shower blessings
on those who are truly devoted to one; it is quite another to buy
pretended devotion by promising rewards and long life to people
who are essentially concerned only for their own pleasures and their
own skins. It is thereupon agreed that Job will be tested. But the
issue is really bigger than that. Job is declared by Yahweh to be a
model of human piety. So it is really Yahweh's entire enterprise that
the satan's counterchallenge puts on trial, though of course
Yahweh, in His wisdom, initiated the affair. If the model Job is a
fraud, Yahweh's relation to the people has failed. If Job is vindicated, we shall have seen the difference between rational self-
interest and true love and fear of God.

It should be remarked, before going further, that the issue from
this heavenly perspective is *not* one that centers on law. It is

acknowledged on all sides, and indeed certified by Yahweh himself, that Job is a man blameless and upright in his *conduct*; the question raised by the satan concerns Job's *motives*. The issue is thus sharply defined in terms of the state of the soul rather than, as in law, the outer man. We, the audience, witnesses to the heavenly deliberations, are allowed at once to see the great issue at trial.[25]

Yahweh authorizes the satan to deprive Job of every possible external good in life except his very life and consciousness. Family, possessions, honor, physical health—all are destroyed, except that Job still lives and is still conscious of himself as one who was upright and true to his God. This formerly great chieftain is now, both literally and symbolically, on the garbage heap beyond the borders of the community.

In the folk-tale prologue, Job—"patient Job"—endures and prays:

> Naked I came from the womb.
> Naked I shall return whence I came.
> The Lord gives and the Lord takes away.
> Blessed be the name of the Lord.[26]

So we have our answer. Job's faith and devotion to the Lord did not depend on rewards. But this answer, true enough in its way, does not give us the kind of answer we want and need. We now know from his behavior that Job's motives were not self-interested and that his worship of God has its own integrity and was not the result of ulterior motives. But the point of the test was to shift attention from behavior to motives, which is to say that we want to understand Job, not merely to observe him. Why does Job still bless God? What are his motives? What is the issue as he sees it? How can he bring himself to such acceptance, given that life under such a God now must seem so arbitrary and mean a thing? Is Job just a thoughtless, blind worshipper? Or did he have inward struggles? Did he come to terms with the truth or succeed in running away from it or in camouflaging it? How does a model man live through such a crisis inwardly able to bless God rather than curse Him? What rational questions, what inner debates, what emotions, what impulse to rebel, and what grounds for final acquiescence play a role in such an ordeal?

We need insight to see with our own inner eye of the soul the reality of this truth. Only if we, too, go through Job's ordeal, at least vicariously, can we be with him at the end when, as he says, he at last *sees* with the eye of religious vision what he had formerly only heard second hand. Only then will *we* see. So far, we have only been told about the bare fact.

And so now the folk-tale characters leave the stage, and the painted backdrop is raised to reveal suddenly the inner world of Job's agony. There is a radical shift from one literary mode to another, from pseudo-primitivist folk-tale to intensely dramatic and passionate poetry, from swift-moving narrative to elaborately reflective and many-sided examination of the issues, from the language of naiveté to the language of heart's agony and blasphemy, and from myth time to the burning present. This shift, and the gap it establishes, serves to induce a kind of aesthetic repression of the prologue, a repression that reinforces the story line: Job and his friends are utterly absorbed in the ordeal as they experience and understand it; no suspicion of the real "cause of action" and the ultimate issue can arise to distort the results of the test.

And so, too, by virtue of the aesthetic repression effect, is the reader's consciousness dominated by Job's and the friends' understanding of the events. Any shadow of consciousness that this scenario is a test of Job's disinterested good faith before the heavenly court would fatally corrupt the experiential validity of the test. For the test has become to see, to live through, vicariously so far as the reader is concerned, the movement from total despair and misery to complete acceptance. Indeed it may be just because the poem-drama so fascinates and dominates attention that many commentators have mistakenly taken the central issue to be that which is defined *within* the poem, the issue as defined by Job and his friends, and have ignored or underestimated the truly central issue, as defined in heaven, and on which the whole book turns.[27]

So now the poem proper begins. Despair, anger, bitterness, fierce attitudes, awful challenges, and radical, tough-minded thought are the stuff of this ordeal. False piety, meekness, or lip service to religious platitudes will not do for Job. In the beginning, it is Job's sheer despair that shatters the silence.

Job's reaction to disaster is to curse the day he was born.[28] But suicidal attitudes, whether retrospective fantasies or prospective actualities, are evasions. The three friends who have come to comfort him will not let him settle for such attitudes. They begin, early on, to insist that he, who has been so strong in regard to the ordeals of others, must be strong enough to face the issues in his own case.[29] Whereupon they define the issues in terms of God's justice, the legalistic terms familiar in the Israelite thought of the epoch:[30] If we walk in His way, observe His law, then of course we prosper; if we stray, however, He makes us suffer, and we perish.[31] Therefore, Job's suffering may not be viewed merely as misery; it must be viewed as punishment. Job must have failed to act righteously, that is, according to law.[32] And until Job does so view his suffering, confesses his guilt, accepts his punishment as such, and repents, he is compounding his guilt, and even more punishment will accrue.[33] For after all, perjury or even evasive silence are in themselves contempt of the injunction that we shall fear and love God and that we shall stand witness in full truth and loyalty toward Him. These precepts, as Job's friends remind him, the wise ancients taught us.[34] They persistently press Job: be honest, confess and repent.[35]

This perspective does indeed arouse Job, even provoke him, out of his blindly suicidal despair. Though intermittently still uttering despairing groans, Job ever more emphatically and outspokenly picks up the challenge. But his response to this challenge is not quite what was expected. He does accept the challenge to face the truth, and he also accepts the legitimacy of the presupposed framework within which the truth is to be understood—the framework of God's law, of His justice, and of consequent human guilt and punishment, or righteousness and reward. But the conclusion that Job reaches is not at all what was intended by the friends.

"O if only my miseries would be weighed in the scales of justice!" he cries, they would outweigh anything wrong I could have done.[36] It is incomprehensible, but God is persecuting me.[37] Why was I ever born? Why does He not finish the job and mercifully put me to death?[38] What have I done to deserve this? You, my friends, have betrayed me: you spout words and theories and chop logic.[39] I can recognize truth from falsehood, right from wrong. You have put my integrity in question. This quality you may not take from me; no one can do that.[40] How can you look at my suffering and blithely say I deserved this? You don't face realities; you just talk old platitudes that in this case are lies.[41]

The friends insist. And, because in their view God does necessarily reward the righteous and punish the wicked, they charge Job with blasphemy for maintaining that the law is on his side as against God! They even accuse Job of specific sins, with no evidence, in order to defend their theory.[42]

Instead of acquiescing, Job presses his understanding of the facts, but with ever increasing explicitness and elaboration of the implications. Indeed Job increasingly commits himself to the proposition that he is not alone in his unfair suffering. In this world we see it all around us, he alleges: it is the wicked who prosper, and it is the innocent, whom they exploit, who suffer.[43] God, the Almighty Ruler, is unjust generally, not merely in Job's case.

Throughout, as we see, Job never really questions the underlying premises of his complaint, the premises he shares with the friends. The world can only be understood in terms of God's law for us, and thus, he believes, in terms of rewarding the righteous and punishing the wicked. And yet, incomprehensibly, the facts show that the rule of law has gone awry. God acts unjustly. Obviously the dilemma arises because he is still assessing the matter in terms of law and the principle of necessary retribution and reward.

Job's premises can lead logically in only one direction: go to law. And Job is the very man to pursue the truth as he sees it in the way that logic requires. Yet he despairs: even if a man would try to appeal his fate and argue his case, God will not answer! How could one summon Him to law?[44] How could one force Him to answer one's charges? Why does He not state His case against me openly, draw up an indictment? I would proudly respond to the indictment. I would present my defense in full, nothing more nor less than the record of my entire life.[45] He, who knows all, should be my witness in my defense.[46] And yet, even if He were to appear, how could I choose the proper arguments and answer His questions, when I am terrified by His awfulness and stand here crushed by His power?[47] If only there could be an arbitrator who could assume authority over us both and hear the case![48] Or if only I had someone strong and free to serve as my advocate![49] I have been on the right side of the law all my life, and I charge that the Judge has turned not merely prosecutor but unjust persecutor![50]

There is courage here, but there is incoherence and blasphemy too. Job's legalistic logic, as he himself sees, leads to its own *reductio ad absurdum;* his integrity, given his beliefs, leads to a kind of moral delirium. And it is his utter truthfulness before God that leads to blasphemy.

It is absolutely essential to be aware that in all this Job is not an inherently presumptuous man before God. "Why do You follow me," he calls to the Lord, "and catch me out in every little thing? I am Your creature, made by You and totally in Your power to the end. Why should You torment Your own creature this way?"[51] He has no false modesty, but neither does he have false pride. Job asks, "What is man that thou makest much of him?"[52] The echo of the psalm[53] whose language he borrows serves as background to Job's humility. The psalm praised God for making His insignificant creatures to be almost as angels in dignity. Job uses the same language but turns it around to challenge God for taking such insignificant creatures as worthy to be targets of His wrath. Although Job apparently rejects the teaching of the psalm, nonetheless the poet, in having Job speak so, has tacitly framed Job's ordeal within the perspective of that psalm and has thereby highlighted the issue of dignity, of the near-divine dignity that God's poor vulnerable creatures can have. And it is this dignity which radiates from Job in his ordeal, the dignity that his integrity affords him, even sitting on the dung-heap, a poor, miserable, intellectually confused, morally disarrayed, physically pustulant, and repellent old man.

The basic conditions that generate Job's dilemma should be summarized in an analytical way so that we will be able to exhibit both the full force of it and the meaning of the resolution. There are, specifically, four conditions that conspire to place him in this dilemma.

First, as we have seen, Job claims complete integrity before the Lord. The Lord's attitude and behavior may be puzzling, but Job's good faith commitment to the Lord is total and unconditional. He will be true to the Lord, and ultimately he will be vindicated before the Lord, Judge of all. He insists on this eventuality, again and again.

Second, we must understand that Job is correct in insisting on his past and present integrity. We know that he is certified at the very outset, by Yahweh Himself, as a blameless servant. But even aside from this, Job's words ring with truth and sincerity. Further-more, and most central to the meaning of his ordeal, were Job not utterly and truly convinced the law was on his side, he would have every reason to follow an easier line. He could follow his friends' ad-vice, confess to the most likely sin, repent, beg forgiveness, and, having now taken a certain amount of punishment, be released from further suffering. After all, Job's fear of the Almighty's wrath and his belief in the Almighty's immeasurable powers to reward far sur-passes any other motives Job might have, except where these con-flict with the demands of his rocklike integrity before God.

The third element of his predicament follows from the firm belief, held by Job as well as his friends, that life on God's earth is life under law, that those who obey God's laws are to be rewarded, and those who transgress are to be punished. It follows logically that there must be a mistake. No, not even a mistake, for inasmuch as God is almighty and all-knowing, this punishment must be willful injustice. This seems especially so when we take into account the more general observation by a candid Job that he is not the only upright person to suffer. He presses the question: have we not all seen wicked people prosper? No wonder that Job, being forced to contemplate God as unjust, feels his dilemma to be unbearable!

Fourth, because the framework of existence is one of law, Job instinctively appeals in the language of law for a personal hearing from the Lord, a hearing at which Job or his advocate could receive the indictment, plead his case, call witnesses, and demonstrate to the Lord the error and injustice in what the Lord has caused to happen. The more this self-incriminating blasphemy is elaborated, the more it also seems sheer madness.

It is the combination of these circumstances that gives power and dignity and necessity to Job's spiritual crisis. But to what extent is Job's dilemma real for us? To what extent can we share, even vicariously, in his ideal? Is there not a quaint archaicism about the notion that God makes the wicked, and only the wicked, to suffer; and that He rewards only the virtuous? Once we readers, by an act of aesthetic suspension of belief, grant to Job and his friends their naive credulity, the dilemmas it creates can elicit our sympathy. But can we truly have empathy, can we participate even vicariously? For many modern readers, the whirlwind at the end of Job can seem more like a tempest in a teapot. Have not even theists in modern times got beyond such primitive notions? Can we take seriously the idea that God's law for us implies inevitable rewards and punishments? And, if not, can even the believer really take the Book of Job seriously?

My own belief is that we are wrong if we are patronizing or condescending to Job and his friends. We should not confuse their technological and scientific primitiveness with spiritual primitiveness. The doctrine that under God's law, He punishes the disobedient and rewards those obedient to His law is not merely an archaic popular belief, a belief in magic, or a tenet of some special theological doctrine. One is tempted to assert that disinterested obedience to law should suffice in itself, at least ideally. Why are Job and his friends so convinced that this is not enough and that rewards and punishments are a necessary corollary of law, even of God's law?

Up to this point I have purposely stated the problem without differentiating such notions as piety, integrity, righteousness, uprightness and obedience. Now, however, I want to press what I consider to be the fundamental issue: the nature of obedience. I propose to restate the Old Testament theme that we are given God's commandments and that our love and fear of God with all our heart and soul is realized in "keeping the commandments of the Lord and his statutes."[54] That demand can be restated in this way: our central spiritual task results from God's laying upon us the requirement that our will shall be in conformity to His Will.

This task is not necessarily a moral task. It has a moral dimension if God's Will is conceived of as a good will. And in the Old Testament, there surely is a moral significance to God's Will; but what needs emphasis here is that whatever the moral status of God's Will, God rules through His Will, that is, the dominion of His Will over ours. The question of reward and punishment has generally been thought to be linked to the moral aspect of the situation, but I think this analysis is in error. We need to recognize the phenomenon of the dominion of one will over another as a distinctive and much more general relationship. Even if it be an evil will that dominates another will, the relation of one will dominating another remains constant. Even more general is the concept of human will being subordinate, whether subject to a dominant personal will or to some other suitable force such as, for example, law or custom. In any case, I want to bring out how and why punishment and reward are inextricably linked to dominion over human will[55] and, more specifically, why it is that the assumption that God is Almighty, far from allowing God to forego punishment and reward to achieve His Will, instead makes the link all the more indissoluble. And I can only allude here to the fact that what we discover to be true of dominion over all is *a fortiori* true of all systems of government.[56]

The concept of dominion over the will and the phenomenon to which it refers are very familiar to us. When one examines the concept, however, a number of paradoxical implications quickly emerge. When the dominion over human will is exercised by an Almighty Will the paradox intensifies. But inasmuch as the basic paradoxes are quite general, we can develop them in more homely and less controversial contexts than that of the Divine Commands and subsequently apply the results of our analysis in the latter context.

Suppose, for instance, that your will is subject to my will. I am, perhaps, your superior officer in the military, your supervisor on the job, or a judge issuing an order to you. The first thing to notice is that I am exercising power over your will, not your body. The difference is this: if I grab you and hold you, I am exercising power over your body, but if I give you an order, the immediate object of my power is your will. Instead of being subject to bodily force, you are to act of your own will as I order you to act. If I give you an order, this act presupposes that you have the power to act on it of your own will. But this act also necessarily presupposes that you have the power to disobey me, to exert your will in a way contrary to what I command. In short, the first paradox of exercising power over someone's will is the presupposition that the subject has the power to disobey.

This paradox necessarily holds true of God's laws, too. God may command us to act in certain ways. In doing so He exercises His dominion over our will. But this exercise of dominion, if it is to make any sense, implies that He does not physically compel us. He requires that our will conform to His Will. And this requirement in turn only makes sense if he leaves us the power to act of our own will, that is, the power to obey or to disobey.

So it is that the central drama of Old Testament history, from the forbidden tree in Eden to the last of the prophets and chroniclers, springs out of this paradox of the dominion over will. It is the drama of the disobedient children of God. But this is a drama inherent in any relationship that turns on exercising dominion over the will rather than over behavior directly.

Now we have to go farther into the paradoxes of dominion over the will because, depending on whether the subordinate will obeys or defies the dominant will, new and differing paradoxes arise. Suppose, first, that you do not comply with my order as your commanding officer. What remains to be done? If I do nothing then my order turns out to have had no force, no power at all over your will. I said, "Do so and so." But you do not do it. Because I do nothing about it subsequently, there is neither constraint of your power at the time of the act nor any constraining consequence for your future power. So the verbal form of what I said may have been that of a command, but apparently it was not seriously meant as an order, or perhaps I changed my mind after giving it and decided it should not be enforced. In any case, although I say you must do it, your power to do as you willed is at no point curbed. But then I do not dominate your will, I do not really exercise power over it; I only talk as if I did.

There is only one way out of this paradox if there is to be such a thing as a command or law having force as such, and it is the universal, age-old way: I must in some way constrain, curb, or humble your will because of your disobedient act. It must be a constraint on your will subsequent to the act because it is essential that you have the power of will at the time the act.

To constrain, humble, or crush the will is, of course, the very core of what is classically meant by suffering. To suffer is to endure that over which our will has no power, that which is against our will. To suffer is to be the patient, not the agent. "Behold, we count them happy which endure. Ye have heard of the patience of Job . . . ."[57]

How does one humble a person's will and make a person suffer? Among the universally effective forms of humbling the will are the infliction of physical pain and the deprivation of access to loved ones or home, of liberty, and of honor or property. These acts are ubiquitous forms of punishment because they are generally contrary to what human beings will. If people generally willed these things, they would not be thought of as suffering. You do not really punish masochists by imposing the kind of pain they relish. Exile would not punish one who longed to shake the home dust from his feet. It is because most of us would will not to be in pain that the infliction of pain is institutionalized as reliably punitive, and so, too, for exile, close confinement, loss of property, and public disgrace.

So the second paradox of dominion over the will is that the dominator's hand is forced; the logic of the enterprise dominates the dominator. There is no meaningful alternative to punishing the disobedient, making them suffer for their disobedience. It is not that punishment necessarily deters future disobedience; it is that the idea of laying down a law, order, or command loses its significance if not conjoined with the idea that the consequence of disobedience will be punishment, humbling of the will.

This paradox intensifies when we assume that God's central relation to us is expressed in terms of His Will or Law. Then even the Almighty is bound by this necessity intrinsic to law. He has no option. He must punish us by making us suffer for disobedience. It becomes empty verbiage if I say that God exercises dominon over my will, that He commands me, if I also acknowledge that I have the power of my own will to act contrary to what God enjoins and if I aver that, if and when I exercise my own will, he does not intend to impose constraints over my will as a consequence. This situation amounts to saying that He leaves me free to do as I will.

The third and largest paradox of dominion over the will is that, because the dominator is dominated by the necessity of imposing punishment, the subordinate will ultimately gains a certain crucial element of control over the dominator, even if the dominator is God. If I will to disobey the Lord, I compel him to punish me. In the case of fallible and finite lawgivers, the element of their fallibility enters, and this element weakens my power. A human lawgiver must, in general at least, attempt to punish, but any of a number of eventualities may intervene to prevent the punishment. But for an allpowerful God who cannot be turned from his purpose, who carries out what He decides,[58] there are no such alternatives once He has decided what His Will is. God then has no choice but to punish me if I disobey. And whether or not I disobey is of course up to me. To suppose otherwise makes the concept of issuing commands incoherent and unintelligible.

A fourth and final result, more interesting yet, is that if I choose to comply with the Lord's Will, He must not punish me; He must not make me suffer as a consequence. He must, in effect, reward me. This idea needs a brief further explanation. Imagine that a professor says to the student: "You are required to turn in a term paper by next week; if you fail to do so, you get an F. On the other hand, if you do turn it in on time, you also get an F." Now what possible sense can be made of that statement? It is an absurd, bizarre way of talking. But if the professor is serious, what we must take it to mean is that the term paper is irrelevant. The professor merely talks as if the F were in some way a consequence of the paper. But what the student is in effect being told is that regardless of whether the paper is turned in, the professor has resolved, for reasons as yet unexplained, that he will give that student an F. The true meaning of the statement is that the paper will have no effect on the grade. By contrast, if one really means to impose a demand upon a person's will, to require a term paper for example, one must be understood to intend to act subsequently in such a way that it will make a difference whether there is obedience; otherwise the command loses its sense.

So, too, even if it is the Lord commanding us how to act, our compliance or noncompliance has to make a difference. Noncompliance must have undesirable consequences; otherwise we are really being left free. But if it is to make a difference whether we comply, it must be the case that the consequence of compliance is that we are not made to suffer, that our will is not constrained. But to say my will is in some respect not constrained, curbed, frustrated, or humbled, amounts to saying that my will is in that regard accomplished or that I achieve what I will. That proposition amounts to saying that as a consequence of obedience I am rewarded for my obedience. For, after all, reward is but the complement of suffering. Reward is the fulfillment rather than the frustration of will in some respect, or it is not reward at all from the subject's standpoint.

It may seem at first that one could escape this logic by distinguishing between moral law, with the consequent moral character of a particular deed, and enforced law, which implies that empirical consequences are visited upon us for our deed. In this view God's will merely establishes the objective norms by which to evaluate conduct. But we still face the fact that if no consequences eventuate, then whatever the right or wrong labels mean, they do not reflect any will on God's part as to how we shall act in this regard. It is unintelligible to say that God, or anyone, wills that someone should will rightly and, then, to assert further that the subordinate will is left the full power to act rightly or wrongly and that it is understood that nothing is ever to be done subsequently by God to affect the will of the subject favorably or unfavorably, depending on how the subject acted. So the proposition that God's commands are to be taken as moral norms but not as enforced by punishment and reward amounts to the odd proposition that God has in reality no will one way or another as to whether the subject shall act rightly or wrongly! If He does not have any will in this regard, why should we? We are left with nonsense.

So, I repeat, the oddity about the Lord's exercise of dominion over our will is that ultimately it puts Him in bond to us. We can, by our conduct, of our own will, manipulate and control His response. This irony is the logic of law, the inner meaning of dominion over a will. If I choose to disobey, I compel Him to punish; and, far more appealing, if I choose to obey, He is foreclosed from making me suffer for it. That is, He must gratify my will by rewarding me. This logic is not God's grace but His necessity. It is not the necessity of magic.[59] It is the necessity internal to the concept of the force of law. Because the Old Testament view is that God's all-powerful, all-seeing Will is at the very center of our existence as His creatures, and because the fear of God and the eschewing of evil as defined by His law is what gives ultimate meaning to that existence, it follows that, if I choose to keep my will in conformity with His commands, my will will be unconstrained or fulfilled. Therefore, I will in all significant ways prosper by being rewarded for obedience to His Will.

I am not, of course, saying that Job and his friends had developed precisely the analysis that I have been presenting. I have given an explicit analysis of what I believe was intuitively perceived by these thoughtful and religious men and by so many other religious persons in the Judeo-Christian tradition.[60] It is a truth that is readily blinked at by those who would at one and the same time hold to belief in God as just lawgiver and judge, and yet remain skeptical about the inevitable triumph of virtue over vice.

Given this insight, then, Job is inevitably driven to the highest pitch of moral despair and confusion. He feels that, if this is a world of law, then his suffering must signify either his guilt or God's failure justly to enforce the law. What does not yet enter Job's mind is the more profound logical possibility suggested by the observation that not only he, but other innocents, suffer in this world, and that the wicked often prosper. On the analysis that I have given, that observation implies that the concept of God-as-Lawgiver is incoherent and inapplicable to the reality of existence. Given lack of symmetry between righteousness and reward, and between wickedness and punishment, the concept of God's injustice loses sense along with the concept of God's justice, because these concepts can only make sense in the context of law, and that concept becomes incoherent where there is no such symmetry in a world ruled by the Almighty. It is this logically implied truth—the irrelevance of the concept of law in relation to God—that Job will eventually see as an experiential revelation.

But we had left Job in that strange abyss of despair in which he charges God with injustice, and yet paradoxically claims confidence that his case will be judged, and judged justly. His faith in God remains, and so does his loyalty, though his logic is hopelessly against him. He has pressed the issues to the limit; the friends, far from succeeding in their aims, have only succeeded in prodding and provoking him into this explicit allegation against God and defense of his own integrity.

It is important to note that by this point Job has ceased to address God directly[61] and has lost hope of a direct response. His efforts on his own have failed, and he has recognized this personal failure. Nevertheless, he maintains his integrity.

Suddenly there appears on the scene a young man, Elihu, unannounced, who was never mentioned prior to this time. He is bursting with the message and succor he brings. He charges Job with presumptuousness: Job, a mere man, accuses the Lord of purposely perverting Justice! What a positive thirst for irreverence![62] Of course we and Job have already recognized this much. Job's agony occurs in part precisely because "though I am in the right, I am condemned out of my own mouth for saying so!"[63]

But Elihu is a transitional figure. Although he expresses many of the now familiar arguments and attitudes, he also introduces important new ones that are not necessarily consistent with the old. In a number of instances he reasserts familiar views and attitudes, but he puts them in a new perspective. Elihu insists that God is just,[64] but his insistence takes on a different color when he takes up a rhetorical question that Job had earlier raised: "If I have sinned, how do I injure Thee?"[65] Elihu repeats this question with a new context and emphasis: "Look up at the sky and then consider, observe the rainclouds towering above you: How does it touch Him if you have sinned? However many your misdeeds, what does it mean to Him? If you do right what good do you bring Him, or what does He gain from you?" And then Elihu gives a flat answer: "Your wickedness touches only men, such as you are; the right that you do affects none but mortal man."[66] So God's justice, or whatever it is, is not a matter of law, because human obedience or disobedience does not touch Him but only human beings.

Elihu, the young man, also announces that wisdom comes in suffering,[67] which not only is a strange thing for a young man to say but contrasts sharply with the idea that suffering signifies guilt. Elihu says we must reach the depths of suffering, hopelessness, and helplessness before God may send a being to intercede or to ransom us for a new life.[68]

This idea, again, is a new twist on an old idea. Job himself had earlier expressed the faith that he would be vindicated by a *goel,* an avenger or ransomer.[69] But Elihu shifts the emphasis, and the transaction takes on a new meaning. Now the suffering is portrayed not as mere grievance to be avenged or righted; it is instead the very holy medium through which God transmits His teaching, and it is only when all hope is abandoned that the message can be effective and the *goel* at last appear.

This teaching raises a puzzle that we must pause to examine. The teaching that we become wise through suffering, and the teaching that we need an intercessor, are familiar enough. But we need to understand how and why this is so. It will not suffice to view these requirements as arbitrary, even sadistic, rules of the game. There is here an intelligible internal necessity, a necessity and a meaning that are again linked to the concept of the will. What is central in the notion that we become wise through suffering is the truth that suffering is, as has been said earlier, the humbling of the will. To suffer is to be compelled to endure, undergo, and experience the humbled will, rather than to be able to act and to accomplish one's will.

The wisdom taught by suffering is the wisdom learned in living, not in books; it is the experience of the finitude and fallibility of the personal will, and also, in the perspective of human morality, of its ultimate impotence and defeat. The message of suffering is thus implicit in suffering itself; it is not a lesson only contingently associated with and conveyed through suffering. The experience gives wisdom when we see the fact for what it is, when we experience the humbled will and see at last the will as humble, inherently finite, and fallible, and when we accept this truth in our very bones and not merely in theory. We can obscure the truth of suffering by inventing false theories to explain away the humbling of the will. We explain it away as a contingent affair, an error, or a failure on our part that can be corrected and obviated by some further appropriate act of our own will.

This wisdom is basic to teachings other than that of the Old Testament Book of Job; it is at the core of the wisdom of the Bhagavad-Gita, Buddhism, Lao Tzu, Confucius, and the teaching of Jesus as well.[70] It is especially relevant to Old Testament theology because of the role of God as Lawgiver. For, as I have pointed out, a deeper implication of this notion is that we human beings have a way of subjecting God to our will and thus infallibly achieving our will. All we need to do is obey His law; by so doing we compel Him to make us prosper.

Elihu does not explain all this, but he announces it. God's message comes in suffering; an appreciation of the meaning of the message comes only when we despair of our own powers, thus accepting the inevitability of the humbled human will and accepting suffering as intrinsic to our mortal existence. The implication of the message is that salvation and reconciliation with creation can not be accomplished by depending fundamentally on our own personal will. There must be a *goel* or an intercession from outside. No *goel* can save us, however, until we have learned the essential wisdom that consists in abandoning hope in our personal power to make things as we will them to be.

This teaching may seem to be grim and despairing. But it is only grim to one who has placed all hope, consciously or unconsciously, in a happiness that relies on the fulfillment of the personal will, and, more specifically, the hope that we can impose our will on existence because our existence is essentially lawlike and because we can manipulate existence through knowledge of its laws. Loss of such hope is "despair" in the literal meaning of that word, without hope; it has this meaning only in regard to the deceptive hope of imposing one's will on life. To surrender that hope, is by no means to surrender all hope. As we shall see, that concept is the truth that the Book of Job teaches.

Elihu also puts another idea in a new way. Eliphaz, Job's friend, had earlier alluded to nightmares that he had had, in which the horror of the idea that a puny man should presume to put himself in the right as against God was revealed to him.[71] And Job, too, had had nightmares that he viewed as visitations or persecution from the Lord.[72] Elihu also says that God speaks to man in dreams, not to announce His own superiority over man, nor to persecute but to teach a great lesson about man's false pride in hoping to master life on his own terms.[73]

This lesson of the night, in dreams, visions, and suffering, is not a lesson that demeans, weakens, or darkens. On the contrary, if correctly attended, it inspires true and ultimate strength, the eternal lifting up of song rather than the precarious mortal security of law.[74] God speaks to us in songs, not law, says Elihu. Once the false hope that our puny will can keep life neatly law-abiding is dashed, our vision is opened to a more magnificent hope in creation, a valid hope.

Listen to the songs in the night, says Elihu, behold the visions of night. Suffer, be passive and open, and endure instead of trying to win your case in life as a matter of rights and fairness. Accept your own ultimate finitude and dependence; accept me, says Elihu, as one who will intercede; surrender your will and instead exalt God and His creation, this life. Be lifted up not by logic but by song; listen, and I will sing.

And then Elihu does sing. At last, and for the remainder of the book[75] we are free of argument and legalistic pleadings, and we move into a totally new mode of engagement. Elihu breaks out into a song of the seasons. This fact seems quite irrelevant to those scholars who want to continue to argue the issues! Indeed Biblical scholars have said that the text of Elihu is an interpolation that interrupts the story. And in a way they are right, but in the way they mean it they are so wrong.[76] Of course it is an interruption, almost overdue one might say, of the legalistic approach to life which has dominated the dialogues.

There is a story, which I cannot help digressing to tell, that most of the newly deceased, as they arrive at the pearly gates, are greeted by the attending angel and directed to a broad avenue that will lead them to the Divine Presence; but on the occasional arrival of a professor of philosophy or theology, the angel obligingly points out, instead, a different path leading to an auditorium where there is a lecture on God. I often think of this story as I see how earnestly and ingeniously many commentators on Job persist in weaving their logical webs of argument as they move into the Elihu and whirlwind passages in the Book of Job. Such readers do not and will not register the fundamental transformation that takes place, the shift to song that transports us and takes us to a profoundly different realm where at last we are granted the manifestation of the Divine. Many readers complain that with the Elihu and the whirlwind passages no new argument is introduced. Such readers are, of course, quite right. What is new, and absolutely central to the book, is the shift from argument as a mode of teaching to direct revelation through poetry. It is incredible but true that there are still commentators who would strip away the poetic quality of the text, as if it were a decorative veneer rather than a mode of communication, and examine only the words.[77] Instead of listening to the music of song and poem and opening the self to what the poet does—in short, instead of suffering—such a reader insists on continuing to act or to impose on the text the old categories and modes of inquiry. From this standpoint God's words can be characterized as a "complete evasion of the issue as Job posed it . . . ."[78] Indeed it has been argued that the Lord so patently fails to refute Job's arguments as to warrant our concluding that the poet's real intention was to make Yahweh the butt of the reader's ridicule![79]

Elihu sings[80] of rains and storms that herald the winter, of the snow, ice, and hail that lead all creatures to withdraw into their dens, and then of the dazzling sun and hot winds of summer. Thus, abandoning the mode of argument, and suiting his actions to his former words, Elihu sings climactically of the radiant light streaming from the northern sky and of the splendor of God.

Suddenly, without warning, and out of nowhere, there is a thundering, shaking, shattering, cataclysmic tempest. The King James translation says that God "answered Job out of the whirlwind."[81] The Hebrew word refers to a rare but terrible tempest of thunder and lightning, great blasts of wind, clouds, and earthquakes, associated in Hebrew literature with the appearance of God.[82] Elihu entirely disappears from the scene as abruptly and mysteriously as he arrived.[83] It is the Voice of Existence that thunders, not a voice in the midst of a thunderstorm, but the self-revealing voice of existence.

Existence does not argue, debate, reason, or adjudicate. It makes no contracts. It issues no commands and promises nothing. Of course, if we read the words of this Voice as if we were reading an argument or debate, we quickly get the impression, as many readers do, that we are now hearing from a blustering potentate, bullying Job into submission in a display of brute power.[84]

But the Voice out of the whirlwind, whose words constitute one of the great poems of literature,[85] reveals to us, not by second hand description, but in direct poetic revelation, the glories, the wonders, the powers, the mysteries, the order, the harmonies, the wildness, and the frightening and amazing multifariousness of untamable existence, and its inexhaustible and indomitable powers and creativity. The Book of Job shatters, by a combination of challenge and ridicule and ultimately by direct experiential demonstration, the idea that the law known to human beings reflects law rooted in the divine or ultimate nature of being, and the idea that the divine or ultimate nature of being is in its essence lawlike. The absurd and fantastic extremes to which Job's belief in a Divine Lawgiver have led him are explicitly taken up by the Voice in the biting rhetorical challenges to Job, ironically echoing Job's challenges to God. If the absurdity into which Job's challenges have tragically led him have not already warned us, the Voice now explicitly reveals that life can be saved from trivialization and futility only if we shift to a radically different understanding than that of Job and his counselors as to the meaning of our existence and the nature of the Divine.

The marvel of the Book of Job is that in the end it does not offer an abstract logical or legalistic argument or a mere assertion of raw, neutral power but instead, and with enormous genius, presents to us a dramatic and poetic vision. In the way that poetry, music, and art present an experience and a vision, and in a way that argument and theory cannot, the poet reveals. The whirlwind passages are not a would-be lecture about the Divine; they are a poem of the Divine.

The truth that is revealed has several dimensions that are especially appropriate to single out here. We are allowed a vision of existence as inexhaustibly rich in creative energies. We see life and death, harmonies and discords, joys and terrors,[86] grace and monsters, the domestic and the wild. We are nothing as measured against the whole; we are puny, vulnerable, and transient. As mere beings we can only be humble. But as beings who are conscious of this miracle, who participate however humbly in it, we are transcendently elevated and exhilarated. We are like unto the angels. The corollary of this vision is not simple minded obedience to some set of rules but integrity. It is consciousness of the wonder of existence, not logic, that induces reverence; and authentic reverence compels utter truthfulness in one's stance toward what is revered. This fusion of authentic reverence and truth in which Job has taken his stand constitutes his integrity. Only now it is lifted to a new and transcendent level.

"I abhor myself, and repent."[87] So read Job's words in the King James text at the end of the whirlwind passages. Indeed, after such stubbornness and such revelation, Job might well feel he has been a blind fool. Nevertheless this translation takes the harshest line, and so far as the Hebrew text goes, the harshness is unnecessary. The original Hebrew may be read as saying something more just and true to the situation: "I melt away, and I repudiate my words."[88]

The point is that Job does achieve humility; the self-assertive "I" has dissolved. But this humility is the very opposite of humiliation. Humiliation presupposes an "I" which exists and is assertive even in its impotence, an "I" that is coerced and self-denigrating. This suffering is what we ordinarily recognize as suffering; it is misery. But authentic humility reflects neither impotence nor self-deprecation; it is as if the self-assertive "I" had been a cloud over the soul that has dissipated. We can see an analogous loss of the self-assertive "I" in contexts other than the religious. For example, it would be absurd if the authentic humility we feel before the sublime late quartets of Beethoven were confused with the humiliation we feel when put down by someone more powerful or ingenious than we. Authentic humility is never associated with being put down, but on the contrary it is an aspect of the transcendent elevation of consciousness. When Opus 130 speaks to us, the "I" has melted away and is not.

This total openness to the music, undistracted by self-assertiveness, is also suffering, but suffering in a significantly new sense, and of course it is not misery. Here is the ultimate wisdom in suffering, a truth that is transforming because this suffering is not the suffering of the oppressed will but will-less suffering. So the ultimate wisdom in suffering is neither the grimness nor the despair that it seems to one who is still in the grip of the will-full self. Where the personal will is at last absent, suffering is simply transparence to reality, whether this be the reality of Opus 130 or even the reality of pain. All reality, joy or terror, appears not as an object of our will but as a consciousness, a gift, the marvel of self-conscious life.

Job's life is now newly and transcendently enriched. I say "enriched"—a cliché. But what words can we use to describe this deep transformation? We have none. Rather, we must revert to naive metaphor. And that, of course, is how the Job story ends, with an epilogue in which we return to the simple language of the folk tale.

Now we can comfortably turn back to the sophisticatedly simple folk tale in which we had left Job, patient, enduring, and unwavering in his acceptance and reverence before Divine Creation. Now we understand who and what he is, and so the folk tale is transformed from a naive tale into a potent and self-conscious myth, a symbol for what is otherwise inexpressible.

Job, we are told,[89] is now graced with redoubled prosperity, realized in completely traditional form. God gives him twice the cattle he had previously owned, twice the number of sons,[90] twice the number of years of life; and as a thoughtful touch, God does not give him twice the number of daughters, which would merely have doubled his burden, but instead bestows the same number of daughters Job had originally had. Each daughter now is gifted, however, and most helpfully, with surpassing beauty and a very substantial dowry.

The Book of Job is thus not an argument but a book of transformed perspectives. As T. S. Eliot wrote, "Everything is true, but in a different sense."[91] Yahweh had said Job was an upright and blameless man, and the satan took this statement to be a measure of Job's beliefs and conduct but not his basic motives. On the contrary, we eventually see that, in God's eyes, Job's beliefs and his obedience were not the core of the matter. Job's blamelessness before God lay in Job's ultimate integrity in spite of his all-too-human stubbornness and constricted view of existence. The satan saw Job as deeply concerned with the good things of life; and the satan was right, as is evidenced by Job's glorying in the memories of his days of prosperity and his groaning over his loss of wealth, status, family, and health. But what the satan did not realize was that the importance all such things had for Job becomes the very measure of his integrity before God, because, when that integrity is at issue, all else, important as it had been, becomes to Job as nothing. Job is unwavering in his refusal to sell out his integrity for the sake of getting back prosperity. Now the good things of life are revealed as having a very different kind of importance for Job. They are, as he thinks, the signs that he has been true to God and God to him, and it is as signs that he mourns them.

"Everything is true but in a different sense." Job had cried out for God to appear and lamented his inability to force God's hand. Job was right in thinking he could not force God's hand, but when he recognizes this fact fully and resigns hope of imposing his will, God does appear. Job says he could never answer one in a thousand of God's questions if God did appear, and how right he was! But he never suspected the nature of the questions nor the topic. Job was awed by God's power and felt he would be struck dumb and terrorized; and he was right in that attitude, too, for the Revelation is a revelation of awesome and fearful powers and beings. There is no blinking the untamed and monstrous in existence, no more than there should be blindness to the wonders and harmonies. But the surprising effect of seeing all this is that in the end God's oppressive hand is taken off Job's shoulder, as Job had pleaded it should be, and Job is elevated to a new level of existence and consciousness.

The Voice at the outset speaks of Job as one whose "ignorant words cloud my design in darkness," as indeed was true. Job had conceived and spoken of God's creation as merely human law writ large. So had the friends, those wise men of the day.[92] But, paradoxically, at the end of the folk tale Yahweh says Job has spoken correctly; the friends have not.[93] And this also is so and is the deepest truth of the book. For Job, unlike the friends, had addressed the Divine in the correct way, with utterly selfless commitment to truth. The friends had addressed the Divine in the wrong way, in that they had been smugly self-satisfied in their assumption that they already possessed all the truth and so could invent realities to fit their theory. They showed neither integrity nor humility in this regard. They were in bad faith before God.

If we turn back now for a last look at what the Book of Job teaches concerning law, we find that it is not all negative. The Book of Job moves from a central concern with rules and laws and their consequent punishments and rewards to a concern with integrity, reverence for creation, awareness of the radical vulnerability of human beings, and as corollary and complement, an awareness of the dignity, only a little lower than the angels, that such consciousness gives even to a Job on the garbage heap.

If we accept this teaching of the Book of Job, what status remains for law? The simplest part of the message is that law is a matter of concern to humanity and not, in any ultimate way, to God. Or, to put this thesis in less theological terms, human existence cannot be encompassingly understood in terms of law and justice, because these things, grand and important as they may indeed be for human beings, are far transcended by the mysteries and many-sidedness of the creative forces that work through us and upon us. We need not diminish the importance of law; we need to magnify human existence.

But if the Book teaches negatively that law cannot possibly suffice as our ultimate perspective, it also teaches positively three theses of fundamental significance to law: the near god-like dignity of the individual, the awful vulnerability of the individual, and the need for reverence and awe before this world in which we exist. Surely these three tenets must be at the foundation of any system of law if it is to abide in the spirit of the teaching of the Book of Job.

Taken as a whole, this teaching leaves open the specific nature of law. The particular system with its procedures, statutes, and other paraphernalia will be related to specific local cultural conditions and will reflect the kind of creativity of legal thinking and practice that emerges under those conditions. In this way, it seems to me, the Book of Job leaves us a desirable freedom; it serves as an intellectual and spiritual weapon with which to fight off dogmatic imposition of specific laws or systems of law presented under the guise that they are divinely inspired, either literally or metaphorically.

On the other hand the lesson of Job is by no means one of pure relativism or positivism. It does not leave the law without roots in the foundations of our existence.[94] True, we have no specific guidelines as to what, in particular, constitutes respect for human dignity, reverence for the wonder of human existence, and compassion and concern for our profound vulnerability. But then who could expect such things to be set out explicitly in abstract terms? Certainly the poet of Job saw the futility of such a hope, for he saw that these three foundations arise out of revelations, human wisdom, and suffering, not out of mere reason. No constitutional provision can guarantee against governors and legislators who have shut out these realities of human existence. Nevertheless, it is no less urgent and fundamental that the law, whatever its local form, must have, as its primary wisdom and inspiration, the consciousness of the mystery, and dignity, and vulnerability of human existence.

Such a thesis may seem so vague and so intangibly spiritual as to lack any genuine, concrete usefulness for the practice of law. And yet this is not the case. It is a preconstitutional thesis that sets the context of deepest principle, as is found in such a basic document as our Declaration of Independence; and it can have a profound political and legal vitality. Such principles, and the spirit they embody, have moved nations, but only when this spirit is alive in the people. It is vision, not legalistic argument, that is the inspiration. Those who think doctrine and administrative structure constitute law fail to understand that when such vision ceases to inspire the people, the best legal institutions become corrupted. Such a threat is not so far away from us today that this prospect should be difficult to see.

Truly, this book must be seen in a context suggested by the poet's own words, a context in which tension is maintained by contrast. Job had said "What is man, that thou shouldest magnify him . . . and that thou shouldest visit him every morning, and try him every moment?"[95] These words mirror and are answered by the words of the Psalmist, "What is man, that thou art mindful of him? And the son of man, that thou visitest him? For thou hast made him a little lower than the angels, and hast crowned him with glory and honour."[96]

NOTES

1. See the discussions of Job, chapters 4-6, 8-9, 13-16, 19, 23 & 31, in S. R. Driver & G. B. Gray, *A Critical and Exegetical Commentary on the Book of Job* (1921) [hereinafter cited as Driver & Gray]; *Job* (M. H. Pope ed. & trans. 1965) [hereinafter cited as Pope]; *The Book of Job* (N. C. Habel ed. 1975) [hereinafter cited as Habel]. See text accompanying note 30 infra.

2. E.g., Deuteronomy 12-25 (specific laws stated); Isaiah 42:6 (God's reasons for giving His law to the Chosen People of Israel).

3. I have not seen any work that takes up the theme of law in Job and subjects the book's treatment of that theme to any extended analysis, or that investigates how the legal perspective bears in any specific, internally related way to the other themes of Job or to the essential structure of the work. Yet many commentators have explicitly noted the frequent and continuing use of law images and terms throughout the book. The major commentaries on Job go no farther in an analytical direction than to remark briefly to the effect that Job talks in terms of bringing God to court, or of forcing God to acquit him, and that Job eventually realizes the impossibility of this approach. Many commentaries do take up the doctrine of retribution and the theme of punishment and reward but only to report that Job learns the falseness of this doctrine. Little or no analysis is offered. But see note 59 infra.

4. "It will be almost universally agreed that in the Book of Job we have the supreme literary masterpiece of the Hebrew genius." T. H. Robinson, *The Poetry of the Old Testament* 67 (1947). Robinson alludes to it as possibly being "second to none in all the range of human writing." Id. Pope says that "A modern man reflecting on the Book of Job from the vantage point of two millenia of human experience must marvel at the religious insights to be found therein." Pope, supra note 1, at LXXVII. Gordis characterizes the Book of Job as "the crowning masterpiece" of the Bible, R. Gordis, *The Book of God and Man* 1 (1965) [hereinafter cited as Gordis], and in his discussion of its status speaks of "untold readers and scholars who have recognized in it one of the supreme human masterpieces." Id. at 3. Such tributes are readily found elsewhere in the literature.

5. See C. J. Friedrich, *The Philosophy of Law in Historical Perspective* ch. 2 (1963) [hereinafter cited as Friedrich].

6. One of the best known texts is that of the so-called "Babylonian Job," also known as "The Poem of the Righteous Sufferer," or "I will Praise the Lord of Wisdom." J. B. Pritchard, *The Ancient Near East* 596-600 (Supp. Lambert trans. 1969).

7. Pope. supra note 1, at 1-LXIV; Gordis, supra note 4, ch. 5; N. H. Snaith, *The Book of Job, Its Origin and Purpose*, ch. 2 (1968) [hereinafter cited as Snaith].

8. See Friedrich, supra note 5, at 8.

9. See Exodus 19-24 (the "Book of the Covenant").

10. See E. Dhorme, *A Commentary on the Book of Job* cxxviii–cxxx (1967) [hereinafter cited as Dhorme]; Gordis, supra note 4, ch. 12; Pope, supra note 1, at lxxiii.

11. Cf. Friedrich, supra note 5, ch. 6 (on Aquinas), ch. 2 at 9 (on Calvinism).

12. See Presidential Address, "Punishment and Suffering" by H. Fingarette to the American Philosophical Association (March 26, 1977).

13. See note 7 supra.

14. Eliphaz: "What innocent man has ever perished? . . . Those who plough mischief and sow trouble reap as they have sown; they perish at the blast of God. . . ." Job 4:7–9 (New English Bible). Bildad: "If you are innocent and upright, then indeed will he watch over you and see your just intent fulfilled . . . your end will be great. . . . The godless man's life-thread breaks off. . . . God will not spurn the blameless man, nor will he grasp the hand of the wrongdoer." Id. 8:6–20. Zophar: "If you have wrongdoing in hand, thrust it away; let no iniquity make its home with you . . . sure of protection you will lie down in confidence. Blindness will fall on the wicked; the ways of escape are closed to them, and their hope is despair." Id. 11:14–20.

15. "O that the grounds for my resentment might be weighed, and my misfortunes set with them on the scales." Job 6:2–3 (New English Bible). "So now I bid you, turn and look at me: Am I likely to lie in your face? . . . Let me have no more injustice . . . for my integrity is in question. Do I ever give voice to injustice?" Id. 6:28–30. "Leave me to speak my mind. . . . I will . . . take my life in my hands. If he would slay me I would not hesitate; I should still argue my cause to his face. This at least assures my success, that no godless man may appear before him. . . . Be sure of this: Once I have stated my case I know that I shall be acquitted." Id. 13:13–18.

16. Good has stressed this idea: "We could say that the book shows Job's movement from a position of magical dogmatism [i.e., that man can by his excellence require God to save and accept him or by his unworthiness require God to damn and reject him] to his ultimate stance in faith." E. M. Good, *Irony in the Old Testament* 197–98 (1965) [hereinafter cited as Good]. For a critique of Good's thesis that what is at issue is a belief in magic, see note 59 infra.

17. Job 38:2 (King James).

18. Habel, supra note 1, at 11. See Driver & Gray, supra note 1, introduction, § 7; Dhorme, supra note 10, introduction, chs. 7 & 12; Job, 8–18 (H. H. Rowley ed. 1970) [hereinafter cited as Rowley]. Pope, in discussing textual problems, states, "The Book of Job is textually the most vexed in the Old Testament, rivaled only by Hosea which has the advantage of being much shorter." Pope, supra note 1, at xxxix. As Pope later adds, the Book of Job "presents formidable linguistic and philological problems." Id. at xlii.

19. Habel summarizes the consensus among commentators in his commentary on Job 1:66–67: "Satan is not a proper name but a title meaning

'the adversary.' Here Satan is not equivalent to the devil of later Christian theology, but functions like a prosecuting attorney in a court of law (cp. Zech. 3:1–2). He also seems to be engaged in espionage activities, ranging the entire earth to check on the lives of men (cp. Zech. 1:10–11)." Habel, supra note 1, at 17. See also Psalms 109:6.

20. Job chs. 1–2.

21. Job 1:8–11.

22. Job 1:11. It has commonly been said that the satan challenges Yahweh and that in Job 1:12 Yahweh accepts the challenge, the two of them thus making, in effect, a *wager*. The present author also thought as much until Professor Good called to his attention the colloquy between Good and Professor David Robertson. Robertson, "The Book of Job: A Literary Study," 56 *Soundings* 446 (1973) [hereinafter cited as Robertson]; Good, "Job and the Literary Task: A Response," 56 *Soundings* 470 (1973). In that discussion, Professor Robertson pointed out that Job is uttering a formal oath in his final defense, Job 29 to 31. Robertson, supra, at 460–61. This fact led Professor Good to remark that the satan, in Job ch. 1, is also using an incomplete form of such an oath. Good, supra, at 475. The full form is one in which one calls down dire consequences upon oneself (as Job does in Job 31) if one's words are not true. This form is the form the satan uses but with the specific consequences left unstated. Thus if this reading is correct (and I accept it as such, and as revealing), the satan and Yahweh are not laying a wager at poor Job's expense; instead the satan is solemnly carrying out his "legal" duty, charging under oath—in what may be a characteristically routine, officially abbreviated form—that Job is a fraud. This charge is a proper way to institute proceedings for which the satan is "professionally" responsible. And so it is proper, under God's justice, for God then to authorize commencing the ordeal or trial. However, I see no good reason to over stress the power of the satan's oath and to say that the magic of such oaths forces God's hand, as both Good and Robertson claim. Later we will realize that God's purposes transcend mere justice, and we will then recall that it was Yahweh, not the satan, who initiated the entire affair by citing Job specifically to the satan, thereby challenging the latter. In short, All-seeing Yahweh wanted Job to be tried, which, as we will see, was ultimately for Job's good, and ours, in a way that explicitly transcends questions of justice.

23. Job 2:4–5.

24. Deuteronomy 10:12–13 (New English Bible).

25. But this issue has commonly been overlooked, in part for the reasons discussed in the text accompanying note 27 infra.

26. Job 1:21 (New English Bible).

27. Most of the commentators have in effect taken the main theme of the entire book to be as understood, more or less, by the participants in the poetic dialogue. See, e.g., Pope, supra note 1, at LXVIII–LXXV: "It has been generally assumed that the purpose of the book is to give an answer to the

issue with which it deals, the problem of divine justice or theodicy," that is, the question "raised inevitably by any and every instance of seemingly unmerited or purposeless suffering, and especially the suffering of the righteous man." Pope himself says that "either the book ends in magnificent anticlimax, or we must see the highlight in the divine speeches. . . . The content of the divine answer is . . . on the face of it, a disappointment. The issue as Job had posed it is completely ignored. . . . The complete evasion of the issue as Job had posed it must be the poet's oblique way of admitting that there is no satisfactory answer available to man, apart from faith." Dhorme, supra note 10 at CL–CLI, ultimately sees the Book of Job as "an important stage" on the road from the earlier Israelite doctrine of "immediate retribution" to the "final solution" of Christianity in which "future retribution" on the Day of Judgment will vindicate good over evil. Rowley, supra note 18, at 19, says that "we can hardly suppose that the principal aim of the book was realized in the Prologue." "It is equally wrong to think that its purpose was to solve the problem of suffering." Instead, says Rowley, "When God speaks to Job from the whirlwind, he does not reveal to him why he is suffering. . . . He reminds Job that there are mysteries in nature beyond his solving, and . . . the mystery of suffering is one of these. . . . It is of the essence of the message that God found Job *in* his suffering. . . . To sufferers in all ages the Book of Job declares that less important than fathoming the intellectual problem of the mystery of suffering is the appropriation of its spiritual enrichment through the fellowship of God." Id. at 20–21. Driver says, "The problem with which [the Book of Job] deals is this: '[w]hy do the righteous suffer?' and its principal aim is to controvert the theory . . . 'that suffering is a sign of the Divine displeasure, and presupposes sin on the part of the sufferer.' " S. R. Driver, *An Introduction to the Literature of the Old Testament* 409 (1956) [hereinafter cited as Driver]. Driver reports that the nineteenth-century scholar Budé saw the question in the Prologue as being whether egoism is the root of piety. Budé, however, held that the deeper and broader question in the book is the one raised in the dialogues about the meaning of the suffering of the righteous. Id. at 430. Gordis believes that the Book of Job is single-mindedly devoted to the theme of the operation of the divine law of justice in the life of the individual, and the doctrine of reward and punishment. Gordis, supra note 4, at 149. Note that in each case the commentators see the question as revolving around suffering, the issue in the dialogues. Perhaps an exception is the ambiguous statement of the matter in Driver & Gray, supra note 1, at LIII–LXIII. Driver and Gray clearly raise the issue of Job's integrity and make the point that Job's conduct in the ordeal proves the satan wrong; they point out that Job never demands the restoration of his goods but, something very different, the vindication of his character. Nevertheless, they speak of the writer of Job as one who, although he emphasizes that Job does not suffer as the result of any sins he has committed, has no positive theory of suffering to propound. All this theorizing adds up, after taking into account the hesitancies and difficulties announced by the authors, to a primary emphasis on vindication of Job's integrity rather than on the problem of suffering. But Driver and Gray fail to bring out the internal connections among the issues. Terrien stands out as one who says definitely that the theme of the Book of Job is not the "problem of suffering." To recognize this notion is to open the way to seeing Yahweh's speeches out of the whirlwind as climactic to the argument of the book rather than as a monumental irrelevance or put-down, as most commentators must take it. Terrien, "The Yahweh Speeches and Job's Responses," 68 *Review and Exposition* 497 (1971) [hereinafter cited as Terrien].

28. Job ch. 3.

29. Eliphaz says, "Think how once you encouraged those who faltered. . . . But now that adversity comes upon you, you lost patience . . . and you are unmanned." Job 4:3-5 (New English Bible). "For my part, I would make my petition to God and lay my cause before him. . . . Do not reject the discipline of the Almighty." Job 4:8, 17 (New English Bible).

30. E.g., Job 4:8, 17. Eliphaz says, "Can mortal man be more righteous than God?" The word "righteous" in the Hebrew text connotes "on the right side of the law" or "having the law on one's side." Dhorme, commenting on Job 9:15, says, "The verb . . . 'to be righteous' . . . has equally the sense of 'to be in the right' in a debate or a lawsuit." Dhorme, supra note 10, at 145. It may be significant, however, that it is in Job's speeches that we find richness and quantity of legal imagery and language, far more so than in the speeches of the friends. He presses and sharpens the issues, while the friends leave the issues confused and cryptic.

31. Although, as remarked supra in note 30, the friends do not stress the imagery and language of law per se, they do unambiguously, emphatically, and persistently put forward the doctrine of retribution and reward. See note 14 supra. It is Job who treats this doctrine as a matter of law, of a covenant between God and man, rather than, for example, as a mere matter of God's pleasure.

32. Job 4:17-19; 5:17; 8:2-7; 22:21-26.

33. Job 15:4-6.

34. Job 8:8; 15:10.

35. Job 5:8, 17-18; 8:5; 11:13-15, 22:21-30.

36. Job 6:2-3. In later passages, Job further expresses his faith that if he could indeed bring his cause to trial and present his defense, God would surely acquit him. Job 19:25-27; 23:2-7; 31:2-6; 31:35-37.

37. Job 6:4; 7:13-21; 9:16-20; 19:6-12.

38. Job ch. 3; 7:15-16.

39. Job 6:14-27.

40. Job 6:28-30; 13:15; 27:2-6; ch. 31.

41. Job 13:1-12.

42. Job 22:5-9.

43. Job 21:7-17. In Job 24:2-17, there is an eloquent portrait of the exploitation of the poor and innocent by the wicked. That the problem, as defined by Job and his friends, is the problem of the meaning of suffering has now become evident. This problem is the problem that most commentators, too, take as central to this work. But this view is mistaken. See note 27 & accompanying text supra.

44. Job 9:3 (New English Bible) (alternatively: "Man cannot answer God."); Job 9:19 (New English Bible: "Who can compel him to give me a hearing?") (King James: "[W]ho shall set me a time to plead?"). According to Dhorme, the language used here "assumes a juridical implication, 'summon,' 'cite,' before a court of law." Dhorme, supra note 10, at 138.

45. "[T]ell me the ground of they complaint against me." Job 10:2-7 (New English Bible). "[L]et me know my offences." Job 13:22-23 (New English Bible). "If my accuser had written out his indictment . . . I would plead the whole record of my life and present that in court as my defence." Job 31:35-37 (New English Bible).

46. Job 16:19.

47. "How much less shall I answer him, and choose out my words to reason with him?" Job 9:14 (King James). Dhorme says that the choice of the Hebrew term "to choose words" indicates concern for "the words which the accused would use before a tribunal." Dhorme, supra note 10, at 135. Pope, who translates the term as "match my words," also says the Hebrew word "is often used as a juridical term." Pope, supra note 1, at 70. Another legalistic phrase, "[i]f I summoned and he responded," appears in Job 9:16a (New English Bible).

48. "For he is not a man, as I am, that I should answer him, and we should come together in judgment. Neither is here any daysman betwixt us, that might lay his hand upon us both." Job 9:32-33 (King James). The term used in the New English Bible and by Dhorme is "arbitrator"; Pope uses "umpire." The custom was that by laying hands on the shoulders of the parties, the arbitrator or judge assumed jurisdiction over the case. See Dhorme, supra note 10, at 144.

49. "For in my heart I know that my vindicator lives." Job 19:25 (New English Bible). The Hebrew word translated as "vindicator" is goel. The goel is an avenger, redeemer, or ransomer, originally the nearest kinsman who acts to avenge or ransom a member of the family.

50. The concluding verses of Job's great oath in chapter 31 of the Book of Job are an eloquent summation of this attitude, with final and ringing confidence in the justice of the claim, along with the background of despair that God will ever answer this appeal and acknowledge its justice. See note 61 infra.

51. Job 10:8-18.

52. Job 7:17 (New English Bible).

53. "What is man that thou art mindful of him? And the son of man that thou visitest him? For thou hast made him a little lower than the

angels, and hast crowned him with glory and honour." Psalms 8:4-5 (King James). Cf. Job 7:17-18 (King James): "What is man that thou shouldst magnify him? and that thou shouldst set thine heart upon him? And that thou shouldst visit him every morning, and try him every moment?"

54. Deuteronomy 10:11-13.

55. See Presidential Address, "Punishment and Suffering," by H. Fingarette to the American Philosophical Association (March 26, 1977).

56. Id.

57. James 5:11 (King James).

58. Job 23:13-14.

59. Professor Edwin M. Good has remarked on the manipulative power that human beings have over God by virtue of the reward-punishment feature of the Divine Will. Professor Good, however, asserts that Job's belief that we have such a power is a belief in magic. He sees the Book of Job as a protest against such "magical dogmatism," the belief "that in the last analysis man has the upper hand over God." Good, supra note 16, at 197. So the sticking of pins into the image of an enemy is in this respect no different from the "pursuit of moral or theological excellence," for both are equally magical in that the aim is man's self-fulfillment by methods that purport to produce inevitably the desired effect. Good sees Job as moving "from a position of magical dogmatism to his ultimate stance in faith." Id. at 197-98. Although I agree and have emphasized that the belief in the necessity of retribution and reward is in effect a belief in our power over God, I disagree with Good's account in two respects. First, and most important, I have tried to show that the belief in the inevitability of retribution and reward is not a primitive, naive, irrational, or magical belief; on the contrary, it reflects insight into a genuine and central logical necessity in that it is unintelligible to assert God has commanded us to act in certain ways and at the same time to deny that He inevitably punishes the disobedient and rewards the obedient. Second, I find Good's account of Job's transformation ambiguously stated in regard to a crucial issue: Good says that Job's sin is his readiness to dethrone God in the interests of his own personal fate. Id. at 238. But in truth Job is not, in his conduct, attitudes, and motives, a man who is committed to self-fulfillment or who is trying to use his moral excellence merely as a device to win benefits for himself; he is a person of true and complete "faith" (to use Good's term here). The honor and wealth with which the pious are to be rewarded are for him the signs of God's good will, not ends in themselves. That lesson is what the whole story is designed to show us: what a truly pious man is and how wrong the satan was in alleging that Job is self-oriented and manipulative. On the other hand Professor Good is right insofar as his claim pertains to Job's beliefs. Though Job was motivated by faith and not by the desire for reward, he did hold the belief, as did his three friends, that God's will and attitude toward man is expressed through reward to the righteous and punishment of the wicked. It is when the facts of life shake this belief that

Job is thrown into moral perplexity and despair. For, although his faith in God never wavers, he no longer understands its meaning. Given the realities that he candidly confronts, Job's belief provides no acceptable interpretation of what life devoted to God can mean; yet the ultimate reality, now intellectually inexplicable to him but nevertheless actual, is his true faith in God, regardless of rewards or theories.

60. This insight is also central to two great strains of Chinese thought, the teachings of Confucius and of Lao Tzu. See H. Fingarette, Evans-Wentz Lectures in Oriental Religion (Stanford University, April 1977).

61. Good brings this fact out and says that Job directly addresses God only twice after chapter 14, very briefly once in 17:3-4 and again in the midst of his final summation in 30:20-23. Good interprets this fact to mean that, although Job can "hope against hope," he basically has given up hope that God will render justice and sees no point in addressing himself to God. Good, supra note 16, at 231-32.

62. Job 34:5-7.

63. Job 9:20.

64. "The truth is, God does no wrong, and the Almighty does not pervert justice." Job 34:12 (New English Bible).

65. Job 7:20 (New English Bible).

66. Job 35:5-8 (New English Bible).

67. "[M]an learns his lesson on a bed of pain. . . ." Job 33:19 (New English Bible).

68. "[H]is soul draws near to the pit, his life to the ministers of death. Yet if an angel, one of thousands, stands by him, a mediator between him and God . . . if he speaks in the man's favour . . . then that man will grow sturdier than he was in youth." Job 33:22-25 (New English Bible).

69. See note 49 supra.

70. See H. Fingarette, Evans-Wentz Lectures in Oriental Religion (Stanford University, April 1977).

71. Job 4:12-21.

72. Job 7:13-14.

73. "In dreams, in visions of the night, when deepest sleep falls upon men . . . God makes them listen . . . strikes them with terror . . . to check the pride of mortal man." Job 33:15-17 (New English Bible).

74. There is debate among authorities on the Hebrew text of the Book of Job as to whether Job 35:10 should read, as in the New English Bible, "But none of them asks, Where is God my Maker, who gives protection by night[?]" Or, as in the King James version, "But none saith, Where is God my maker, who giveth songs in the night[?]" The problem arises because there are two very similar root-forms, one meaning to "make music," and the other meaning "strong," "protect," "mighty." Compare the commentaries on this passage of Dhorme, supra note 10; Driver & Gray, supra note 1; Gordis, supra note 4, and Rowley, supra note 18, with that of Pope, supra note 1. I see no reason why the ambiguity evident to these scholars should

not also have registered in the mind of the poet himself even as he wrote. Regardless of whether he had "song" or "support" uppermost in his mind, the two senses reenforce each other wonderfully in this context where suffering, visions, dreams, and angelic intercession are so prominent and where strength is what is needed. It is song and vision rather than physical might or legal reasoning that are here the media for receiving God's strength. Accordingly, I have tried to work my paraphrase in the text in a way that retains the ambiguity.

75. Job 36:26 et seq. It is true that the New English Bible reads the horatory phrase of Elihu at 37:14 as "Listen, Job, to this argument. . . ." But all other versions merely have "Listen," or "hear." The insertion of the word "argument" in the New English Bible seems to be an interpretative elaboration which, if I am right, is misleading; it reflects the inclination to insist that we are to continue reading the Book as an argument, the very inclination which is fatal to a correct understanding of the Book from this point onward.

76. There has been extensive dispute about the textual status of the Elihu speeches. The views of the commentators range from the claim that the speeches are a very alien interpolation by a later scribe who intended to undercut or oppose themes in the original text to the claim that they are by the same poet who wrote all the rest of the Book of Job, though possibly written and interpolated at a date later than that in which the dialogues were written. Certainly the Elihu speeches are in some important sense an interpolation. Elihu appears out of nowhere and disappears into nowhere so far as the rest of the text is concerned. He alludes to things said in the dialogues and adumbrates some of the speeches of Yahweh out of the whirlwind. But no one else ever alludes to him or to what he has said. I do not aspire to enter the debate about the historical origin of these Elihu speeches. But I view the appearance and the utterances of Elihu as integral to the aesthetic and religious meaning of the Book of Job. In Elihu we have just the link that is proper and essential to move Job and us from the deadend of Job's beliefs and logic to a new stance, rooted in suffering, song, and visions, towards our life, our existence, and the Divine.

77. A revealing example of the way in which the content of the book is distorted as a result of this fallacy of taking the "poetry" to be mere "emotional" coloring is the approach of J. Kahn, who attempts a psychiatric analysis of Job's suffering. Kahn says, "It is not our chosen task to comment on the poetic quality of Job's speeches. The language is appropriate to the intensity of the emotion which is being experienced. It is our purpose to draw conclusions about these experiences using the kind of reasoning which would be available to a clinician. . . ." This approach, says Kahn, will provide us with a "modern perspective" in which we will "deal with Job's experiences and feelings as being the equivalent of symptoms." J. Kahn, *Job's Illness: Loss, Grief, and Integration* 24 (1975).

78. Pope, supra note 1, at LXXV. Pope says this "must be the poet's oblique way of admitting that there is no satisfactory answer available to man, apart from faith." See note 27 supra.

79. Robertson, supra note 22, at 468. Robertson also says, "It is clear that in these two speeches [by Yahweh, out of the whirlwind] God is trying to convince Job and us of his innocence, that is, of the fact that he is a wise and just ruler of his world." Id. at 462. I would have said that, to the contrary, it is clear that God is not trying to do this. What Yahweh says, as well as the mode of His speech, speaks eloquently to the irrelevance of the issue of justice as it is raised by Job. Surely the fact that Yahweh does not offer arguments designed to meet Job's case head-on ought to lead to the hypothesis that, for reasons we need to try to understand, God takes Job's charges to be irrelevant. Robertson's hypothesis is, in my view, a fantastic hypothesis. It is utterly incongruous, in the face of the magnificent poetry of the whirlwind speeches, that the poet intends Yahweh to be the butt of our ridicule!

80. "Remember then to sing the praises of his work." Job 36:24 (New English Bible).

81. Job 38:1.

82. See Psalms 18; Habakkuk 3; Nahum 1:3; Zechariah 9:14; Ezekiel 1:4. See also Terrien, supra note 27, at 500 n.4.

83. From the standpoint of textual analysis, this fact, along with Elihu's totally unexpected appearance on the scene, tends to support the thesis that the Elihu speeches are an interpolation. See note 76 supra. This fact is in no way inconsistent with the thesis that, from an aesthetic and religious standpoint, the interpolation is supremely apt. It certainly fits the view that he is a transitional figure, one who appears only after all hope is lost and who comes to intercede. He does intercede, both by making cryptically illuminating remarks to Job and by singing the praises and wonders of the Lord (rather than by arguing a case or challenging the Lord); and his song, like the small fire that sets a forest ablaze, is swallowed up in the storm it has evoked. It is common for such intermediaries in religious and spiritual crises to appear from outside, perform their role, and disappear again, not being interested parties in the particular crisis. This role is well-established in a number of traditions, from that of the psychoanalytic therapist to that of the boddhisattva in Mahayana Buddhism. See H. Fingarette, *The Self in Transformation* ch. 6 (1963).

84. Robertson's views along this line have already been discussed. See note 79 supra. Archibald MacLeish also portrays Job as the moral victor over a tyrant god: "I will not duck my head again to thunder—that bullwhip crashing at my ears. . . . Neither the Yes in ignorance . . . the No in spite . . . neither of them!" A. MacLeish, *J. B., A Play in Verse* 106–7 (1956). Jung took a similar view of Yahweh as the amoral bully-tyrant. C. G. Jung, *Answer to Job* ch. 2 (1960). And Kallen concludes that in the Book of

Job God's "justice is his wisdom, and this again is nothing else than power, force, the go and potency, generative and disintegrative, in things. It possesses nothing of the moral or the human. . . ." H. Kallen, *The Book of Job as a Greek Tragedy* 71 (1959).

85. See note 4 supra. It is a notable fact about the literature on Job that even though the magnificence of its poetry, and especially of the Yahweh passages from the heart of the tempest, has been so widely acknowledged, there is so slight attention paid to it as a poetic statement. It is treated as if its ideas could be extracted for logical analysis, while the poetic decorativeness and the emotion it conveys can be set aside. This naive approach to the way in which poetry communicates, and to its content, is crippling in reading a work such as Job. The poet presents not arguments but images. I choose at random two out of innumerable amazing ones: "Canst thou bind the sweet influences of Pleiades, or loose the band of Orion?" Job 38:31 (King James). "Canst thou send lightnings, that they may go, and say unto thee, Here we are?" Job 38:35 (King James). The commentators betray what is communicated in these passages by stripping off the decorative language and taking the message to be: "Are you as powerful or knowledgeable as I am? No!" One might as well discuss the meaning of Shakespeare on the basis of plot summaries.

86. Terrien remarks on the significance of Behemoth and Leviathan as "symbols of cosmic evil." Terrien, supra note 27, at 504. He also speaks of the attitude of "self-loss which opens itself to the infinite wonder of holiness." Id. at 499.

87. Job 42:6 (King James).

88. The New English Bible reads, "I melt away; I repent. . . ." There are differences as to how to render this passage, the idea of "melting away" or "sinking away" being one possible rendering, favored for example by Dhorme, supra note 10. The rendering "abhor" is common. It is important to note that in several of the principal early texts the verb has no object, the word "myself" being an interpretative elaboration added in the translations or later versions. Pope, in a commentary on this passage, says the verb in question is not used in terms of self-loathing and that the object of the verb is not "myself" but "my words." He translates therefore as "Recant." What seems most plain is that there is recantation or repentance; what is most doubtful is that there is self-abhorrence. Terrien translates as "I lose myself into nothing" and stresses that the Hebrew word used here, which is usually translated as repent, has the meaning of intense pain at the thought of displeasing another. Terrien, supra note 27, at 505. Terrien says that the idea expressed is, specifically, that of "dying to his old self" and later refers to the "evocation of self-death" in Job 40:6. Terrien, supra note 27, at 507. See also note 86 supra.

89. Job 42:7 et seq.

90. Although most translations give Job seven sons, the New English Bible allows a variant reading to the effect that Job has fourteen sons at the

end of the story, double the number he had at the outset. The form of the numeral used in the original text is unusual and permits this alternative reading.

91. T. S. Eliot, *The Family Reunion*, Part 2, Scene 2, reprinted in *Complete Poems and Plays* 275 (1952).

92. "Wisdom" was a fairly specific school or tendency of thought, identifying a certain kind of teacher in the Near East. There were "wise men" not only in the southern Mediterranean countries but also in Greece—the Sophists. The wise men taught young men, generally the more well-to-do, giving them what purported to be some practical intellectual skills and practical principles of life. Generally the wisdom teachers were concerned with the pragmatic and naturalistic lessons to be learned from life. They did, however, also teach more metaphysical, even religious beliefs. The poem to Wisdom, chapter 28 in the Book of Job, is one of the great utterances in this tradition. Socrates can be viewed as a more philosophical and spiritually concerned sophist, a sophist who in truth represented a profound attack on the general run of worldly sophistic thinking. The three friends of Job are presumably wise men of the more prosaic kind. Job, one may suspect, was thoroughly acquainted with the Wisdom thought as well as the legalistic thought, that permeated intellectual and upper class circles in the Hebrew world. But he, too, represents a profound attack on these current intellectual fashions. See the discussion of the Wisdom movement in Gordis, supra note 4, Chapter 4.

93. Job 42:8-9. Although I do not think the issue rests on the exact words used in the text, I do think it worth noting that my interpretation of this statement of Yahweh's, which he repeats, is not what the words of most translations suggest. The common translation is to the effect that Yahweh charges the friends with not speaking the truth about him, while asserting on the other hand that Job did. However, I have read the passage to mean that the Lord wrathfully accuses Eliphaz and the two friends of failing to address themselves to Him correctly, as Job did. The usual translation thus emphasizes the truth content of what Job's friends say *about* God; my translation emphasizes the manner in which they address themselves to God. In the text I explain why the latter is to me more plausible. I found, on inquiring into the linguistic aspects of the matter after reaching this view, that there are indeed grounds, based on textual scholarship, for the reading I prefer. It was actually proposed long ago by Budé. See Driver & Gray, supra note 1, vol. 1, at 374, vol. 2, at 348. The word translated as "truth" or "rightly" has the basic meaning of "correct," and this meaning includes the relevant ambiguity at issue here. There are differences among the classical textual sources as to the exact word and grammar, and the differences bear on just this ambiguity. See Habel, supra note 1, who notes that there are versions that do in fact use language more akin to my interpretation. Dhorme, supra note 10, at 648, is illuminating as to the extent to which the passage is ambiguous in respect to this issue. My

own feeling is that we probably have to do with an idiomatic use that overlaps with several similar English idioms; we, for example, speak to a question; we address the question. That is to say, we concern ourselves with the issue, as the friends and Job were concerned with God. This concern is to be talking about God, but also to be talking to Him, before Him and not merely about Him, as of an absent party.

94. There is expressed in the text above a conception having interesting affinities to the view of Hart as to what he calls the "minimum content of natural law" (H. L. A. Hart, *The Concept of Law* 189 [1961]), especially when this view is taken in conjunction with his theses about respect for the individual as central to our notion of justice. See H. L. A. Hart, *Punishment and Responsibility* 49 (1968).

95. Job 7:17–18 (King James).

96. Psalms 8:4–5 (King James).